EARTH TIME

DAVID SUZUKI

Essays

Stoddart

Published in 1998 by Stoddart Publishing Co. Limited
34 Lesmill Road, Toronto, Canada M3B 2T6
180 Varick Street, 9th Floor, New York, New York 10014
Email customer.service@ccmailgw.genpub.com

Distributed in Canada by:
General Distribution Services Ltd.
325 Humber College Blvd., Toronto, Ontario M9W 7C3
Tel. (416) 213-1919   Fax (416) 213-1917
Email customer.service@ccmailgw.genpub.com

Distributed in United States by:
General Distribution Services Inc.
85 River Rock Drive, Suite 202, Buffalo, New York 14207
Toll-free Tel. 1-800-805-1083   Toll-free Fax 1-800-481-6207
Email gdsinc@genpub.com

02   01   00   99   98   1   2   3   4   5

Canadian Cataloguing in Publication Data

Suzuki, David, 1936–
Earth time: essays

ISBN 0-7737-6009-1

1. Human ecology.   2. Social ecology.   3. Social change.
I. Title.

GF47.S89 1998   304.2   C98-931476-6

Cover Design: Angel Guerra
Text Design: Tannice Goddard

Printed in Canada on recycled paper

*We gratefully acknowledge the Canada Council for the Arts and
the Ontario Arts Council for their support of our publishing program.*

My career as a columnist and broadcaster has been made possible by the support of people who are variously referred to as "the general public," "ordinary people," or "the grass roots." By whatever name, they are people who care about the kind of world we are leaving for our grandchildren, the community we live in, and the things in life that really matter. I thank them for listening to my ideas and thoughts, and for the support and inspiration they've provided.

CONTENTS

Introduction   vii

PART I — TAKING STOCK
1 From Superman to Superspecies   3
2 The Trumpet of Science   7
3 Exponential Growth and the Impact of Population   17
4 From Rural Creature to City Dweller   26
5 Consumption   30
6 The Information Revolution   35
7 Global Economics: In Conflict with the Earth   44
8 Human Borders, Nature's Boundaries   50
9 The Bottom Line Is the Starting Line   58

PART II — CHANGING PERSPECTIVE
10 Economics: Out of Balance with the Earth   63
11 Consumption: Beyond Need   90
12 Exponential Growth and Its Consequences   109
13 Information: A Shattered World   127
14 Politics: From Old-Fashioned to Green   142
15 Science and Technology: Limits, Benefits, and Costs   159
16 Who Needs Nature? We Do!   182
17 Finding Solutions and Taking Action   213
18 Learning From the Past to Shape the Future   242

Conclusion   259
References   263
Credits   271

INTRODUCTION

Viewed through a geological and evolutionary time frame, our species is a very recent arrival on this planet, an infant species. And for the first 99.9 percent of our brief existence on Earth, we have been deeply embedded in the natural world, completely dependent on intact Nature whose abundance provided all that we needed for survival.

Our secret for survival has always been our brain. The human brain has contributed to our resourcefulness and our ability to adapt to many different ecosystems — from desert to arctic tundra, fetid tropical rainforests to wetlands, grasslands, and temperate rainforests. We are a resilient species. With the discovery of the efficacy and efficiency of farming a mere ten to twelve millennia ago, we were able to abandon nomadic life to dwell in fixed domiciles and to develop social hierarchies and accumulate possessions. With agriculture, humanity embarked on a path that has culminated in the twentieth century's explosion in population, consumption, and technology.

Now we can see our century as a moment, a moment when human time is completely out of synchrony with Earth time. Most people alive today have known only rapid change in technology, the economy, and material consumption. Change is a normal part of our landscape. But as forests and fish disappear while air, soil, and water accumulate toxins, all parts of society strive to continue the spurt of growth. If our species is to return to a balance with the things that sustain us, we have to see the present moment in geological time and understand the context of this spasm of ecological destruction.

From 1985 to 1996, I wrote a weekly column, first for the *Globe and Mail* and then for a syndicate. In all those years, I never once missed a deadline, although there were a few close calls getting columns sent from Okinawa, Siberia, and the Amazon. This book contains a selection of columns from the last two and a half years that I wrote them and a long essay that was written in 1997.

Although I was glad finally to have the weekly responsibility lifted from my shoulders, it was a great privilege to share my thoughts week after week. In my columns I tried to look beneath the waves of information that wash over us and identify what is truly important.

In the 1980s, my essays dealt with subjects like genetics, which is my area of training, and science in general. The articles in this collection reflect my increasing preoccupation with the growing intensity of the global ecocrisis and its major root causes.

Once one looks at the world through the perspective of environmentalism, the speed and the scale of the looming disaster are crystal clear. The capacity of people to deny or ignore it is at once mystifying and frightening. What will it take to jar people out of their apparent lethargy?

As we approach the end of this millennium, it's important to take stock of where we are and how we got here. Only then will it be possible to chart a course into the future. That's what I hope these essays will help us do. The first part of the book is a critique of what is blinding us to the real crisis, while the remainder looks at specifics from different angles.

Amanda McConnell used her wonderful writing skills to help me spruce up Part I. I thank Victor Vesely for his diligence in seeking authors' permissions to quote from their works. Lisa Hayden assisted me in innumerable ways both large and small. I'm grateful to my family, especially Severn and Sarika, for tolerating my inattentiveness as I was constantly preoccupied with "next week's column."

PART I

TAKING
STOCK

1

FROM SUPERMAN
TO SUPERSPECIES

"What has evolved on our planet is not just life, not just grass or mice or beetles or microbes, but beings with a great intelligence, with a capacity to anticipate the future consequences of present actions, with the ability even to leave their home world and seek out life elsewhere. What a waste it would be if, after four billion years of tortuous biological evolution, the dominant organism on the planet contrived its own annihilation. No species is guaranteed its tenure on this planet. And we've been here for only about a million years, we, the first species that has devised the means for its self-destruction."

— CARL SAGAN, ASTRONOMER AND AUTHOR

FACING THE FACTS

Popular folklore abounds with warnings about the perils of acquiring power or station beyond human capability. Those who exceeded human limitations were, like Icarus, brought down. But where once we aspired to be supermen, we now are transforming ourselves into something even more awesome, a superspecies.

The enormity of the global ecological crisis — from species

> *"The clever are adept at extricating themselves from situations that the wise would have avoided from the outset. Unfortunately, our cleverness as a species has gotten us into a situation from which the same faculty can no longer free us. Cleverness has its limit. Wisdom is now needed."*
>
> — DANIEL HILLEL,
> OUT OF THE EARTH

extinction to overpopulation, deforestation, toxic pollution, and climate change — often overwhelms us, leaving us with a sense of impotence in the face of the scale and the scope of issues. "It's too depressing" is often the reason given for a disinterest in environmental issues. Individuals and groups who raise the environmental alarm are regularly criticized for being "too negative" or dismissed as "prophets of doom and gloom" — another case of messengers being blamed for the news they bear.

As we approach a new millennium, there is an urgent need to establish a new foundation on which to create a sustainable future, a future that satisfies our basic requirements and offers the opportunity for fulfilment and happiness. I don't believe that such a future can be found by simply propping up the current institutions and building on present economic and social assumptions and values, when they are at the core of much of our destructive inclination. The search for alternatives must be inspired by a recognition of the full extent of the crisis humankind now confronts.

Facing up to the facts is often uncomfortable, even frightening, but what makes it bearable and necessary is a belief that there is still time and there are solutions. Numerous examples exist of nature's incredible resilience, regenerative capacity, and generosity, if given a chance. Besides, we have no choice but to try; it is our children's future that is at stake. But to find an alternative, we must face the full dimensions of the crisis and learn to recognize its root causes. As Henry David Thoreau wrote, "there are a thousand hacking at the branches to one who is striking at the root."

For most of our history, we humans have been bound up with the natural world, part of the planet's community of life, depending on our immediate surroundings for every single thing we needed to live and to enjoy our lives. Nature has been our home, our parent, and our god. Today that relationship has been transformed. We are still totally dependent on the Earth and its gifts, as we always will be, but our attitude to the natural world and our impact on it have been altered radically.

The momentum of social change has been building exponentially for centuries, but in the past hundred years several trends have accelerated with lightning speed. Together they have created a species whose impact is now global and explosive. The rate of this transformation has prevented us from developing a new ethic, an appropriate way to act under these novel conditions. We are still occupied, as were our ancestors in Africa's Rift Valley, with acquiring knowledge of and control over our surroundings, collecting material goods for comfort and protection, gathering food, raising our families, sitting by the fire and listening to stories. But the consequences of those age-old activities have been grotesquely amplified by modern technology, a massive growth in human numbers, and a globalized economy that demands ever-increasing consumption.

OUT OF BALANCE

When a species is introduced into a novel environment, it usually soon dies for lack of an appropriate habitat or the conditions necessary for survival. In those rare circumstances where a new arrival does find conditions conducive to growth, such an "exotic" species may run amok in the absence of natural counterbalances. Thus, the introduction of European diseases to aboriginal human populations in the Americas, and the arrival of placental mammals in Australia where previously there had been none, had catastrophic social and ecological effects.

As a species, human beings have had a similar impact. As we have spread and multiplied over the Earth, we have gone from being creatures dependent on planetary forces over which we had little control or effect to being a superspecies with the capacity to alter, whether deliberately or unintentionally, the Earth's biophysical features. This change in human power has occurred so suddenly that, like an exotic species, we have not yet encountered the limiting factors that will bring us back into balance with our surroundings. Or perhaps we are just starting to encounter them, in the devastating and possibly irreversible effect we are having on the planet's ability to support us.

The existence of limits and our hitting them can be seen all around the planet. Globally, almost all of the major food fishes are being harvested at the maximum sustainable level or are already in serious decline. We had a graphic illustration of this when the fabled northern cod, which sustained Europeans and North American migrants for more than five centuries, was declared commercially extinct in 1992. A two-year moratorium on fishing for northern cod has been extended to the present, but there is still little indication that the fish is making a comeback. Thailand, once a major exporter of tropical wood, has been a net importer for several years. The total web of biodiversity on the planet, which is the critical element in providing so many services to all of us, is undergoing an extinction spasm that exceeds the last great episode, which witnessed the disappearance of the dinosaurs.

It is not pleasant to confront the reality of any crisis. But sooner or later, we have no choice or else a situation gets beyond influence. Many believe we have already reached this stage ecologically, although too often those who are describing the problems are urged to "stress the positive" or to "get on with the solutions." This can become an excuse to avoid facing up to the magnitude of the problem. But we can't come up with serious solutions until we do. The good news is that most scientists and experts still believe there is time to change without total devastation of the way we live.

2

THE TRUMPET
OF SCIENCE

*A*t the end of the sixteenth century, Francis Bacon, one of the originators of modern experimental science, recognized that knowledge (*scientia*) is power. He wrote frequently of the "advancement of learning" as if it was a way to invade and conquer nature, stealing her secrets and carrying off treasure. But he had no expectation that science would fracture the comprehensive way human beings had integrated their observations, insights, and speculations and eliminate the sacred. On the contrary, he saw the investigation of nature as a profoundly religious act. He believed that through science, we might glimpse the inner workings of God's creation and worship Him all the more.

But scientists assumed a very different reality. They saw the world as open to the human brain, as ripe for exploration, and as raw material for speculation and enquiry. Armed with powerful new tools, they rapidly accumulated startling insights into nature's laws and regularities. Biologists, for example, discovered myriad living creatures invisible to the naked eye, recognized the cellular basis of all life, and developed rules of classification to introduce order to the bewildering variety of living things. The new sciences, together with the technology they made possible, have taken the path Bacon

> *"The cosmic religion's experience is the strongest and oldest mainspring of scientific research. My religion consists of a humble admiration of the illimitable superior spirit who reveals himself in the slight details we are able to perceive with our frail and feeble human minds. That deeply emotional conviction of the presence of superior reasoning power, which is revealed in the incomprehensible universe, forms my idea of God."*
>
> — ALBERT EINSTEIN,
> PHYSICIST AND
> NOBEL LAUREATE

anticipated, storming the citadel of nature and plundering its precious secrets. But the consequences have been far from what he expected. Instead of inspiring awe for God's creation, the practice of science, after four hundred years, has made us feel like gods ourselves — and the plundering has become a way of life.

The Industrial Revolution accelerated the pace of human social evolution, amplifying our strength and productivity, and creating new kinds of work in factories and mines. Most of all, it enhanced our sense of our own power. If scientific information could be applied through technology, then the biblical injunction to subdue the Earth seemed achievable. While astronomy had relegated us to the cosmic boondocks, and evolution seemed to render us the products of chance, science and technology put us back at the centre as masters of our destiny. Instead of managing our own behaviour, employing ritual, prayer, and taboo to keep the world we belong to intact, as the old-world views prescribed, this time we had real power at our disposal. The Earth's productive systems, upon which we depend, could finally be brought under our control. Forests, fisheries, freshwater systems, insects and the plants they feed on — instead of being subject to the vagaries of weather, natural cycles, and planetary change — could all be planned and regulated by human science to meet human needs. In modern technical jargon, this dream of domination is called *management*. And so far, in spite of all the money and time we have invested in it, it remains a dream.

THE NEWTONIAN REVOLUTION — REDUCTIONISM

The great physicist Isaac Newton likened the universe to an immense clockwork mechanism whose properties were an expression of the totality of its constituent parts. He believed that scientists could focus on fundamental components and properties of the cosmos and gather information that could be added together like the pieces of a jigsaw puzzle to provide a comprehensive picture of the whole. That is the fundamental premise of reductionism, a theory whose goal was the ultimate predictability of the behaviour of whole systems through a complete understanding of their parts.

At the most elementary level of matter, physicists examining parts of atoms created a solar-system-like model with discrete protons and neutrons analogous to the sun at the centre and electrons orbiting the nucleus like the planets. Quantum mechanics destroyed this comforting model by replacing it with an atomic image whose components could be predicted only

"It seems to me certain that it will always be impossible to explain the mind on the basis of neuronal [nerve cell] action within the brain."
— WILDER PENFIELD, BRAIN SURGEON

statistically. That is, a particle's position could be defined only by probability, not by absolute certainty. If at the most elementary level there is no absolute certainty, then the notion that the entire universe could be understood and predicted based on the knowledge of its components becomes absurd.

It could be argued that even if statistical uncertainty and synergism prevent a complete exposition of the universe, scientists can nevertheless continue to search for universal principles that apply within each level of organization, thereby giving power to control within each domain — subatomic, atomic, molecular, cellular, etc. The problem is that despite the impressive scientific gains made in this century, our knowledge base is minuscule compared with all that is yet unknown or not understood. As the ecologist Edward O. Wilson writes:

How many species of organisms are there on earth? We don't know, not even to the nearest order of magnitude. The number could be close to 10 million or as high as 100 million. Large numbers of new species continue to turn up every year. And of those already discovered, over 99 percent are known only by a scientific name, a handful of specimens in a museum, and a few scraps of anatomical description in scientific journals. . . . I recently estimated the number of known species of organisms, including all plants, animals, and microorganisms, to be 1.4 million . . . evolutionary biologists are generally agreed that this estimate is less than a tenth of the number that actually live on earth.

"After the sun's energy is captured by the green plants, it flows through chains of organisms working dendritically, like blood spreading from the arteries into networks of microscopic capillaries. It is in such capillaries, in the life cycles of thousands of individual species, that life's important work is done. Thus nothing in the whole system makes sense until the natural history of the constituent species becomes known. The study of every kind of organism matters, everywhere in the world."

— HOWARD T. ODUM,
ECOLOGIST

It should be pointed out and emphasized that "identification" of a species means merely that the taxonomic position of a specimen has been tracked down and it has been given a name. It does not mean anything is known about its numbers, distribution, basic biology, or interaction with other species — studies that might take a human lifetime to complete *for each and every species.*

The Nobel laureate Richard Feynmen once said that the process of attempting to understand nature is like trying to figure out how to play chess by watching a game while being able to see only two squares at a time. We are a very long way from knowing enough to understand, let alone "manage," anything in nature. We lack even the crudest kind of inventory of all species and their distribution and behaviour to make even educated guesses as to how to manage natural systems, especially ones as complex as forests, wetlands, prairies, oceans, or the atmosphere.

Each detail of nature's secrets revealed by scientific persistence exposes layer upon layer of complexity. A good example is Lyme disease. First reported in the 1970s in Lyme, Connecticut, this condition, which was new to medicine, afflicted its victims with symptoms of arthritis, aches, and loss of energy. It was found to be caused by a spirochaete bacterium, with an incidence that fluctuated on a three- to five-year cycle. The transmitting agent of the disease was quickly found to be the black-legged tick.

Biologists gradually uncovered a complex life cycle in which the tick and spirochaete intermeshed unexpectedly with oak trees. Eastern oak forests periodically produce bumper crops of acorns in a process called *masting*. Mast years are interspersed with two to four years of poor or no acorn production. In the fall of a mast year, the forest floor is covered with acorns, and animals like chipmunks, deer, and mice gorge on them. The white-tailed deer is particularly fond of acorns, and large numbers of the animals are drawn to oak forests they normally avoid.

White-tailed deer provide an ideal target for black-legged ticks and thousands may cover a single victim at a time. On the deer, the ticks feed and mate. Females engorge themselves with blood, growing from the size of a poppy seed to a small jelly bean, then drop onto the forest floor, where the ticks lay their eggs in the leaf litter.

The following summer, the tick eggs hatch into a horde of larvae. But the spirochaete that causes Lyme disease is not transmitted from mother ticks to their eggs, so the larvae are not infective. There is another component. Rodents, including white-footed mice, also love acorns. In a mast year, the mice gather large quantities of acorns and store them for consumption during the winter. As a result, the mice remain well-fed and continue to mate through the winter. In the spring following a mast fall, white-footed mice are abundant and undergo a population explosion that peaks in the summer — at precisely the time the huge population of black-legged tick larvae hatches. The ticks parasitize reptiles and mammals but acquire the spirochaetes only from the white-footed mice. Oak trees, deer, mice, and ticks are all part of the cyclical outbreak of Lyme disease in people.

Our knowledge about the make-up and behaviour of the biophysical elements of the planet is minuscule and fragmentary. Scientists are sometimes criticized because they can't make up their minds about the rate and intensity of the global warming currently under way, for example, but our knowledge base is so primitive that merely tweaking assumptions here or there in computer models of climate change can alter predictions from an impending ice age to catastrophic heating. That is not an indictment of scientists; instead, it indicates gaps in our knowledge large enough for the future of the planet to fall through.

TECHNOLOGY — CRUDE BUT POWERFUL

This lack of even a basic inventory of the biophysical characteristics of the Earth, to say nothing of the underlying principles that govern their interaction, should temper our claim to be able to manage our surroundings. The earliest widespread attempt to manipulate nature for human purposes was in agriculture. Humanity has been incredibly successful at domesticating plants and animals and exploiting heredity by selecting useful stocks. The process transformed human existence from nomadic hunter-gathering to settled farms. But it did have consequences. England and Europe were once covered by a vast ancient forest, the Sahara was covered with lush vegetation, and Lebanon was famous for its forests of cedar. "At the height of the Roman Empire," says Wilson, "North Africa was covered by fertile savannas, and it was possible to travel from Carthage to Alexandria in the shade of trees."

Until very recently, agricultural methods were circumscribed by nature — weather, climate, pests, and the biological complexity of domesticated plants and animals. Modern agribusiness has radically shifted farming from a modest local, small-scale, and diverse enterprise to a massive,

"In human medicine the loss of skin from whatever cause is a serious threat to life: the loss of more than 70 percent of the skin by burning is usually fatal. To denude the Earth of its forests and other natural ecosystems and of its soils is like burning the skin of a human. And we shall soon have destroyed or replaced with inefficient farmlands 70 percent of the Earth's natural land surface."
— JAMES LOVELOCK, ORIGINATOR, GAIA HYPOTHESIS

uniform, technologically driven activity. Often a single strain of plant is sown over large tracts of land and then water, nutrients, and pests are monitored and controlled. By creating such a *simplified* system, in which all of the major components are known, agricultural scientists perpetrate an illusion of control. Inevitably, however, reality intrudes when nature breaks through with storms, cold spells, heat waves, diseases, or parasites, but now havoc breaks out on a grand scale. Simplification ends in collapse because diversity and interdependence are the critical survival mechanisms in any natural system on Earth.

Agricultural management provides a model often used to control populations of wild organisms. Thus industrial forestry classifies the complex community of organisms that make up an ancient forest as "wild," while the drastically simplified tree plantations resulting from massive clearcutting, tree planting, fertilizing, and pesticide spraying, are called "normal" forests. This perspective leads to old-growth forests being denigrated as "decadent" and an ancient tree as "overmature"; commercially useful trees are reduced to "stems," while non-useful trees are "weeds." It also leads to plantations of trees that are vulnerable to disease and insect attack and to poisoned waterways, eroded soil, and massive loss of other life forms — in other words, to collapse. According to Chris Maser, a forester in Oregon:

> Liquidating old-growth forests is not forestry; it is simply spending our inheritance. Nor is planting a monoculture forestry; it is simply plantation management and plantation management is all we are currently practising. . . . Restoration forestry is the only true forestry. We use the forest — remove products and nutrients

"Under the philosophy that now seems to guide our destinies, nothing must get in the way of the man with the spray gun. The incidental victims of his crusade against insects count as if nothing; if robins, pheasants, raccoons, cats, or even livestock happen to inhabit the same bit of earth as the target insects and to be hit by the rain of insect-killing poisons no one must protest."
— RACHEL CARSON, BIOLOGIST AND AUTHOR

— and then we restore its vitality, its sustainability, so that we can remove more products in time without impairing the forest's ability to function. . . . Anything else is not forestry.

SALMON — A CASE STUDY OF THE HAZARDS OF "MANAGEMENT"

Our lack of detailed knowledge and our deliberate simplifications of wild populations have turned out to be a terrible hazard in many different areas. For example, in salmon hatcheries on the Pacific Coast of British Columbia, eggs fertilized with milt in tanks are reared to fingerling size and released by the millions. Early in the program on the river, tens of millions of the prized sockeye salmon were incubated and released at a place in the river where their run to the ocean would be shortened. Years after the program began, biologists discovered that, unlike other species of salmon, sockeye fry move to lakes, where they spend a year before going to sea. Furthermore, hatcheries may provide no more than an illusion of increased productivity: as the hatcheries enhance the total numbers with fingerlings created from selected eggs and the sperm of fish from a major river, the natural populations that are genetically programmed to return to small tributaries are swamped out, thereby reducing the gene-pool diversity critical for maintaining healthy runs.

From the modern human economic perspective, the fabulous numbers of Pacific salmon that spawn and die are a "waste" because more adults return to spawn than are necessary to lay the number of eggs that will survive. If there is an "excess," then "harvesting" up to 80 percent of a run is rationalized as acceptable to maintain the "stock." But once again this way of looking at salmon grotesquely oversimplifies their "uses." Scientists have only recently begun to realize that the returning salmon do more than deposit eggs: after death, their carcasses provide a significant portion of the nutrients required by the surrounding scavengers — bear, wolf, seal, eagle, and raven — as well as by the baby salmon themselves.

Science has given us a glimpse of a world that is endlessly complex and full; in studying it, our chief lesson is how much more there is to study. We're like mountain climbers who scale the first ridge, only to see range after range of rugged peaks sweeping to the shadowy horizon. Undaunted, we have set out to conquer the mountains, doing what we are uniquely equipped to do — make sense out of chaos, tease meaning out of confusion. But the order we end up imposing is extremely limited and narrowly human. Using the inadequate knowledge base of our science, and viewing the world through the distorting lenses of our own desires, we try to force nature to conform and produce according to our rules. We act as though the natural world belongs to us, instead of remembering where we belong — like all other living things on Earth.

> "If enough species are extinguished, will the ecosystems collapse, and will the extinction of most other species follow soon afterward? The only answer anyone can give is: possibly. By the time we find out, however, it might be too late. One planet, one experiment."
>
> — EDWARD O. WILSON, THE DIVERSITY OF LIFE

TECHNOLOGY'S HIDDEN COSTS

Scientific knowledge is fragmented into disconnected bits and pieces that provide little insight into how they fit together and behave as a whole. Nevertheless, a fragment may be exploited to design powerful technologies. This harnessing of scientific knowledge can be impressive, especially in warfare and medicine. Thus the development of technologies such as weapons, airplanes, and computers, antibiotics, organ transplants, and oral contraceptives has been a stunning achievement in this century. Difficulties arise from the scale and speed of adoption and the way innovations are used.

Technologies are developed to perform a very specific function and usually provide immediate and obvious benefits. However, given our underlying ignorance of the historical, economic, social, and ecological context within which they will be applied, we cannot anticipate the other consequences of innovations. The atomic bomb is a case in point. The rationale for its development in the United States was defensive: the threat from Germany's first-rate physics community had to be countered. Once the Allies had the bomb, a new argument was made to put this unmatched power to use: it would accelerate the end of the war, thus avoiding a prolonged and costly invasion of Japan and saving countless lives on both sides. But at the time the bombs were dropped, no one had any idea of the potential wider consequences because radioactive fallout, disabling electromagnetic pulses, and nuclear winter were all discovered after 1945.

In the same way, antibiotics were remarkably effective when they were first employed. But the pharmaceutical industry saw such opportunities for profit in these new wonder drugs that they began to be prescribed inappropriately and excessively, even being put to work in animal feed as growth promoters. It was only decades after the widespread use of antibiotics began that microbiologists discovered multiple-drug resistance factors that can be exchanged between different species of bacteria. Now new antibiotics soon become ineffective, as resistant mutations develop and spread.

As we approach a new millennium, futurists pronounce the possibilities of limitless energy from nuclear fusion, computers that can think, cloning, and genetically engineered life forms. From the development of the internal-combustion engine to the synthesis of the chlorofluorocarbon (CFC) molecule, the Earth has paid a great price to teach us that every technology, no matter how beneficial, has costs *and many of those costs cannot be anticipated beforehand*. Unfortunately, learning that lesson does not seem to have made us any wiser in the ways we introduce and regulate new technologies today.

3

Exponential Growth
and the Impact
of Population

$\mathcal{T}$he math is inescapable; anything growing steadily at a constant rate will double in size. The process is called *exponential growth*, and no matter what it is that is growing — the annual output of garbage, the gross domestic product (GDP), the energy consumed per capita, or growth in city populations — the doubling time is predictable.

TABLE 1
EXPONENTIAL DOUBLING TIMES

Percent Increase/Year	Doubling Time in Years
1.0	70.0
2.0	35.0
3.0	23.3
4.0	17.5
n	$70/n$

In the initial stages of exponential growth, doubling is hardly noticeable because the numbers are small. If you begin cutting trees in a forest, first cutting one tree a year and doubling the number cut each year, even after six years you still only cut 64 trees. In the same way, at the start of the AIDS outbreak in the early '80s, doubling time was frighteningly short, but even now the total percentage of affected people remains relatively small. But at some point, when hundreds of thousands are infected, the numbers will take off with further doublings.

In the past century, many different factors have affected the rate at which the planet's human population increases — most of them the consequences of science and technology. Public-health measures, improved food supplies, advanced medical care, better transportation, and rapid communication have all helped reduce infant mortality and increase the average human life span. After millennia of a slow but steady rise in human numbers, this century ushered in an unprecedented period of spectacular growth. Viewed through the lens of our evolutionary history, the change in human numbers is imperceptible over 99 percent of our existence. Only in the last few thousand years do we see an inflection, and in the last pencil width of time, the numbers leap straight off the page.

Like Rachel Carson before him, Paul Ehrlich became a controversial prophet when he issued one of the first widely heard warnings about population pressures with his famous book *The Population Bomb,* written in 1968. Cataclysmic growth, he pointed out, can overwhelm all of the technological progress in agriculture and medicine by the sheer weight of the numbers. The demand for space, land, water, forests, and resources will soon exceed the Earth's capacity to provide. His predictions raised an enormous controversy, as rich and poor nations strongly disagreed on whether consumption or population were the most destructive factors. As well, debates raged over birth control and abortion as methods to bring down population growth. All the while, human numbers and misery continued to grow rapidly.

WORLD SCIENTISTS WARN OF POPULATION'S DANGER

In October 1993, eminent scientists from around the world gathered in New Delhi, India, and issued a terrifying statement:

> If current predictions of population growth prove accurate and patterns of human activity on the planet remain unchanged,

science and technology may not be able to prevent irreversible degradation of the natural environment and continued poverty for much of the world.

In February 1994, fifty-eight of the world's scientific academies, representing their leading scientists in the respective countries or regions, simultaneously released a statement on population. Signatories included academies from all the industrialized nations (except Japan) and academies from Russia, India, China, and Brazil, as well as federations of Caribbean, Asian, and Third World scientists. The facts are clear:

> It took hundreds of thousands of years for our species to reach a population level of 10 million, only 10,000 years ago. This number grew to 100 million people about 2,000 years ago and to 2.5 billion by 1950. Within less than the span of a single lifetime, it has more than doubled to 5.5 billion in 1993. . . . We face the prospect of a further doubling of the population within the next half century.

Even with massive and immediate reductions in fertility rates, our numbers will continue to rise. Barring major epidemics, wars, or starvation, scientists calculate that if the current worldwide average of 3.3 children per female is reduced to the "replacement level" of 2.1 within sixty years, world population will level off at 11 billion by 2100. If an average of 1.7 is reached early in the next century, population will still rise to 7.8 billion by the mid-twenty-first century and then begin to decline slowly. If fertility cannot be brought lower than 2.5 children per woman, human numbers will reach 19 billion by 2100 and 28 billion by 2150.

The impact of humanity is not simply a reflection of numbers; the other crucial factors are per capita consumption of the planet's resources and our technological capacity to extract more. As human demands extend beyond the primary requirements of adequate diet, clothing, and shelter to the excesses of entertainment, consumer goods, recreational shopping, and the global economy, our species' impact is amplified many times. The statement of the world's scientific academies warns that rising human numbers and rising rates of consumption are together causing ecological changes that may ultimately be irreversible, including "loss of biodiversity, increasing greenhouse gases emissions, increasing deforestation worldwide, stratospheric ozone depletion, acid rain, loss of topsoil and shortages of water, food and fuel-wood in many parts of the world."

IPAT — INCLUDING GROWTH AND CONSUMPTION

Although population increases in developing nations create massive environmental destruction and vast human misery, the industrialized nations of the North have a far greater impact on the Earth. Ehrlich has developed an equation to explain the total impact of our species on the planet. The extent of the impact (I) is affected by our number (P), affluence or consumption (A), and the technology we possess (T). The equation is $I = P \times A \times T$, or IPAT. Since they possess 85 percent of the world's income, but only 23 percent of its population, the wealthy countries have an environmental impact that extends far beyond their own borders. It is their powerful technology that has emptied the planet's oceans of fish, felled its tropical forests, and altered the chemical constituents of the global atmosphere. A country like Canada, the second-largest nation on Earth, has a population of only 30 million, but its high consumptive culture means the average Canadian consumes sixteen to twenty times as much as the average Indian or Chinese and eighty to one hundred times the average Bangladeshi or Somalian. Canadians, then, have the global ecological impact of up to 600 million Chinese or 3 billion Somalians, while Americans have an effect that is at least ten times greater. We in the rich countries cannot, therefore, avoid responsibility merely by blaming the poor countries for their rapidly growing populations.

There is a second way that the rich countries affect the planet. Our obvious wealth and continuing growth encourages the developing nations to aspire to the same goals. Taken together, two countries — India and China — have populations twice the size of the entire

North. If they continue to try to enter the twenty-first century following the same route as the industrialized nations, using nineteenth-century technology like coal-burning power plants to generate electricity, the repercussions for the rest of the world will be catastrophic. The world academies state:

> In the last decade food production from both land and sea has declined relative to population growth. The area of agricultural land has shrunk. . . . The availability of water is already a constraint in some countries. These are warnings that the earth is finite and that natural systems are being pushed ever closer to their limits.

Leading scientists believe the quality of life can be improved for everyone alive today, and for their descendants, while still maintaining the environment. But it will require an immediate and all-out mobilization of resources, personnel, and finances to meet the challenge. They warn that zero population growth globally must be achieved within the next generation's lifetime. Such a rapid and massive reduction in fertility rates cannot be accomplished by simply distributing contraceptives. There must be a broad strategy for raising the quality of human life, the key to which is improving the social and economic status of women. The focus must be on reduction and elimination of gender-based inequalities in sexual, social, and economic matters; provision of convenient family-planning and other reproductive-health services; and meeting basic needs for clean water, sanitation, accessible health care, and education.

The scientists point out that the ability of governments to alter population growth appears to be limited by economic resources and the will to do something. But the inexorable growth in population and its inevitable ecological impact will destabilize the earth's human support systems. In this new territory of change, all bets are off because we have no solid basis for maintaining any human activity without a rich environment.

No Time to Waste

The challenge, according to the world scientists, is for all nations to use resources more efficiently, to protect the environment more scrupulously, and to reduce frivolous and wasteful consumption.

And here the news is encouraging. Air, water, and soil have been used as if they are virtually limitless or endlessly self-replenishing resources, and so they have not been properly accounted for in the economy. Similarly, the exploitation of fossil fuels has been subsidized through exploration incentives and the public payment to the build the infrastructure for automobiles, such as roads, police and ambulances, and so on. Thus many of the social and ecological costs of using fossil fuels are not reflected in their real price. This has meant that the efficient use of materials and energy has not been a high priority. We already know that a toll placed on each bag of garbage is a strong incentive to waste less. So when efficiency becomes a driving force to reduce waste output and energy and materials used through the entire life of a product or process, there are vast savings to be made. Indeed, von Weizsäcker et al. suggest in their book *Factor Four: Doubling Wealth — Halving Resource Use* that the economy could be quadrupled on half the current energy and resource use. In addition to the immediate environmental and economic benefits of better use of non-renewable resources in industrialized countries, it frees up more for use by the developing nations.

Industrialized countries are the major consumers of energy and materials, and they also produce the bulk of the waste products. Scientists believe the wealthy nations must not only increase efficiency, but also provide funding and technical expertise so that developing nations can leap-frog over the polluting, destructive technologies to the most advanced, efficient technologies available. Scientists urge governments to incorporate an environmental ethic into all legislation, economic planning, and priority setting, and to encourage greater responsibility in the private and public sectors. They continue:

> As scientists . . . it is our collective judgment that continuing population growth poses a great risk to humanity. It is not

prudent to rely on science and technology alone to solve problems created by rapid population growth, wasteful resource consumption and poverty. . . . Science and technology can only provide tools and blueprints for action and social change.

The document of the world academies of science echoes an earlier document, entitled "World Scientists' Warning to Humanity," that had urgently called for a global initiative on population and sustainable development in 1992. The world academies of science report stated:

We urge [governments and international decision-makers] to take incisive action now and to adopt an integrated policy on population and sustainable development on a global scale. With each year's delay the problems become more acute. Let 1994 be remembered as the year when the people of the world decided to act together for the benefit of future generations.

But years have passed since 1994. On September 30, 1997, 98 out of 171 living Nobel prize winners were signatories to a document called "World Scientists' Call for Action at Kyoto" that was presented to President Clinton. The scientists warned that at the global conference on climate to be held in Kyoto, "there is only one responsible choice: act now." The final agreement in Kyoto to limit greenhouse gas emission was so weak and full of loopholes that few believe it will reduce greenhouse gas output.

Numerous, ubiquitous, and burdened with an insatiable appetite, human beings have become a new force on Earth. Armed with the formidable tools of science and technology, we now have the capacity to eliminate whole ecosystems almost overnight. The one thing we seem incapable of is imposing limits on ourselves.

THE ECONOMIC GROWTH IMPERATIVE

Exponential doubling also characterizes the global economy. Since the end of the Second World War, the global economy has undergone a spectacular expansion, but its benefits have not been evenly distributed. Today the 1.2 billion people in the industrialized nations consume most of the planet's resources, create the bulk of its toxic waste, and possess more than 82 percent of its wealth. Claims that economic growth is necessary so that wealth can "trickle down" to those who need it have been revealed as a grotesque scam, both nationally and internationally.

TABLE 2
GLOBAL INCOME DISTRIBUTION, 1960–1989
SHARE OF GLOBAL INCOME

Year	Richest 20%	Poorest 20%	Ratio of richest/poorest
1960	70.2	2.3	30 to 1
1970	73.9	2.3	32 to 1
1980	76.3	1.7	45 to 1
1989	82.7	1.4	59 to 1

Source: UNESCO, *Sources 58, May 1994*

Are we better off now that we've become professional consumers, driving economic growth endlessly ahead of us and possessed of all the disposables we are ever likely to want? It depends what you consider "better." Even within the industrialized nations, wealth is distributed unevenly. The United States best exemplifies the full-fledged consumer society. How do its citizens measure up to their national ideals? The nation that values youth and thinness is the most obese in the world. The place where the dollar rules has more disparity between rich and poor than any other industrialized nation. That peaceful, democratic country has a unique reputation for violence. And more people per capita are imprisoned in the land of liberty than in any other industrialized country. Longer working hours, higher levels of stress, failing families, drug addiction, children at risk — these may be manifestations of a pathology of consumerism. Let loose in the world's biggest store, people suffer from various ills: the plague of having too much, the frustration of unsatisfactory ownership, the rage and jealousy of those who cannot afford the merchandise.

DOES ECONOMIC GROWTH MAKE EARTH SENSE?

Nevertheless, governments of all countries continue to hold up economic growth as the key to their well-being. Nations such as India and China are determined to achieve our level of affluence — a sixteen- to twentyfold increase in consumption. Imagine those populations with the same per capita car ownership as the United States; the ecological consequences would be catastrophic. Yet why should they set their sights lower than we do?

When increasing consumption is part of our definition of progress, and ownership of objects is perceived to be the chief path to happiness, no nation can ever call a halt, or contemplate the revolutionary thought, "We've got enough. Let's remain here, at this level, in balance with the world we inhabit."

Many have recognized that increased consumption is not the key to happiness or satisfaction. Way back at the beginning of the American experiment in democracy, one of the authors of the Constitution, Benjamin Franklin, said:

> Money never made a man happy yet, nor will it. There is nothing in its nature to produce happiness. The more a man has, the more he wants. Instead of filling a vacuum, it makes one.

The contemporary religious historian Robert Bellah wrote with a similar sentiment:

> That happiness is to be attained through limitless material acquisition is denied by every religion and philosophy known to humankind, but is preached incessantly by every American television set.

4

FROM RURAL CREATURE TO CITY DWELLER

*E*xponential growth has characterized another remarkable change in this century — the way most of humanity lives. At the turn of the century, more than 95 percent of all people on Earth lived in rural, village communities. At that time, only sixteen cities contained a million or more people and none had more than 7 million. Most large cities then were in industrialized countries.

TABLE 3
WORLD'S LARGEST CITIES IN 1900

City	Population	City	Population
London	6,480,000	Birmingham	1,248,000
New York	4,242,000	Moscow	1,120,000
Paris	3,330,000	Beijing	1,100,000
Berlin	2,707,000	Calcutta	1,085,000
Chicago	1,717,000	Boston	1,075,000
Vienna	1,698,000	Glasgow	1,015,000
Tokyo	1,497,000	Osaka	970,000
St. Petersburg	1,439,000	Liverpool	940,000
Manchester	1,435,000	Constantinople	900,000
Philadelphia	1,418,000	Hamburg	895,000

City	Population	City	Population
Buenos Aires	806,000	Ruhr	766,000
Budapest	785,000	Rio de Janeiro	744,000
Bombay	780,000		

Today, Canada has three cities with more than a million people, while Australia has five. There are at least 400 cities of a million or more globally, and the fourteen largest all have more than 10 million inhabitants.

TABLE 4
WORLD'S LARGEST CITIES

City	1994 Population	2015 Population (Projected)
Tokyo	26,518,000	28,700,000
New York	16,271,000	17,600,000
Sao Paulo	16,110,000	20,800,000
Mexico City	15,525,000	18,800,000
Shanghai	14,709,000	23,400,000
Bombay	14,496,000	27,400,000
Los Angeles	12,232,000	14,300,000
Beijing	12,030,000	19,400,000
Calcutta	11,485,000	17,600,000
Seoul	11,451,000	13,100,000
Jakarta	11,017,000	21,200,000
Buenos Aires	10,914,000	12,400,000
Osaka	10,585,000	10,600,000
Tianjin	10,376,000	17,000,000
Rio de Janeiro	9,817,000	11,600,000

Over half of all humanity now lives in cities, and since most people in the industrialized nations are already urbanites it is in the developing countries where the greatest growth of cities is occurring. China alone plans to build 200 brand new cities for a million or more inhabitants within the next fifteen years.

Efficiencies of scale and distance can be achieved through urban living. Multiple-dwelling units have a smaller outside surface-to-volume ratio, so compared to free-standing single homes, the average heat loss per unit is less. When people live closer to where they work, play, and shop, cheaper, convenient rapid transit and walking can compete with automobiles as a means of movement. However, cities have evolved in a helter-skelter fashion, with little attention paid to such environmental issues as toxic waste, garbage, and transportation, while the car has been excessively served. Thus as cities have grown, they have absorbed resources from vast distances while returning waste and toxic chemicals.

CUTTING THE NATURE CONNECTION

But the most destructive aspect of most modern cities is the profound schism they create between human beings and nature. In a human-created environment, surrounded mainly by fellow human beings and a few animal and plant species of our choice, we feel we have escaped the limits of nature. Weather and climate impinge on our lives with far less immediacy. Food comes in packages, disguised from its origins in the soil and cleansed of telltale biological signs of blood, feathers, and scales. The source of our water and energy and the destination of our garbage and our sewage become distant and obscured. We forget that as biological beings, we are as dependent on clean air, water, soil, and biodiversity as any other creature. Cut off from the sources and the consequences of the way we live, we imagine a world under our control and will risk or sacrifice almost anything to make sure our way of life is maintained. As cities continue to grow around the world, policy decisions will reflect more and more the illusory urban bubble that we believe is reality.

In cities we are far less free to act on our own impulses. We have to conform to the demands of our surroundings lest they become chaotic. Thus we become domesticates of our own creations, our technology, docilely waiting for traffic lights to change, responding to ringing telephones and sirens, and tailoring our behaviour to conform to the specific demands and limitations of computers. As John Livingston says in his book *Rogue Primate: An Exploration of Human Domestication*:

All domesticated animals depend for their day-to-day survival upon their owners. . . . The human domesticate has become equally dependent, not upon a proprietor, but upon storable, retrievable, transmissible technique. Technology provides us with everything we require. Knowledge of how-to-do-it sustains us utterly. And since none of us knows how to do *everything*, we are further dependent upon the expertise of countless others to provide even the most basic of daily necessities. Like that of a race horse or a Pekinese, our dependence upon agents external to ourselves is total. Without knowledge of how-to-do-it, or access to someone else who does know how, we are irretrievably helpless.

The inexorable result of exponential growth is that at some point, the numbers after each doubling become enormous while the social, economic, and ecological consequences increase even more. Humanity has reached that point in its evolution. The speed with which we have achieved global dominance in numbers, technological prowess, consumption, and urbanization has been so sudden and vast that we have created novel terrain for which there is little precedent to help us navigate the future. To compound the difficulties, we have become increasingly driven by economic, political, and social demands that are too short-sighted to get us onto a path of genuine sustainability. By stepping back, we acquire a broader and longer perspective within which to assess this unique moment in time.

5

CONSUMPTION

$\mathcal{U}$nderlying the destructive way resources are being exploited is a mind-set that can be traced to the Age of Exploration and Discovery. Since Christopher Columbus's "discovery" of the New World, European societies have colonized much of the rest of the planet. Like most newcomers, they lacked respect for what they found: they were generally unable to recognize the indigenous wisdom within the societies they conquered, or to appreciate the elegance and complexity of the ecosystems they encountered. In Africa, North America, South America, Australia, and New Zealand, indigenous people were eliminated, enslaved, or oppressed while the newcomers ransacked their new territories, destroyed or sent home the treasures they encountered, and worked to transform an alien terrain into the landscape of home.

CONSUMPTION AND HABITAT PRESERVATION

As human numbers and consumption rise, we require more space in which to live and from which to extract the food and products that we demand. As we invade areas that were once unoccupied and clear wild forests, dam watersheds, drain wetlands, and cultivate new soils, we take over space that was once habitat for other creatures. Some of our largest, most charismatic species, like grizzly bears, bison, whales, cheetahs, and tigers, are severely impacted because they can no longer range across the vast expanses of terrain they evolved with. Our approach tends to be to set aside areas of wilderness as parks or reserves within which wildlife is presumed safe. But many wild animals require vast areas encompassing diverse and contiguous ecosystems, which are accessible only in exceptionally large parks. Most animals and plants cannot change their genetically programmed behaviour and needs to adapt to human-created conditions, so they gradually diminish in numbers or disappear altogether.

When the natural world is seen as a source of "resources" or "wealth," it becomes an aggregate of commodities — a collection of objects and materials that can be removed, bought and sold, possessed. The process breaks apart the complex relationships of nature; it simplifies them into a conduit for feeding human appetites. Population growth and increased technological power thus put pressure on both the planet's land base and the habitat of wild plants and animals. We have assumed the planet is ours for the taking, and we dole out small pieces of it as parks and reserves for wildlife. In the process, we chop what should be continuous habitat for animals and plants into minute fenced-off islands of wilderness. Extinction usually follows.

CONSUMPTION AS A DELIBERATE GOAL

Our use of resources, from oil, gas, wood, and minerals to air and water, has escalated dramatically in this century. Both individually and collectively in cities and nations, the consumptive demand has magnified our impact on the planet. But this rise in consumption has also been an integral part of the economy. It wasn't always this way. As early as 1907, the economist Simon Nelson Patten was severely criticized for his prescient warning of a change that was taking place: "The new morality does not consist in saving but in expanding consumption."

Consumption, a word that once meant to waste away under the effects of disease, now affects the planet as a central part of our economic system. What makes it insidious is that our own identities have become tied up in the need to have more. As Paul Wachtel says in *The Poverty of Affluence*, "Having more and newer things each year has become not just something we want but something we need. The idea of more, of ever increasing wealth, has become the center of our identity and our security, and we are caught up by it as the addict by his drugs."

I am often told, "Well, it's human nature to want more. You can't buck that." It's true that when members of the Kayapo tribe from the Amazon visited me in Vancouver, they saw a lot of things they wanted. If they didn't find anything they wanted, it would be a terrible indictment of a total emptiness of the way we live. But the Kayapo lived deep in the Amazon forest in complete self-sufficiency. In contrast, our consumption is far beyond anything necessary for survival, and society's hyperconsumption is driven by billions of dollars spent annually to make us want things. Bill Gates spent more than one billion dollars in advertising alone for the product Windows95.

> *"The purchase of a new product, especially a 'big ticket' item such as a car or computer, typically produces an immediate surge of pleasure and achievement, and often confers status and recognition upon the owner. Yet as the novelty wears off, the emptiness threatens to return. The standard consumer solution is to focus on the next promising purchase."*
> — ALLEN D. KANNER AND MARY E. GOMES, "THE ALL-CONSUMING SELF"

It is instructive to remember that the Great Depression of the 1930s came to an end because the Second World War provided a massive economic jolt. American industrial might was fanned to white heat to support the war effort, but as victory began to loom the business community worried about how to keep the economic boom going. The solution was *consumption*. Shortly after the Second World War, the retailing analyst Victor Lebow declared:

> Our enormously productive economy . . . demands that we make consumption our way of life, that we convert the buying and use of goods into rituals, that we seek our spiritual satisfaction, our ego satisfaction, in consumption. . . . We need things consumed,

burned up, worn out, replaced, and discarded at an ever-increasing rate.

By 1953 the chairman of President Eisenhower's Council of Economic Advisors would state that the American economy's "ultimate purpose" was "to produce more consumer goods."

But there's a problem. When products are made to be durable, industry will eventually saturate the market. Solutions such as planned obsolescence and constantly expanding new markets to the Third World, elders, yuppies, children, ethnics, and so on have worked well to overcome this defect, at least temporarily. Coca-Cola president Donald R. Keough expressed a religious attitude to market opportunity: "When I think of Indonesia — a country on the equator with 180 million people, a median age of 18, and with a Moslem ban on alcohol — I feel I know what heaven looks like." The ultimate innovation to ensure an endless market has been *disposability*. Citing convenience or hygiene to justify products that are used once and thrown away, industry creates an endless market for that product.

OUR ROLE AS CONSUMERS

There is a plethora of ways that each of us may be viewed — by gender, nationality, relationship to others, skills, education, religion, hobbies, hopes, activities, and so on. But today we are increasingly looked on by governments and business in one way — as *consumers*. When a recession strikes, government analysts often blame the public for "lack of confidence" and call for programs designed to stimulate the economy by encouraging people to spend more. The rationale for the demand for constant growth in consumption and the economy is that growth increases wealth which, through the market system, satisfies all human needs. The consumer-driven way of life is a far cry from the lessons our grandparents acquired about the virtues of thrift, and the ecological and social consequences of profligate consumption are devastating.

But is this the key to personal happiness? Try this visualization exercise. Imagine you have reached the end of your life. On your deathbed, you reflect on the things that really mattered, that brought happiness, pleasure, and fulfilment. Would they really be those once sought-after brand-name items like cars, TV sets, clothes, or even a big home? Somehow, thought of this way, those "things," that "stuff," fade into insignificance. Because what really matters in the end are human relationships — family, friends, neighbours, community — and activities that fulfil us, like gardening, hobbies, volunteering, and reading. They add richness to our lives far beyond the "necessities" that we all need money to buy.

6

THE INFORMATION REVOLUTION

We are able to confront and resolve our problems, we believe, if we are provided with enough information to choose rationally from a number of options. That is the basic assumption of participants in a democracy, or in what is popularly referred to as civil society, in which ordinary citizens drive social agendas. The problem today is that information no longer serves the function of clarifying choice and permitting better informed decisions.

Information is touted as the wave of the future by media pundits, government leaders, businesspeople, and educators. And certainly it will play a critical role in future economic growth, jobs, and leisure. Furthermore, as global ecological problems, such as global warming, species extinction, toxic pollution, and topsoil degradation, become more acute, solid information will be needed to make sense of them and find real solutions. But the highly hyped explosion in information actually overwhelms us, and renders us even less able to apply common sense.

Each of us now has access to more information than at any other time in human history: it thunders at us from every direction. But the flood of information monkey-wrenches the average person's ability to assess it. For example, information these days tends to be validated merely because it exists. Often, after describing an astonishing phenomenon such as the Bermuda Triangle, a UFO, or spontaneous combustion, the storyteller will punctuate the account by stating "I saw it on TV," or "I read it somewhere," as if that's sufficient authority to validate its repetition as fact.

People frequently stop me on the street to congratulate me for doing a program on a topic like breast cancer or a new technology. "But we've never covered that topic," I often have to reply, only to hear, in an embarrassed stammer, "Oh, maybe it was on *Oprah* or *Nova*."

Most of us are now informed primarily through television or newspapers, and we assume that they present us with the way things are. But the media do not so much reflect reality as *create* it. The priorities of media owners are reflected in what is considered newsworthy in the first place. Thus the O. J. Simpson trial or President Clinton's alleged sexual behaviour is inordinately reportable while the World Scientists' Warning to Humanity, which was signed by more than half of all Nobel prize winners and suggested we may have as little as ten years to avoid a global catastrophe, is not. When newspaper reporters attend a public lecture, they often must squeeze an hour-long speech into six inches of a newspaper column. They cannot possibly capture the thrust of the entire speech. Instead, they search for a "hook" from which to hang the report: often it is a throwaway line or some irrelevance or irreverence tossed in to hold audience interest. But the bait also catches the reporter's interest, and the goal in reportage is numbers, not veracity.

Again, I can give an example from personal experience. Back in the 1960s, I gave a public lecture for an hour and a half on genetics. During the question-and-answer period, someone asked what I thought about cloning. I answered the question, then flippantly threw in the aside that I hoped the prime minister wasn't contemplating it. The next day, the newspaper headline announced "Suzuki Warns PM: 'Don't Clone Yourself!'" even though I hadn't mentioned cloning at all during the main body of my speech.

VIRTUAL REALITY

Does television do the job of reporting any better? Surely documentary programming presents the reality of the world that is covered. After all, pictures never lie. Of course, that cliché is no longer true, as the line between photographs and computer-generated images is getting harder to discern. Imagine this scene from a nature documentary: *Deep in the heart of the Amazon rainforest, a troupe of howler monkeys swings through the treetops, 100 feet from the ground, hooting like a football crowd as it passes. A sloth hanging from a lower branch is shaken from its lethargy and starts to climb slowly down the great buttressed trunk. Out of the shadowy recesses of the forest two giant butterflies appear, huge, iridescent blue wings flapping in synchrony as they circle a brilliant shaft of sunlight.* The scene is meticulously accurate: all these animals live in that region of the Amazon; they are in the place they belong, doing what they normally do. But the documentary form has its own way of recreating reality. This two-minute scene is selected from hours of footage that took days or even weeks to shoot. The magic of editing creates a flurry of activity in the forest, puts together a crowd of creatures in a place that in reality is mostly silent and still.

As the flow of information continues to increase, newspapers compete for our attention by compressing reports into single paragraphs. Radio and television stories chop "interviews" up into sound-bites, leaving a personality or politician just time to say, "I don't agree," or "there is no cause for alarm." News reports may range from fifteen to forty seconds in length, while an "in-depth report" might last for two whole minutes.

The overabundance of information is reflected in the tidal wave of brief fragments coming at us. According to Theodore Roszak, writing in *The Cult of Information: The Folklore of Computers and the True Art of Thinking*, a single weekday edition of the *New York Times* newspaper contains more information than the average person in seventeenth-century England would have encountered in an entire lifetime. The amazing eruption of the information industry is reflected in the fact that computer processing speed has doubled every two years for the past thirty! As a consequence, information has become compressed. So between 1965 and 1995, the average length of a TV commercial shrank from 53.1 to 25.4 seconds, while the average news sound-bite was reduced from 42.3 to 8.3 seconds! At the same time, according to *TV Dimensions '95* and *Magazine Dimensions '95*, the number of ads squeezed into a minute went from 1.1 to 2.4.

I was confronted with a striking confirmation of the compression of information in 1992 when we were preparing a program on the Earth Summit being held in Rio. By then, *The Nature of Things* had been an hour-long program for thirteen years. In the archives, I looked up the report done in 1972 on the UN conference on the environment held in Stockholm. The program was still a half-hour long back then, and to my amazement it contained three- and four-minute interviews with Paul Ehrlich and Margaret Mead. Today we never put on an interview longer than thirty to forty seconds. And it was clear my expectations and interest span had changed, because I found the 1972 interviews slow.

Thus, the shorter, punchier accounts we are now getting are stripped of any kind of historical or contextual material that might make the news event more understandable in a larger sense. Each night a stream of unrelated stories gives us a glimpse of a fractured, puzzling, often frightening universe. There are battles being fought by mysterious factions in countries whose past is a blank. Violence and misfortune are the normal state of affairs, forest fires rage, trains crash, and deficits rise. Studies are reported on subjects we have never thought about, and politicians announce decisions without rhyme or reason. Modern life exists in a confusing, chaotic world that is much as it must have seemed before people were formally educated.

THE HIDDEN MESSAGES

The media are fascinated by the newest member of their group, the information superhighway, marvelling at its apparently limitless potential. Cyberspace, virtual reality, the World Wide Web, 500 channels of interactive television — what a brave new world this is to be. U.S. vice-president Al Gore, a committed environmentalist, is also a strong supporter of the limitless benefits of the information super-highway.

But beneath the hype and techno-adulation, there are troubling questions. Theodore Roszak's book *The Cult of Information* raised some of them:

> For the information theorist, it does not matter whether we are transmitting a judgment, a shallow cliché, a deep teaching, a sublime truth, or a nasty obscenity. All are information. . . . Depth, originality, excellence, which have always been factors in the evaluation of knowledge, have somewhere been lost in the fast, futurological shuffle. . . . [T]his is a liability that dogs every effort to inflate the cultural value of information. . . . We begin to pay more attention to "economic indicators" than to assumptions about work, wealth and well-being which underlie economic policy. . . . The hard focus on information that the computer encourages must in time have the effect of crowding out new ideas, which are the intellectual source that generates facts.

Here is another take on the so-called benefits of information and the computer revolution from Allen D. Kanner and Mary E. Gomes, authors of "The All-Consuming Self":

> Priority is being given to the technology necessary for around the clock interactive shopping. Television sets are being transformed into electronic mail catalogues. The goal is to allow viewers to buy anything in the world, any time of day and night, without ever leaving their living rooms.

Clifford Stöll, author of *Silicon Snake Oil: Second Thoughts on the Information Highway*, has been deeply immersed in the information network since its inception. His five modem-equipped computers are plugged into the info world, he surfs the Net regularly, and he loves his cyber-community. Nevertheless, he has profound misgivings about the technology:

They [computers] isolate us from one another and cheapen the meaning of actual experience. . . . [M]ore than half of our children learn about nature from television, a third from school and less than 10 percent by going outdoors. . . . [N]o computer can teach what a walk through a pine forest feels like. Sensation has no substitute.

Curious students who are excited about learning will take to computers as readily as they do to literature, history, and science. But Stöll reminds us that

isolated facts don't make an education. Meaning doesn't come from data alone. Creative problem solving depends on context, interrelationships, and experience. The surrounding matrix may be more important than the individual lumps of information. And only human beings can teach the connections between things.

We are surrounded by information and information technology. But they do not tell us what we need to know: how to live in balance with the natural systems of the planet. Ecological issues require a different kind of information: material we can use for long-term thinking, for seeing connections and relationships, and for acting in cautious, conservative ways.

> "We have transformed information into a form of garbage."
> — NEIL POSTMAN,
> UTNE READER

Computers have been pushed as one of the great revolutionary hopes for education, and Steven Jobs, the fabled co-creator of the Apple computer, has been one of the strongest advocates of this notion. But even he has had second thoughts, according to an interview he gave to *Wired* magazine's Gary Wolf in 1996:

I used to think that technology could help education. . . . I've had to come to the inevitable conclusion that the problem is not one that technology can hope to solve. . . . Historical precedent shows that we can turn out amazing human beings without technology. Precedent also shows that we can turn out very uninteresting human beings with technology.

The reason that computer technology fails to deliver on its expectations is that while information can be accessed in vast quantities and with great speed, education is about sifting through it, making sense of ideas and what we perceive. No computer can do that, as Alan Kay, one of the pioneers in personal computing, testified before Congress in 1995:

> Perhaps the saddest occasion for me is to be taken to a computerized classroom and be shown children joyfully using computers. They are happy, the teachers and administrators are happy, and their parents are happy. Yet in most such classrooms, on closer examination I can see that the children are doing nothing interesting or growth-inducing at all! This is technology as a kind of junk food — people love it but there is no nutrition to speak of. At its worst, it is a kind of "cargo cult" in which it is thought that the mere presence of computers will somehow bring learning back to the classroom.

Even a big booster of the information revolution like U.S. president Bill Clinton warns us, "In the information age, there can be too much exposure and too much information and too much sort of quasi-information. . . . There's a danger that too much stuff cramming in on people's minds is just as bad for them as too little, in terms of the ability to understand, to comprehend."

In our infatuation with the seemingly wondrous possibilities the computer creates, we welcome it into the school only to find that it has become another vehicle for marketing opportunities. Marketing companies like Lifetime Systems design commercial packages to look like educational material, wrote David Shenk in a 1994 article for *Spy* magazine. The company points out the opportunities to prospective clients: "Kids spend 40 percent of each day in the classroom where traditional advertising can't reach them. Now you can enter the classroom through custom-made learning materials created with your specific marketing objectives in mind. Communicate with young spenders directly, and through them, their teachers and family as well."

The highly fragmented offerings in an ever-increasing menu of television channels has been paralleled by a growing number of both news channels and news programs. Along with CNN, MSNBC, SKY, BBC World, and CBC Newsworld, we have the analogue of print tabloids in *Hard Copy* and *Cops*. As Shenk says:

> the news-flash industry supplies us with entertainment, not journalism, and as such is part of the problem of information glut. . . . Our fundamental understanding of Bosnia or the stock market is not going to change, no matter how many news-bites we hear about them. To actually learn about the subject requires not a series of updates, but a careful and thoughtful review of the situation.

As the quality of air, water, and landscape degenerate from the assault of human activity, more and more of our fellow human beings find themselves in sprawling megalopolises. In cities we are distanced from the natural world, spending more and more time in search of stimulation in shopping malls, electronic games and television. In lieu of the experiences of the real world, we now have all of the gut-wrenching, adrenalin-rush, sensory overload of "virtual reality." The truly horrifying aspect of the cyber-world is that it appears to be *better* than the real world. After all, one can access the virtual world of sex and experience every kinky possibility without fear of contracting AIDS, feeling guilty, or being caught by one's partner. We can take part in a gunfight, lose, and live to shoot again; race a car, crash, and walk away; or get blown up or beaten to a pulp without pain or injury. Who needs a real dangerous world when all of our sensations can be zapped to the max without risk?

During the '70s, on a noon-hour television talk show, the host asked me, "What do you think the world will be like in a hundred years?" I replied: "Well, if there are still people around then, I think

> *"Superabundant information is grand, until we understand that it can rob us of the peace that is our spiritual birthright. We have only recently realized our need to develop an ecological relationship with the natural world. Perhaps we must also realize our need for inner ecology, an ecology of the mind."*
>
> — PHILIP NOVAK,
> DOMINICAN QUARTERLY

they'll curse us for nuclear power and television." The host did a double take and, ignoring my caveat about still being around, asked, "Why television?" My answer was as follows: "Well, Bob, you just asked me a pretty tough question. If I had answered, 'Gee, I'll have to think about that for a minute,' and then proceeded to think without saying a word, you'd cut to a commercial in less than five seconds. Because television cannot tolerate dead space. It demands instant response. There's no room for reflection or profundity. It's not a serious medium."

Reflecting now on that answer, I wouldn't change my assessment. However, that response was given years before the multi-channelled universe of cable, which demands even faster, snappier programming to keep our attention. The one element that the real world of nature requires for us to experience it is *time*. So the more our children experience nature through television and films, the more they will be disappointed when they encounter the real thing. Wild things don't perform on cue. They are shy. Often they are active only at night or underground. Nature allows us only rare moments when there might be a flurry of activity. And the waiting makes the experience all the more satisfying when nature does reward us.

7

GLOBAL ECONOMICS: IN CONFLICT WITH THE EARTH

"*Oikos* is the Greek word meaning household, estate or domain and is at the root of both *economics* and *ecology*. *Economos* is the rules and regulations for running the domain while *eco-logos* is the reason for it all, the underlying principle, the spirit. Normally, the *logos* should determine the *nomos*, but in the late 20th century, this is not the case."

— SUSAN GEORGE, ECONOMICS CRITIC

Throughout history, people created economies to serve the needs of individuals and their communities. Those economies were diverse and local; each was profoundly rooted to a place and culture. But today the relationship between people and economies is upside down and back to front. One form of economics now blankets the world, and we are told that we must serve the economy, that we must sacrifice for the sake of the economy, that communities must give up social services for the sake of the economy. Where once the human world trembled at the prospect of demons and dragons, today it's the economy that strikes fear into people's hearts.

The economic system dominant today is so fundamentally

disconnected from communities and the Earth that it has become inevitably destructive to both. Economics is predicated on the notion that such fundamental human activities as caring, co-operating, and sharing are emotional and irrational, and in contrast to "rational self-interest." Economists boast that their profession is based on the inherent logic of *selfishness* and *greed*. Yet the quality that acts most powerfully in everybody's life, that gives individuals hope and courage and holds families and communities together, is generosity in all its forms: volunteerism, compassion, kindness, and affection.

Conventional economists are infatuated with what they call human capital: the tremendous inventive and consumptive capacity of people. Thus population growth is celebrated by economists because it increases the "greatest natural resource of all — the human brain." More people, it is argued, mean more creative minds to invent new sources of wealth and resources. This means, by a breath-taking reversal of common sense, that countries like Japan, China, and India, which are poor in the necessities of life but rich in human beings, are considered rich or potentially wealthy; in the current frenzy of deficit reduction and downsizing, economists pronounce nations like Canada and Australia, which have plenty of resources but a sparse population, economically precarious.

ECONOMICS AND THE REAL WORLD

Everything we depend on for survival, including air and water, soil, plastic, energy, glass, metal, and food, comes from the Earth and represents "natural capital." Yet we are led to believe it is a strong growing economy that ensures their deliverance. In the looking-glass world of economics, human capital is overvalued, while natural capital and the processes by which the living world maintains itself are undervalued or considered irrelevant.

A schematic representation of the economy is filled with items and arrows indicating the intricate relationship between resource extraction, processing, manufacture, retailing and regulations, taxes, and incentives. But the ozone layer, underground aquifers, topsoil, biodiversity, and freshwater are depicted as *externalities*: outside the

> "The wider human habitat, far from being humanized and ennobled by man's activities, becomes standardized to dreariness or even degraded to ugliness. All this is being done because man-as-producer cannot afford 'the luxury of not acting economically' and therefore cannot produce the very necessary 'luxuries' — like health, beauty and permanence — which man-as-consumer desires more than anything else. It would cost too much; and the richer we become, the less we can 'afford.'"
>
> — E. F. SCHUMACHER, ECONOMIST

realm of the economy. But that means the economic system is no longer grounded in the real world, since those so-called externalities are actually the life-support systems of the planet. Without them, there could be no life — and certainly no economy.

In the "household" of the living world, each system, each entity, has a part to play in the "economy" of the whole. A standing tree performs numerous "services" for the Earth — removing carbon dioxide from the atmosphere and sequestering it, breathing out oxygen, transpiring water to affect weather and climate, holding soil to prevent erosion and flooding, providing habitat to plants and animals — yet none of these services has economic worth according to the way our system does its accounts. As the CEO of a multinational forest company once said to me, "A tree only has value when it's cut down." In our economic system, he is right. Of course, economics recognizes other values in a forest, such as its recreational and medicinal properties, but all value is still defined in terms of human use, not in terms of the entire living world.

Progressive economists like Herman Daly are attempting to include factors that were previously thought to be outside the boundaries of the economy — that is, to internalize what were once considered external. In fact, nature performs many "services" that benefit humankind yet are lost or discounted in our current economic system. Now ecologists are attempting to document and evaluate those vast services rendered by nature.

If we try to replace or substitute a natural service with a human-created technology, we may get an estimate of its economic worth.

Thus we can compute the worth of water purification by a watershed by the calculated cost of doing the same thing with a purification plant. Some of nature's services can never be replaced because we simply don't have the technological competence to even try. For example, David Pimentel calculates that on a sunny day in New York State, insects pollinate a trillion flowers, a feat no human technology can reproduce. Nevertheless, it is possible to make crude attempts at putting a dollar value on much of what nature does. When Bob Constanza and his associates did this, they came up with an annual economic value of about $30 trillion, an amount that is almost twice the collective annual GDPs of all the countries in the world! In our economic systems, these services aren't even part of the discussion, so it's no surprise we are so ecologically destructive. Critics, of which I am one, of this economic assessment of ecological services warn that there are some things that are beyond economic worth, that might be considered sacred. In imposing an economic value on all parts of nature, there is a danger that economists will simply factor everything in, including air, water, and biodiversity, as if it can all be rationally calculated.

Nevertheless, by trying to estimate the economic worth of nature's services we quickly realize its enormous "value," a value that dwarfs our economies yet is currently unacknowledged. So we continue to push the limits of a finite planet. And still the process continues: the underlying assumptions and priorities still drive us on towards disaster.

SPREADING THE MESSAGE OF ECONOMICS' ENDLESS BENEFITS

Economic growth promoted by global free trade is the only path proposed by the vast majority of the world's leading economists. According to them, productivity can be increased forever using scientific innovation and the techniques of management and control; this road to progress will produce more wealth, which will trickle down to the less fortunate in society; bigger is better because it produces economies of scale, and so the biggest of all — the global market — is the best; naysayers and doomsayers are forgetting the

"More people and increased income cause problems in the short run. These problems present opportunity, and prompt the search for solutions. . . . In the long run, the new developments leave us better off than if the problems had not arisen. . . . We now have in our hands — in our libraries, really — the technology to feed, clothe, and supply energy to an ever-growing population for the next 7 billion years. . . . Even if no new knowledge were ever invented . . . we would be able to go on increasing forever, improving our standard of living and our control over the environment."

— JULIAN L. SIMON,
ECONOMIST

endless ingenuity of the human brain.

The planet's human societies are now being overwhelmed by one model of progress and development. Global media networks spread the cultural values and perspectives of a limited number of centres around the world, while transnational corporations saturate the globe with uniform mass products.

A NEW COURSE — ECOLOGICAL ECONOMICS

A few economists are starting to chart a new course, however, working out ways to base economic theory on ecological principles. Herman Daly is one of the most eminent; he was a senior economist with the World Bank for six years and is the co-author, with John Cobb, of *For the Common Good: Redirecting the Economy Towards Community, the Environment and a Sustainable Future*. He proposes to correct the errors, biases, and accounting mistakes of conventional economic theory so that sustainability, rather than growth, is the key value. His central proposal attacks the ideas at the heart of modern economics and politics, suggesting that governments should

move away from the ideology of global economic integration by free trade, free capital mobility, and export-led growth — and toward a more nationalist orientation that seeks to develop domestic production for internal markets as the first option, having recourse to international trade only when clearly much more efficient. . . . [T]o globalize the economy by the erasure of

> *"If a high-growth economy is needed to fight the battle against pollution, which itself appears to be the result of high growth, what hope is there of ever breaking out of this extraordinary circle?"*
>
> — *E. F. SCHUMACHER,*
> *ECONOMIST*

national economic boundaries through free trade, free capital mobility, and free, or at least uncontrolled, migration, is to wound fatally the major unit of community capable of carrying out any policies for the common good.

In 1933 John Maynard Keynes, one of the founders of the World Bank, wrote from a very similar point of view:

I sympathize with those who would minimize, rather that those who would maximize, economic entanglement between nations. Ideas, knowledge, art, hospitality, travel — these are the things which should of their nature be international. But let goods be homespun whenever it is reasonably and conveniently possible; and, above all, let finance be primarily national.

Daly has constantly attempted to remind his fellow economists that all people, including economists, live in a finite world on which they totally depend for all life's needs. It is a delusion to assume that the economy can grow indefinitely while allotting the environment a small corner of it. In fact, it's the other way around. The environment defines the limits within which we live, and the important question we should be asking is, How big can the economy grow without compromising its carrying capacity?

Life is local. Each locally adapted community of life is the *oikos*, a household, estate, or domain of the living world. Its *ecology* determines its *economy* — the rules by which it runs, survives, thrives. The rest, as Hamlet said, is silence.

8

Human Borders, Nature's Boundaries

"*Ecology* has caught us by the throat."
— Mikhail Gorbachev, former premier of the Soviet Union

With the shattering of the Soviet Union and its empire and China's entry into new international trading relationships, the "free world" led by the United States is trumpeting the triumph of democracy and the supremacy of the global marketplace. But the worldwide collapse of communism means institutions of democracy must undergo more scrutiny, since they now hold even greater sway over our lives. Such examination reveals enormous shortcomings and problems that prevent us from establishing policies that will protect the Earth's future.

Political Horizons Are Too Short
Immediately upon election to office, politicians must be concerned with re-election: their decisions and actions must pay dividends before another vote. Making massive investments and sacrifices today for benefits that may accrue decades later (as in the case of climate change, for example) holds little attraction for politicians, since they

are the ones who will have to defend the imposition of immediate costs and then watch others years later reap credit for the benefits. Furthermore, when faced with a choice between doing the right but unpopular thing or doing nothing and hoping catastrophe will somehow be averted, politicians will *always* opt to do nothing. The tragedy of Newfoundland's loss of northern cod is a classic example.

The time frame that defines human priorities in modern society has been drastically reduced. Aboriginal people speak of making decisions only after reflecting on seven generations of ancestors and seven generations into the future, but today our bottom line is often a weekly paycheque or an annual return on investment.

Political reality is dictated by a horizon measured in months or a few years. However, in nature, time scales are on a different order of magnitude, which explains why it is difficult to mesh economic and political deadlines with nature's time needs.

An illustration of how fleeting political commitment can be is seen by the shifting position of ecological priorities over the past decade. Fuelled by Rachel Carson's book in 1962, the environmental movement gathered strength and became a global force. By 1988, public anxiety had pushed the environment to the top of the political agenda. That year, U.S. presidential candidate George Bush declared that if elected, he would be an "environmental president"; Britain's prime minister, Margaret Thatcher, announced she was a "greenie"; and Canadian prime minister Brian Mulroney elevated the minister of the environment to the exclusive inner Cabinet and appointed a rising political star, Lucien Bouchard, to the post.

Public demand for leadership and direction in protecting the environment culminated in the largest gathering of

"In a week's time all cleaning up work will halt on the massive Exxon Valdez *oil spill in Alaska. . . . While green issues promise to be increasingly important, President Bush, who declared his passion for the environment during his election campaign, has failed to visit Valdez or declare a national emergency. Now, a planned visit after Exxon's departure has been cancelled as a political 'downer.'"*
— CHRISTOPHER REED, THE GUARDIAN

heads of state in human history, at the Earth Summit in Rio de Janeiro in 1992. The Rio conference was intended to signal a dramatic shift in human activity: from that point on, economics and the environment would be inseparably linked and humanity would seek a way to live in ecological balance through "sustainable development."

Yet by the early 1990s, the environmental movement was already being pushed to the periphery by economic problems. Only two weeks after the Earth Summit, the Group of Seven (G-7) industrialized countries met in Munich. The environment and Rio were not even mentioned. The economy had reclaimed its dominant role, and it knocked environmental issues off political platforms everywhere. The young U.S. presidential candidate Bill Clinton proudly displayed his "It's the economy, stupid" reminder of the only campaign issue. (Many of us think he left out a word. It should have read "It's the economy *that's* stupid!") During the federal election in Canada in 1993, a major newspaper editorialized that the three issues of the election were "the economy, the economy, the economy."

When I interviewed Lucien Bouchard shortly after he had been appointed environment minister, he declared, with passion and sincerity, "Global warming threatens the survival of our species. If we don't act now, it will be a catastrophe." In 1993, the all-party Standing Committee on Environment released *Our Planet . . . Our Future*, part of which was a section entitled "No Time to Lose: The Challenge of Global Warming." The report asserted that the potential threat posed to humanity by global warming was "second only to all-out nuclear war." Both Sheila Copps, who became deputy prime minister and environment minister, and Paul Martin, the future finance minister, were on that committee. Yet today Bouchard's priority is Quebec sovereignty, while Copps has defended the government's failure to reduce Canada's carbon-dioxide production, even though it is an international commitment as well as a campaign promise. As finance minister, Paul Martin's sole concern now seems to be the economy. Electing people who *say* an ecological threat is of paramount concern does not, unfortunately, ensure action to prevent that threat.

There is no politician more informed and more passionately concerned about the global environment than U.S. vice-president Al

Gore. His best-selling book, *Earth in the Balance*, outlines in detail the crisis we face and the action needed to avoid a catastrophe. Yet in office, he has been hamstrung in his efforts to make the environment a top concern for the administration. Perhaps a clue to the problem is provided by Gore himself. When I interviewed him in 1988, I asked how people can help informed politicians like him. He replied that we shouldn't look to people in politics or industry to lead the way. "If you want change, you have to take it to the people," he told me, "and convince them there's a problem. Explain the options so they demand action. Then," he continued, "people like me will trip over ourselves to climb aboard the bandwagon." Without broad public commitment to the environment and continuous pressure on governments, business will successfully continue to corner political debate and protect its own in-terests, even at the expense of the global environment on which we all depend.

SKEWED REPRESENTATION, UNBALANCED PRIORITIES

Running for political office costs a mint; people from most sectors of society cannot afford to stand for election and lose. Consequently, most individuals who choose a political career are business-

> *"I have never pondered such matters . . . nor do I ever intend to."*
> — ENOCH POWELL, LATE SENIOR BRITISH POLITICIAN, ON ENVIRONMENTAL ISSUES

people or lawyers. It is therefore not surprising that governments are obsessed with matters jurisdictional or economic. Businesspeople and lawyers are unlikely to have much understanding of scientific, ecological, or technological matters. Yet in political office, these businesspeople and lawyers are legislating or not acting on issues such as climate change, species extinction, deforestation, and ozone depletion.

MISSING THE REAL CONSTITUENCY

In principle, politicians are elected to act on behalf of their constituencies. But although elected by the public at large, politicians of all parties respond primarily to the needs of big business and industry, which provide the bulk of a candidate's funding. Of course, politicians must acknowledge voters as well, especially during an election. However, what of all those who do *not* vote? Children don't vote. Future generations don't vote. How can a politician obsessed with re-election care about those who aren't even on the voters' lists?

For that matter, trees don't vote, and neither do fish, rivers, oceans, or the air. Ministers of forests, natural resources, oceans, fisheries, or agriculture don't speak on behalf of forests, resources, oceans, fish, or soil, respectively. They represent human beings who exploit those resources. Looked at closely, the phrase *representative democracy* takes on a whole new meaning.

"We borrow environmental capital from future generations with no intention or prospect of repaying. They may damn us for our spendthrift ways, but they can never collect on our debt to them. We act as we do because we can get away with it: future generations do not vote; they have no political or financial power; they cannot challenge our decisions. But the results of the present profligacy are rapidly closing the options for future generations."

— OUR COMMON FUTURE, THE BRUNDTLAND REPORT, *1987*

FORCING NATURE INTO HUMAN BORDERS

Human political boundaries do not coincide with those that make ecological sense — mountain tops, valley bottoms, watersheds, river systems, etc. Migratory animals do not stay within human borders any more than plants, air, and water do. But we continue to try to shoehorn nature into our bureaucracies and borders.

The incompatibility of human borders and natural boundaries is illustrated by a map of the Pacific Northwest. The coast is one continuous marine ecosystem, reaching from the Bering Sea of Alaska down thousands of kilometres to California, yet it is fragmented by the administrations of two countries, one province, and four states.

A fish that hatches in the upper waters of the Taku River in British Columbia passes through the Alaska panhandle on its way to the sea, then spends years traversing Russian and Japanese waters before returning back through Alaska to its Canadian birthplace to spawn. Along the way, the fish runs a gauntlet of natural and human predators. Each group of human fishers views salmon passing through their territory as "their" resource and a legitimate prey as separate international, federal, state, provincial, and municipal governments attempt to "manage" these wild creatures.

Fish, plants, insects, mammals, and birds live and travel across human boundaries driven by their innate needs and instincts. But political priorities are determined by human demands that pay scant attention to other species' biological requirements. The incompatibility of such a piecemeal management policy and the long-term sustainability of biological beings is easily seen by inspecting the migratory patterns of different organisms.

The jewel-like monarch butterfly wreaks political havoc as the insect moves from Canada through the United States to a winter destination in tiny patches of forest in Mexico before turning back to move north again. Genetically programmed to follow this path, the insects are not able to adjust when deforestation and agriculture remove critical parts of their migratory route. In the same way, shorebirds have long followed paths that extend from the Arctic to the tip of South America. Their flyway has been determined by critical points at which the birds can rest and feed before continuing their monumental travels. Deprived by human activity of those fuelling and resting spots, the birds are too finely honed by evolution to seek alternative routes. Clearly, as long as human priorities dictate the fate of land development or resource utilization, the very real biological needs of the animals will be compromised.

It has been my experience that when economic pressures build up, we almost always expect nature to fit the mould of our needs. A good example was the economic downturn in the province of British Columbia in 1998. Beset by a massive deficit and a stagnant economy, Premier Glen Clark took action that only exacerbated an already unsustainable history of forest practices. The ministry of forestry's data indicate that a sustainable rate of logging in B.C. would be a volume of 51 million cubic metres a year (a figure ecologists suggest might be 40 percent too high). For decades, the industry has exceeded this volume by a large margin. After years of confrontation and dispute over the forest industry's habit of creating massive clearcuts with little regard for biodiversity, topsoil, and riparian zones, a previous NDP government under Mike Harcourt developed a Forest Practices Act that was reputed to be as stringent as any in the world. In an effort to boost the flagging economy and stagnant sales of logs, Harcourt's successor, Clark, has carried out a series of actions to stimulate the economy while increasing the assault on the forests. Many of the regulations of the Forest Practices Act were removed, ostensibly to improve government efficiency, but in fact freeing the industry to lapse into past behaviour. The stumpage rate — that is, the tax paid by industry to log crown land — was reduced, thereby encouraging greater removal of wood. And finally, in the most cynical move of all, Clark, going against the government's vow to add value within the province to each tree cut, allowed the export of raw logs, thereby exporting all the jobs that could have been made to process the wood from log to finished product. With each step, pressure on the forest has been increased to fulfil the human need for economic growth.

In fact, nature's complexity has much to teach us and, in view of how little we know, ought to be a reference against which we shape and limit our activities. Instead of attempting to overpower or engineer nature by straightening rivers, cutting across watersheds, dragging nets across ocean floors, etc., we should respect the inherent wisdom in nature and follow its contours.

DIVIDING THE WORLD INTO HUMAN COMPARTMENTS

Bureaucratic subdivisions within governments make as little ecological sense as political boundaries. Thus, to return to the example of the Pacific salmon, it is "managed" by international, federal, and provincial committees, as well as representatives of sport, commercial, and aboriginal fishers. But the interests of the salmon as a sustainable biological entity are not the uppermost concern. Furthermore, activities covered by other portfolios such as urban development, agriculture, forestry, and energy impinge on the well-being of the salmon. But with the issue of salmon management fractured by bureaucratic subdivisions, the fish can never be dealt with as a single biological entity.

We have it all wrong. It is the natural world from which we derive a living. The attempt to force parts of our surroundings to conform to our borders and to serve our needs invariably shatters the interconnections and balance that are the basis for nature's productivity.

"*A* human being is a part of the whole, called by us the 'Universe' — a part limited in time and space. He experiences himself, his thoughts and feelings, as something separated from the rest — a kind of optical delusion of his consciousness. This delusion is a kind of prison for us, restricting us to our personal desires and to affection for a few persons nearest to us.

Our task must be to free ourselves by widening our circle of compassion to embrace all living creatures and the whole of Nature in its beauty."

— ALBERT EINSTEIN,
PHYSICIST AND NOBEL PRIZE WINNER

9

THE BOTTOM LINE IS
THE STARTING LINE

*S*cience, technology, population, urbanization, information over-load, economics, globalization: these are immense obstacles to our ability to see with clarity and act decisively to achieve ecological balance. We are lost in a maze of misconceptions and false assumptions; faced with what seem to be unstoppable processes, we attempt solutions that make things worse. Yet we must continue to seek a way out; there is no alternative.

The environmental movement, launched by Rachel Carson's seminal book *Silent Spring*, was immensely successful at raising the alarm and galvanizing public concern about species extinction, toxic pollution, deforestation, and so on. Environmental issues have been impelled by a sense of crisis and by opposition to the forces that are creating the problem.

Is there a way to get everyone to agree on the basic needs that must be assured for all people in order for us to have a truly sustainable future? The critical point in our search for a new path is the establishment of the real bottom line. What are the irrefutable biophysical,

> *"When man becomes greater than nature, nature, which gave him birth, will respond."*
> — LOREN EISELEY,
> ANTHROPOLOGIST

social, and economic needs that form the foundation of sustainable living? Phrased this way, it becomes clear that the ancients knew very well that the four elements of crucial importance for all of us are air, water, earth, and fire — the sacred foundations of everything in their universe. Out of a combination of these elements were created the stars, Earth, and life itself.

> *"Man's conquest of Nature turns out, in the moment of its consummation, to be Nature's conquest of Man. Every victory we seemed to win has led us, step by step, to this conclusion."*
> — C. S. LEWIS,
> THE ABOLITION OF MAN

A new perspective would enable us to see that boundaries cannot be drawn between us and air, water, or soil — in fact, we are, quite literally, air, water, soil, and sunlight and remain so with every breath, drink, and mouthful we take. And it has been life, the entire diverse make-up of living things, that has created and continues to cleanse and replenish the air, water, and soil to sustain us. Every bit of the energy (wood, peat, coal, oil, gas, and food)

> *"We are at a moment both of profound change in the scientific concept of nature and of the structure of human society as a result of the demographic explosion. As a result, there is a need for new relationships between man and nature and between man and man. We can no longer accept the old a priori distinction between scientific and ethical values."*
> — ILYA PRIGOGINE, PHYSICIST
> AND NOBEL LAUREATE, AND
> ISABELLE STENGERS, CHEMIST

on which we depend to keep us alive was originally sunlight that was converted into and stored as chemical energy by the web of living things on Earth. Whatever we do to the air, water, soil, energy, and biodiversity, we also do to ourselves because there is no separation. And to top it off, the web of life that makes earth, air, fire, and water accessible to us is composed not of "resources," but of our biological *kin*. All other life forms are genetically related to us through our shared evolutionary history. Once regarded as relatives, all other species become at the very least worthy of respect and love.

Once we define our place this way, the way we act towards the environment is the way we act towards ourselves. If we are air, water, and soil and we proceed to use those elements as a dumping ground for our toxic effluent, it means we are pouring those toxins directly into ourselves, our children, and future generations. And when we tear at the web of life on Earth, we alter the resilience and adaptability of the only system able to cleanse and replenish our inescapable needs.

PART II

CHANGING
PERSPECTIVE

10

ECONOMICS: OUT OF BALANCE WITH THE EARTH

What is it about this economy that preoccupies us so? At its core, it fails to appreciate natural services, local communities, employment, and values of sharing, caring, and co-operating. The economic system that is being pushed around the world is highly destructive of the most important things in our lives.

IRRATIONAL ECONOMICS DICTATING FUTURE

My newspaper column is on the environment, but I keep coming back to economics because the rapid degradation of the planet's life-support mechanisms and the unsustainable depletion of potentially renewable resources are driven largely by the workings of the world economy. Populations are impoverished by transnational corporations pursuing profits without concern for the long-term survival of local communities and ecosystems.

Increasingly, business reporters and pundits reify the economy and its components as if they are real things that behave rationally. In February 1995, we were told that "the market is skittish" and "the economy is weakening." When Paul Martin released his budget, an economist commented, "It's going to take a while for the market to stabilize, before it really understands the situation at hand." A Wood Gundy economist observed, "The market seems to be reacting well to the budget," which "is going to play well internationally." A front-page headline in the *Globe and Mail* said, "Currency Markets Give Thumbs Up." But neither the economy nor the market are living beings or single objects; they are the collective result of myriad individual acts.

We also heard that "the peso has lost investor confidence" and that the budget "had to satisfy investor demands." "Investors," or "speculators," are not a rational, like-minded group whose behaviour makes sense. Instead, they are millions of people around the world from different educational, cultural, ethnic, and religious backgrounds, whose judgement and actions are affected by all kinds of foibles, prejudices, and blinders.

In a program we did for *The Nature of Things* on the subject of statistics and probability, Jade Hemeon, a business reporter for the *Toronto Star*, described a fascinating game in which twenty people in her office threw darts at the stock-market listings. The names "selected" this way were then put in a hat and five drawn as companies for a paper investment. She also asked five investment experts for their recommendations. The first time the game was played, the companies chosen by darts returned 186 percent on the investment, handily beating all the experts!

The next year, when Hemeon tried again, most "experts" were reluctant to play, but five were eventually found. This time, in a period when the market was down by 10 percent, the darted companies returned 16 percent and again beat all five experts. Of course, the dart results are just a fluke, but the game shows that so is the work of the experts! It is bizarre that the behaviour of such an irrational collective as "the market" should so profoundly influence governments.

When a spokesperson for a New York–based bond-rating agency, Moody's Investors Service, suggested that Canada's credit rating might be downgraded, Paul Martin was forced to respond defensively in Parliament. With that implicit threat, investors began to dump Canadian dollars, thereby forcing the executives of the Bank of Canada to raise interest rates by half a percent.

Excuse me, but is our government sovereign or not? On the day of Moody's pronouncement, the Spanish peseta, the Italian lira, the Mexican peso, and the American dollar were all sliding, and pundits declared it was because investors "expressed confidence" in the German mark and the Japanese yen.

Governments around the world are now being held hostage to "currency speculators," whose sole contribution to society or the world is buying and selling money on the open market simply to make more money. Where I come from, wealth is generated by working at something tangible, whether it is in the creation of a product or the extraction of something of value from the Earth. These days, money seems to be a commodity with intrinsic value and no longer has to be connected to anything real.

Canadians are highly educated and have access to unprecedented amounts of information, yet the mere rumour of lost faith in the Canadian economy or the opinion of some self-proclaimed Bay Street expert that the Canadian dollar is overpriced creates wild swings in the market. And we're not the only hostages to this phantom market. The Mexican government and its national bank were unable to halt the slide of the peso until the U.S. president declared his confidence in the country and promised to invest in it.

It is true we have a crisis of debt that consumes much of each tax dollar merely to pay the interest. But when federal and provincial governments alike beg for foreign loans and investments, they forfeit control over their own economies. The global market, so beloved by transnational corporations and free traders, exacerbates the debt crisis by diminishing the power of local businesses and communities. How can our leaders believe they are securing a future for our children when they don't get at the root of our insecurity, namely, an irrational global economics that has been reified into a monster that dictates our actions?

AN *"ETHNIC"* LAMENTS OUR LOST VALUES

Jacques Parizeau's bitter remarks about "ethnics" on referendum night in 1995 were rightly condemned both inside and outside

Quebec. But as a third-generation ethnic Canadian, I find myself increasingly alienated by what is happening in English Canada.

My parents were children of immigrants who came to Canada early in this century. Those were not easy times for Asians in Canada. Neither my grandparents nor my Canadian-born parents were able to vote, own property in much of British Columbia, or enter a profession such as pharmacy, law, or medicine. They endured, overcoming racism, discrimination, and the Great Depression by hard work, frugality, and the support of family, friends, and community. Even after the terrible trauma of the Second World War, when they were incarcerated, then expelled from B.C., my parents believed they were fortunate to be in Canada. This was their home, and we all had a duty to strive to make it better.

My sisters and I were taught that although we had to earn money, it was only the means for obtaining the necessities of life. Money was to be shared with family or friends in need, not hoarded, flaunted, or bragged about. We felt sorry for people who were "money crazy," or showed off with flashy clothes or cars.

I have clung to those values all my life, yet these days they seem anachronistic and corny. Nowadays the media revel in billion-dollar wheeling and dealing and lionize the fabulously rich. We celebrate the obscene levels of wealth and consumption by a tiny fraction of the world's people and rationalize insensitivity to the predicament of growing numbers of poor, unfortunate, and disadvantaged fellow citizens by accusing them of sloth, deception, or lousy genes.

This is not a Canada I recognize or want. I don't feel comfortable in it, nor do I think this kind of country can attract the love of people who are inspired by a far more uplifting vision of culture and community.

What the Quebec referendum revealed was that strategies and promises are being made up on the spot to respond to an immediate problem, criticism, or demand. Politicians do not "lead" so much as lurch from one predicament to another, improvising responses to deflect the media or quell the crisis. Their response is not based on principle, thoughtful reflection, or the recognition that many assumptions are no longer valid in a profoundly changed world.

The spectre of Newfoundland should haunt us all. It was political-economic agendas that drove the northern cod to extinction and destroyed the very basis of Newfoundlanders' culture and economy. Now unprecedented numbers of the province's people are leaving their island for other parts of the country. They are Canadian "refugees," forced to flee their homeland by the catastrophic consequences of ecological collapse.

Nothing illustrates our surface, Band-Aid approach to societal problems better than government action on the economy. In an effort to crank up the economy and reduce the debt, governments from the right of the political spectrum to the left slavishly follow prescriptions imposed by the World Bank on developing countries and the mean-spirited legacy from the Reagan years.

We are told that for the sake of the economy, we must make reductions in many of the things that make Canada a nation worth fighting for — social safety nets, the arts, education, universal medical care, the National Film Board, scientific research, the CBC, and the tradition of sharing between the have and have-not provinces. Often what are being called cuts are, in fact, mortal amputations.

The solution to Canada's fragile economy, we were told in the late 1980s, was free trade. Prime Minister Brian Mulroney and most large corporations promised "more and better jobs" after the enactment of the Free Trade Agreement (FTA) with the United States. The Canadian Centre for Policy Alternatives (CCPA) has kept track of job-creation performance by forty-eight representative corporations belonging to the Business Council on National Issues, an organization made up of the 160 largest corporations in Canada.

In the October 1995 issue of *Monitor*, the CCPA reported that eleven of the forty-eight corporations had created a mere 11,993 jobs between the beginning of the FTA and the end of 1994. The other thirty-seven "downsized" their workforce by a total of 215,414 jobs, even as revenues were rising from $141.9 billion to $174 billion! The CCPA reports that corporations have "slashed their workforces by nearly 30%. Little wonder that Canada's official unemployment rate remains close to 10% and its real unemployment rate at 18% or more."

The promises of free trade haven't been realized for most Canadians, yet politicians continue to push for more. Our obsession with debt and cost-cutting measures are undermining the very heart of what makes this country special. The spirit of meanness epitomized by Thatcher, Reagan, Bush, and Mulroney was based on the glorification of money, free enterprise, and the global market. They encouraged transnational corporations, currency speculators, and stock-market manipulators at the expense of small businesses and local communities. Where corporations once contributed half of Canada's tax revenues, they now pay a mere 10 percent!

This policy has been calamitous in the United States, reported John Cassidy in the *New Yorker* on October 16, 1995: "Until recently, it was an empirical law of American politics that the majority of citizens . . . received steadily rising earnings." And during the post–Second World War boom years (often referred to by economists as the Golden Era), this was true. From 1945 to 1973, "The rich got richer, but almost everybody else got richer with them and at roughly the same pace." Cassidy says that from 1947 to 1973, "the annual growth rate of family income was between 2.4 and 3% regardless of where the family stood in the income distribution." If the distribution of incomes is divided into fifths, or quintiles, then the incomes (in constant inflation-adjusted dollars) in each quintile doubled.

But since 1973, says Cassidy, "The bottom two-fifths of American families saw their income fall." Even with more working mothers, the average incomes of the middle 20 percent barely rose, from $36,556 in 1973 to $37,056 in 1993. Only the top 40 percent had any real growth in income, with the very rich doing the best.

The median annual salary of all Americans in 1979 was $25,896, but sixteen years later this had shrunk to $24,700, a 4.6 percent wage drop. In contrast, the top third increased by 7.9 percent over the same period. Incomes of the richest 5 percent grew from $137,482 in 1973 to $177,518 in 1993, an increase of 29.1 percent, while the top one percent skyrocketed from $323,942 to $576,553, a 78 percent rise! It's what we've long suspected: most people are working harder but going backwards, while a tiny fraction at the top is becoming spectacularly richer.

Cassidy says, "In the past three years, wages have continued to fall while productivity, profits and stock prices have all soared." Thus, for example, "output per man-hour in the non-farm business sector of the economy grew 3.1% between March 1994 and March 1995. Both theory and history suggest that this . . . should have led to rising wages and salaries. Instead, average wages and salaries fell by 2.3% during the same period."

Over the past two decades, there has been a massive transfer of income from the middle and lower classes to the tiny percentage of extremely wealthy citizens. Cassidy reckons that about $275 billion in annual income has been shifted from the middle class to the rich.

The result is an extremely wealthy elite and an underclass "increasingly divorced from the rest of society." Between these two extremes, Cassidy sees two groups: "an upper echelon of highly skilled, highly educated professionals, who are doing pretty well; and a vast swath of unskilled and semiskilled workers who are experiencing falling wages, stagnant or declining living standards and increased economic uncertainty."

Today the number of families with young children in which both parents work has steadily risen while middle-income families are spending an ever-increasing proportion of their earnings on housing, utilities, and health care. Twenty years ago, the average CEO of a large corporation earned forty times as much as the average employee. Now the differential is 190!

Cassidy states: "The free traders argue that trade increases the prosperity of the country and raises everybody's welfare. . . . No politician can make median incomes start climbing again. . . . So all sides promise what they know they can't deliver: a return to the Golden Era."

He concludes: "The only thing that could be guaranteed to diminish the effects of rising inequality quickly is a steep increase in taxes on the rich. With the top 5% of American households receiving 20% of the country's income, and the top fifth receiving almost half, there is now a lot more rich income to tax."

Canadian politicians seek to emulate policies that have proved disastrous for most people in the U.S. The challenge for English

Canada is to inspire us with a vision of the country that we will fight to maintain for all Canadians.

REPORT FINDS CHILLING FLAW IN ECONOMIC GROWTH CLAIM

Governments on all sides of the political spectrum, at the federal, provincial, and local levels, are obsessed with cutting costs and becoming competitive in the global marketplace. In a debt-preoccupied time, it seems strange to hear it said that culture should be a major economic focus, as former UN secretary-general Javier Pérez de Cuéllar believes. He was appointed president of the World Commission on Culture and Development (WCCD), which was established by UNESCO in 1993 with a mandate to "seek new ways of linking culture — in its broadest sense — to a form of development that goes beyond mere economic growth."

Pérez de Cuéllar writes, "Culture is the key to development . . . the dimension that has been missing from the dominant model of development; a model based solely on economic growth and which, from all available evidence, has failed." Pérez de Cuéllar points out that while economies are growing in most parts of the world, jobs are not. Every country in sub-Saharan Africa has double-digit unemployment, and even developing countries with high economic growth like India and Pakistan have 15 percent unemployment. As Canadians and the British well know, double-digit unemployment is not peculiar to developing nations.

Pérez de Cuéllar insists that "the gap dividing our societies, in North and South alike, cannot simply be overcome by injecting capital, infrastructure, technology or expertise. Solutions are needed that are not solely reliant on classical economic theory and unlimited growth — but take people and their cultures into account and do not endanger the environment — solutions that give the notion of development more 'soul.' This will require a radical change in our behaviour and soon."

The WCCD has documented, in a 1994 UNESCO report, the shocking disparity between rich and poor countries. Ever since the

1950s, as the global economy grew at an unprecedented rate, businesspeople, economists, and politicians have repeated like a mantra the belief that steady economic growth in the industrialized nations is the means whereby wealth will "trickle down" to the poor. The UNESCO report's headline torpedoes that rationale: "Despite Growth — The Disparities Are Increasing."

In the interval during which the gross national product (GNP) per capita has risen worldwide at an unprecedented rate, "inequalities have also increased — between rich countries and poor, between affluent populations and those who are impoverished, and more recently, between those who have a job and the ever-swelling ranks of those who don't."

When the world's population is ranked by wealth and subdivided into five groups of equal number, then "in 1990, the richest group received 59 times more than the poorest. Despite growth of almost three percent per annum worldwide of per capita GNP over the past three decades, this is almost double the ratio of 30:1 in 1960. In that year, the richest 20 percent already controlled 70.2 percent of global GNP. In 1990 this had climbed to 82.7 percent. In 1960 the poorest 20 percent had to get by with only 2.3 percent, which by 1990 had fallen to 1.4 percent."

The report goes on to state that "these figures conceal the true scale of injustice since they are based on comparisons of average per capita incomes of rich and poor *countries*, and do not take into account the wide disparities between rich and poor people in each of those countries. . . . The absolute difference in per capita income between the top 20 percent and the bottom 20 percent of world population, expressed in 1989 U.S. dollars, increased between 1960 and 1989 from $1,864 to $15,149."

The growing disparity in wealth demands an overhaul of the trickle-down notion implicit in the current model of economic development, especially given the widespread phenomenon of *jobless growth*. "Everywhere without exception, the quantity of goods and services has increased faster than the number of people working to produce them. We are seeing growth with proportionally less job creation, due mainly to the scientific and technological revolution."

The most chilling parts of the report are graphs showing employment and GDP from 1975 to 2000 for the Organization for Economic Co-operation and Development (OECD) countries, Latin America, South Asia, and sub-Saharan Africa. In every case, the GDP rises faster than the number of jobs created, so unemployment rises! By the end of the century, a billion more jobs will be needed to reach full employment. WCCD experts agree this is "mission impossible." The long-held notion that profits become investments in future jobs is not borne out. Instead, "investment goes first to increase productivity, which means reducing the size of the workforce." The gap between economic growth and employment, and in the wealth of the industrialized and developing nations, is growing. Pérez de Cuéllar and the WCCD believe we must rethink the fundamental relationship between culture, development, and economics.

THE HUBRIS OF GLOBAL ECONOMICS

FROM PORT MORESBY, PAPUA NEW GUINEA — What is poverty? In urban Canada in 1994, the low-income cut-off line for a family of four was $31,071. Canadians living on social assistance often manage to have a TV set, a telephone, a refrigerator, even a car, commodities that are beyond the dreams of most people here in Papua New Guinea. Laura Martin, minister of finance and planning in East Sepik province, told me that "the official average PNG [Papua New Guinea] income is about $500 (Can) but it's really more like $300." A poor Canadian would be wealthy here.

Today Papua New Guineans appear destitute. Yet not long ago, in this unique place, poverty was virtually unknown. The University of Papua New Guinea social scientist Nick Faraclas writes:

> Imagine a society where there is no hunger, homelessness or unemployment, and where in times of need, individuals can rest assured that their community will make available to them every resource at its disposal. Imagine a society where decision makers rule only when the need arises, and then only by consultation, consensus and the consent of the community. Imagine a society

where women have control over their means of production and reproduction, where housework is minimal and childcare is available 24 hours a day on demand. Imagine a society where there is little or no crime and where community conflicts are settled by sophisticated resolution procedures based on compensation to aggrieved parties for damages, with no recourse to concepts of guilt or punishment. Imagine a society . . . in which the mere fact that a person exists is cause for celebration and a deep sense of responsibility to maintain and share that existence.

Such a place is not fiction, says Faraclas:

When the first colonisers came to the island of New Guinea, they did not find one society that exactly fit the above description. Instead, they found over one thousand distinct language groups and many more distinct societies, the majority of which approximated closely the above description, but each in its own particular way. These were not perfect societies. They had many problems. But after some one hundred years of "Northern development" . . . nearly all of the real developmental gains achieved over the past 40,000 years by the indigenous peoples of the island have been seriously eroded, while almost all of the original problems have gotten worse and have been added to a rapidly growing list of new imported problems.

When Columbus "discovered" the New World, the people he encountered were better off physically, materially, and spiritually than his crew members' families back in Europe. Poverty is a state of mind, and people may discover they are poor only when others tell them or when they see immense wealth flaunted by others.

The anthropologist Helena Norberg-Hodge told me that when she first arrived in Ladakh twenty years ago, her first impression was of overwhelming hardship and poverty. Yet when she asked a boy to show her the poorest family in a village, he looked puzzled and finally replied, "There are no poor people here."

Over time, Norberg-Hodge came to appreciate the incredible

wealth of kinship and community and the richness of culture and tradition in Ladakh. However, urged by industrialized countries, the government decided that the country needed "development." So a road was built across the Himalayas to open the tiny nation to the outside world and bring in money, goods, and tourists. Norberg-Hodge watched stable communities break down as young people left for the allure of city life and material goods. She saw the same village boy, now a man, living in the capital city and begging for money from tourists because "we are poor."

World leaders who met in Bretton Woods, New Hampshire, in 1944 envisioned a new economic order, and to help achieve it they created the International Monetary Fund and World Bank. Now we can see they were astonishingly successful. A mere fifty-one years later, the planet has been saturated with a single notion of development and economic progress. Governments big and small, from socialist to capitalist, military dictatorships to kingdoms and democracies, repeat like a mantra the faith that the global market and economy will improve living standards and bring wealth and opportunity.

Yet global economics is ultimately destructive because it is fatally flawed: it externalizes the natural capital and services that keep us alive, while glorifying human inventiveness as if it allows us to escape finite limits and manage our biophysical surroundings; it assumes that endless growth is possible and necessary and represents progress; it does not value long-term social and ecological sustainability; it rejects caring, co-operation, and sharing as irrational, while promoting selfishness; and it cannot incorporate the reality of spiritual needs.

It is breathtaking hubris to force this single, monolithic concept as salvation into every part of the world.

ECONOMICS NO MEASURE OF PROGRESS

FROM WEWAK, PAPUA NEW GUINEA — One of the most profound discoveries in evolutionary biology is the key role of diversity. Within a species or ecosystem, variety confers the plasticity and resilience that have allowed life to flourish. The fate of monocultures in agriculture, fisheries, and industrial forestry has taught us that homogeneity creates extreme vulnerability to perturbations or change. Human social diversity confers a similar flexibility and is critical for our long-term survival in many different environments.

When we define some countries as "developed," we relegate the rest to being underdeveloped. If some are "advanced," others must be backward; when there are rich, the rest become poor. The International Monetary Fund (IMF) and World Bank have created such categories by imposing a concept of "development" and "economic progress" appropriate for the North.

Originally, the IMF and World Bank were created to hasten the economic recovery of Europe after the Second World War. But once that job was completed, they targeted the elimination of poverty and discovered the nations of the South. In the resource-poor, technology-rich countries of the North, economic growth may be a valid measure of development and progress (although there are many who would argue it is a false indicator there too), but in the South it has proved unbelievably destructive.

The IMF/World Bank notion of development means spurning what worked in the past, ignoring the knowledge of elders and indigenous experience, and rejecting cultural roots and tradition. It demands appraisal of everything by standards of material possession and money. A woman in Colombia once told me that twenty years ago, when you asked about someone, he or she was described in terms of character and personality. "Now," she lamented, "people say, 'He's got a new car,' 'He owns a big house,' or 'He makes a lot of money.'"

People in industrialized countries are beginning to realize there are social, spiritual, and ecological costs to evaluating everything in terms of money. Here in PNG, the global economy has been slow to arrive, but it's looming like a tornado. The detritus is already here — Coke, Pepsi, and Fanta; plastic litter on the beach; Madonna and Michael Jackson blaring from tape decks; Nike shoes, Adidas shorts, and Japanese cars.

Subsistence agriculture, like subsistence forestry and fishing, has sustained families and local communities for thousands of years. But it doesn't generate quick revenues for government or corporations. People and communities who have always grown or gathered their own food are being deceived, seduced, or bribed into becoming part of the global economy. Cash crops like coffee or palm oil provide money, but then food must be bought from somewhere else. The lunacy of such economic progress is described by Richard J. Barnet and John Cavanagh in *Global Dreams: Imperial Corporations and the New World Order*: "Sabritos [Pepsico] buys potatoes in Mexico, cuts them up and puts them in a bag. Then they sell the potato chips for a hundred times what they paid the farmer for the potatoes." Here in PNG, the waters teem with fish, yet the country is a major importer of canned mackerel from Taiwan.

Only a few decades ago, many communities in PNG still lived as they had for thousands of years. Even now, 97 percent of the land is demarcated for extended families according to custom and 85 percent of the population still lives in the forest, with direct access to traditional land. People in towns and growing shanty towns can still return at any time to ancestral areas and use the land.

Consequently, most of Papua New Guinea's vast tropical rainforest — home of the fabled birds of paradise — is still intact. Since 1950, two-thirds of the planet's forests have been degraded by logging and other forms of development. As the world's forests shrink, pressure on the remainder intensifies. By the end of the century, it is expected there will be only four large areas of intact primary forest left. One of them is here in PNG.

In traditional systems of land tenure, people usually think they belong to the land as much as it belongs to them. The social scientist Nick Faraclas says: "In most Papua New Guinean languages, people's relationship to land is not normally expressed in terms of alienable (commodifiable) possession, but rather in terms of an inalienable, that is, familial or even corporal, association. Instead of referring to themselves as 'landowners', Papua New Guineans traditionally refer to themselves as the children, siblings or parents of the ground. In the customary conceptual framework, it is as impossible to envision the buying or selling of ground as a commodity as it is to envision the buying and selling of one's mother or child, or a piece of one's own flesh." The global economy is changing that and all of humanity is impoverished by the loss of traditions and other social systems.

THE DEADLY WAYS OF THE WORLD BANK

FROM PORT MORESBY, PAPUA NEW GUINEA — Papua New Guinea offers a classic illustration of what is happening in countries found predominantly in the southern hemisphere. On becoming independent of Australia in 1975, PNG was encouraged to accept development loans from the World Bank, invite foreign investment in mines and logging, and generate revenue from coffee and oil-palm plantations. But can one set a "fair market price" for land that is sacred — the source of life, history, and spiritual sustenance? And if so, who does it?

After the Arab oil embargo, energy prices and interest rates leapt skyward in the late 1970s, while world coffee prices collapsed in the 1980s. By 1989, the global economy had impoverished PNG and the country was forced by the World Bank to accept a Structural Adjustment Program. World Bank advisers were sent to oversee cut-backs in education, health, and other social services. Yet the debt has grown to $1,000 (U.S.) per capita and now consumes a quarter of the national budget for interest alone.

Mining and logging generate enormous sums (one member of Parliament told me the market value of logs alone was between $10 billion and $20 billion U.S. a year), but most of the money flows directly or indirectly out of the country.

Now the World Bank is pushing a Land Mobilization Program (LMP) to encourage more of its notion of development, as if land that has supported a rich variety of human cultures for 40,000 years is not already well and appropriately "developed." The LMP will allow people to use the land as collateral for loans, thus plugging them deeper into an economy that has already made them poor.

Money is a new and alien concept to many of these tribal people and, even where they still live traditionally, clan leaders can be bought off by western companies for a fraction of the value of the trees and minerals ultimately extracted. Denuded land and polluted rivers are often the legacy left after the companies move on.

It is criminal. People from foreign-owned companies lie, bribe, and cheat landowners to gain access to resources for a pittance. I met people whose leaders had sold logging rights for 500 kina ($500 Can) per family, when a single tree fetches far more than that. Most skilled mining and logging jobs go to outsiders. Most politicians turn a blind eye to what is going on and are among the country's wealthiest people.

In a speech in Port Moresby, I suggested that by any objective assessment of natural resources, PNG must rate among the wealthiest nations on Earth. If Papua New Guineans could push the World Bank and the transnational companies off their backs, I suggested, they could define what development means to them and in a way that fits their culture. That way, they could chart their own course into the future.

My remarks were covered by the media, and the next day I was challenged by Ajay Chhibber, World Bank division chief for Indonesia and the Pacific Islands. He told me I was completely misinformed and demanded an opportunity to set me straight.

At 6 a.m. the next day, I met with him and Pirooz Hamidian, a senior country economist in the East Asia department of the World Bank. Chhibber began by saying, "You and I are well off. We don't have the right to deny the poor people of the world an opportunity to improve their lives."

I agreed, but asked who is really "poor" and how do we define "improvement." What are the fundamental assumptions underlying the kind of economics the World Bank is forcing onto the so-called developing world?

I suggested that global economics overvalues human capital while externalizing natural capital. That's why forests and rivers, for example, which have provided a living for people for millennia, have economic value only when humans "develop" them.

There are alternatives to the World Bank's ideas. All nations share the same biosphere. Since PNG forests remove greenhouse gases that industrialized countries produce disproportionately, it is in *our* interest to pay PNG to maintain their forests. We can encourage forest protection by ensuring that PNG gets full value for wood cut sustainably. And by our experience we can inform people in countries of the South of the enormous social and ecological costs of a high-consumption, profit-driven way of life.

To this, Chhibber retorted, "People are better off now than they have ever been. There's more food than ever before in history and it's because of economic development." Chhibber's statement encapsulates the belief that has concentrated wealth in a few hands while creating ecological degradation and poverty for many, from Sarawak to Brazil to Kenya. But, I countered, leading scientists of the world are warning about ecological catastrophe.

Chhibber replied: "Scientists said twenty years ago there would be a major famine and large numbers of people would die. It never happened. They often exaggerate." I had been referring to a number of statements in press releases, articles, and stories supported by *thousands* of eminent scientists. I have no idea how many scientists Chhibber was referring to. His facile dismissal of scientific expertise and some 10 million deaths by starvation annually reveals why the World Bank mentality is so deadly. Canadians support the World Bank with their tax dollars and ought to take a greater interest in how that money is spent and the values it is promoting around the world.

ECONOMIST SEES ERROR OF OUR WAYS

Living in a way that ensures a future for generations yet to come will require major changes in the way we organize ourselves and live. But at present, all our political and economic leaders are taking us down the same destructive path, towards maintaining growth, overexploiting renewable natural resources, and overseeing economic growth while employment declines. How can we bring the global economy that enmeshes all of us into alignment with the natural world on which it depends? Few economists even consider the question.

An exception is Herman Daly, who left his position as senior economist with the World Bank after six years. On returning to academia, Daly delivered a remarkable farewell speech full of important suggestions for the World Bank.

His first suggestion? "Stop counting the consumption of natural capital as income. Income is by definition the maximum amount that a society can consume this year and still be able to consume the same amount next year. That is, consumption this year, if it is to be called income, must leave intact the capacity to produce and consume the same amount next year. Thus, sustainability is built into the very definition of income."

Conventional economics forgets or ignores the fact that everything we depend on for survival, including air and water, soil, plastic, energy, glass, metal, and food, comes from the Earth and represents "natural capital." Fiscal responsibility dictates that we live on interest and not touch the capital. But Daly points out that economists focus on the notion that wealth is created by human beings, so "productive capacity that must be maintained intact has traditionally been thought of as manmade capital only, excluding natural capital. We have habitually counted natural capital as a free good. . . . [I]n today's full world it is anti-economic."

Daly tells us that the error of considering natural-capital consumption as income is built right into our system of national accounts, in the evaluation of projects that deplete natural capital and in the accounting of international balance of payments. He says the accounting "biases investment allocation toward projects that deplete natural capital, and away from more sustainable projects." Clearly this bias must be corrected if we are to have a sustainable future. Depletion of nonrenewable resources, or their exploitation beyond a sustainable yield, should be counted as user costs. So should the ability of air, water, or soil to act as a sink for the absorption of products of human activity, such as excess CO_2.

Daly says, "In balance of payments accounting, the export of depleted natural capital, whether petroleum or timber cut beyond sustainable yield, is entered in the current account, and thus treated entirely as income. This is an accounting error. Some portion of those nonsustainable exports should be treated as the sale of a capital asset. . . . If this were properly done, some countries would see their apparent balance of trade surplus converted into a true deficit, one that is being financed by drawdown and transfer abroad of their stock of natural capital." Had this been done for the northern cod or B.C.'s old-growth forests, our economic and political decisions might have been very different.

His second recommendation is to "tax labor and income less and tax resource throughput more. [The matter and energy that go into a system and eventually comes out is what goes through — the throughput.] In the past it has been customary for governments to subsidize resource throughput to stimulate growth. Thus energy, water, fertilizer and even deforestation are even now frequently subsidized." In most countries, labour and income are taxed, but in so doing we merely exacerbate the pressure towards higher levels of unemployment. Instead, Daly says, we should be moving our tax base *away* from labour and income.

Daly goes on: "Income tax structure should be maintained so as to keep progressivity in the overall tax structure by taxing very high incomes and subsidizing very low incomes. But the bulk of public revenue would be raised from taxes on throughput either at the depletion or pollution end." He points out that such changes must be instituted in the North first. The problem is that the World Bank has leverage to encourage environmentally sustainable development only in the countries it gives loans to, namely, the poor countries of the South; it does not have influence over the rich industrialized nations.

Herman Daly's perspective enables us to see the distortions built into conventional economics and explains why the current thrust towards economic globalism is so dangerous. Here's another proposal in his parting shots: "Maximize the productivity of natural capital in the short run and invest in increasing its supply in the long run." Any economist knows that when there is a factor that limits production, we should make maximum use of what we have and invest in increasing its supply. But many economists don't look on the "natural capital" that comes from the Earth as a limiting factor.

Economics is based on the notion that human inventiveness can overcome any limits in nature, creating more or finding substitutes. Daly knows this assumption is a mistake. "In the past, natural capital has been treated as superabundant and priced at zero. . . . Now remaining natural capital appears to be both scarce and complementary, and therefore limiting. For example, the fish catch is limited not by the number of fishing boats, but by the remaining populations of fish. Cut timber is limited not by the number of sawmills, but by the remaining standing forests. . . . The atmosphere's capacity to serve as a sink for CO_2 is likely to be even more limiting to the rate at which petroleum can be burned than is the source limit of remaining oil in the ground."

But since, by definition, natural capital cannot be made by us, how do we invest in protecting it or actually increasing it in amount? According to Daly, we can do this by encouraging different kinds of policies such as "following investments, allowing this year's growth increment to be added to next year's growing stock rather than consuming it. For nonrenewables . . . how fast do we liquidate? . . . how much of the correctly counted income do we then consume and how much do we invest? . . . The failure to charge user cost on natural capital depletion surely biases investment away from replenishing resources."

Finally, Daly makes the radical suggestion that we "reverse direction from globalization to more national economies. It will not be easy because, at the present time, global interdependence is celebrated as a self-evident good. The royal road to development, peace, and harmony is thought to be the unrelenting conquest of each nation's market by all other nations. . . . [T]he word 'nationalist' has come to be pejorative."

Daly points out the strange fact that "the World Bank exists to serve the interests of its members, which are nation states, national communities, not individuals, not corporations, not even NGOs. It has no charter to serve the one-world-without-borders cosmopolitan vision of global integration."

We often see this destructive impact of the global economy in Canada, where logging, fishing, or mining policies that may foster sustainable communities and ecosystems are opposed by transnational corporations whose goal is to maximize returns for investors. When international agreements are made for global environmental problems, national governments must be able to enforce them. As Daly says, "If nations have no control over their borders, they are in a poor position to enforce national laws, including those necessary to secure compliance with international treaties."

Daly also makes the daring warning that "Cosmopolitan globalism weakens . . . the power of national and subnational communities, while strengthening the relative power of transnational corporations. . . . It will be necessary to make capital less global and more national. . . . [T]en years from now the buzz words will be 'renationalization of capital' . . . not the current shibboleths of export-led growth stimulated by whatever adjustments are necessary to increase global competitiveness. 'Global competitiveness' usually reflects . . . a standards-lowering competition to reduce wages, externalize environmental and social costs and export natural capital at low prices while calling it income."

Daly forces us to question our current economic paradigm. He brings a welcome dose of common sense to counter the barrage of mindless repetition of the belief and value systems implicit in globalization.

WALL STREET JOURNAL'S *CRITERIA ARE INSANE*

I've long argued that global economics underlies the current wave of ecological destruction and must be altered if we are to have a sustainable future. On January 12, 1995, in an editorial headlined "Bankrupt Canada?" the *Wall Street Journal* declared that Canada "has now become an honorary member of the Third World in the unmanageability of its debt problem." It warned that without heroic measures, Canada might have to call in the International Monetary Fund to stabilize our falling currency.

In fact, our resemblance to less-developed countries extends beyond the deficit. We manufacture very few of the products used extensively in our homes, garages, and workplaces. Most of our major industries are branch plants of transnational corporations whose head offices are located elsewhere in the world. Nevertheless, we live like an advanced nation and finance the illusion with income generated by exporting raw materials.

The patronizing attitude towards Third World countries implicit in the *Wall Street Journal*'s editorial reflects the belief in the superiority of the industrialized world and the global economy. Canada has already lost a triple-A credit rating. The federal government, advises the *Wall Street Journal*, should emulate the provincial premiers who cut rural hospitals, chopped school boards, and slashed welfare rolls.

Before our finance minister follows the prescription of the business community and the *Wall Street Journal*, let's try a suggestion once made to me by the eminent economist Kenneth Boulding. I was describing the scary rhetoric used to "persuade" Canadians to adopt the Free Trade Agreement (FTA) with the United States. Without the FTA, we were being told, Canada would be an "imminent economic basketcase." Boulding responded that to get an idea of how rich we really are, just imagine the consequences for Canada if all other countries vanished, leaving only our country and two hundred miles of ocean. What would happen?

Canada is one of the two major grain exporters in the world, so we would not lack for food. Our natural resources of land, water, timber, and minerals make us the envy of most people on the planet. Furthermore, we have an educated, literate public, capable of creating the most advanced technology desired. Boulding's thought exercise reveals that we are extremely well off.

If we apply the same exercise to Japan, for a long time considered one of the world's economic giants, and China, now roaring into economic prominence, the result is very different. Either country, if left alone, would be in immediate difficulty. Japan has little energy and few natural resources beyond trees, and its population is able to live high on the ecological food chain only by exploiting waters and resources far beyond its borders. China, on the other hand, does have energy, but also has major problems with pollution and limits on agricultural land and resources. Each country, if alone, would be plunged into desperate straits.

There is something absolutely perverted in a system, then, that renders Canada a poor country requiring external economic institutions to stabilize its economy while Japan and China are awesome colossi. Global economics grossly undervalues the air, water, soil, and species diversity that keep us alive while vastly overvaluing human intellect and activity. That's what creates the dichotomy in wealth between Canada, Japan, and China.

On the same day the *Wall Street Journal* was making its pronouncements, U.S. president Bill Clinton declared American confidence in the Mexican economy to help stabilize the calamitous plunge in the value of the peso. For weeks the Mexican government tried frantically to stabilize its currency. Pundits declared that the Mexican economy had not inspired "investor confidence."

Even if we overlook the glowing promise that seduced Canada and Mexico into the North American Free Trade Agreement (NAFTA), what does the peso's plummet reveal? It informs us that currency speculators are now more powerful than governments. The Mexican government dipped deeply into its reserves to buy up pesos, all in a vain effort to halt its slide, just as the French government and banks had done two summers earlier to halt the plunge of the franc. Few governments can stand up against more than $600 billion in daily currency speculation on stock markets around the world!

It is an insane game in which money can be bought and sold to make more money! In this kind of game, money can be created faster than things in the real world, and the players don't have to worry about long-term sustainability. Currency is a human invention, and when it is no longer anchored to anything more tangible than "investor confidence," then we enter an Alice-in-Wonderland fantasy world. It is a realm that relegates Canada to Third Worldhood and has little value for the future of communities or ecosystems.

GDP-DRIVEN VISION IS AN EMPTY ONE

I returned to Canada in 1962, after eight years of college and graduate school in the United States. I had turned down several academic offers there and had come home instead. Canada to me meant the CBC, Tommy Douglas, the National Film Board, medicare, and Quebec — things that made this country both different from the U.S. and, for me, preferable to it.

I once asked a Japanese politician what he felt Japan's main long-term goal was. He replied, "We want our economy to be number one." When I suggested that being number one must be a means to some more inspiring end, he didn't understand what I was talking about.

In the Canada I chose to return to, politicians spoke with sincerity and passion of a just, more equitable society, of a secure future for all Canadians, of protecting a heritage of rich and diverse flora and fauna for our children. Those were the ideals for which I came home, and I have never regretted it.

But the Quebec referendum exposed the enormous changes that have taken place since the 1960s. Increasingly, political rhetoric revolves around matters economic. Our leaders and the media now present the deficit, the debt, and economic growth as the dominant issues of our time.

If we learned anything from the ulcer-inducing debate in Quebec before the referendum, it was that political "leaders" outside that province lack an uplifting vision of Canada. While Quebeckers were being inspired with a sense of history, culture, and belonging, and were expressing their desire to support their elders and their medical and educational systems, the rest of Canada was being told that Quebec separation would be too costly, threatening the economy, jobs, and the value of our dollar.

What an empty vision. Yet more and more we are bombarded with the message that we need to cut government services, to reduce our debt, to increase foreign trade and investment from other countries, and to keep the GDP rising. Those are the very same measures the World Bank imposes on impoverished developing countries under the title of Structural Adjustment.

Canada's crisis over Quebec offered us an opportunity to re-examine what this country stands for, what we value most, the things that make us proud and are worth preserving. The Canada that I chose to return to had a belief in sharing between the have and have-not provinces. There was pride in the notion that all Canadians deserved the best education and medical care. Communities boasted about their neighbourhoods, local merchants, and small businesses.

Today growth in the GDP has become the measuring-stick of

"progress," the standard of well-being that governments and industry do all they can to keep raising. But it is an insane and destructive gauge of the things that really matter — family, community, and ecosystems. Consider this:

Mary and Bob live on the family farm in a small Prairie community. Bob's parents live with them and help to care for the children. Mary home-schools the children and the family lives frugally, sharing farm machinery, labour, and farm produce with their neighbours. Mary volunteers her time with the community centre and hospital, while Bob is a Boy Scout leader and coaches his son's hockey team. Bob and Mary are classed as underproductive members of society because they contribute little to the GDP.

Bob and Mary's son is hurt in a terrible car accident. His need for an ambulance, intensive-care unit, hospital personnel, and medicine all contribute to a rise in the GDP. The boy dies. Bob and Mary must pay for the funeral home, flowers, and gravediggers. It's good for the economy — the GDP goes up.

The tragedy puts a strain on the marriage. Bob places his parents in an old-age home. The GDP grows. Bob moves to the city, rents an apartment, buys a car, gets a job. The GDP increases. Mary stays on the farm, takes out a mortgage, puts the children in day care, hires a farm-hand, takes a job in the grocery store. She is also helping to build up the GDP. Bob and Mary have become contributing, productive members in a society that measures progress in terms of the economy.

The No vote in Quebec gave us a reprieve, an opportunity to reflect on what Canada is and rethink what we want it to be. If we don't, why should the Québécois want to remain a part of us?

A PROGRESS INDICATOR THAT'S REAL

The GDP, now routinely measured instead of the GNP, is an economic register of the total value of goods and services bought and sold. It has become the key indicator of the health of our national economy and, for some, a measure of progress.

But the GDP only adds and never subtracts; that is, no distinction is made between destructive and productive activities. An industry that makes a profit while polluting a stream adds to the GDP. People poisoned by the polluted water and hospitalized will need the services of doctors, nurses, and lawyers, as well as goods like medicine and flowers, all adding to the GDP. When the polluter is made to clean up the problem, often with government subsidies, that too is added to the GDP!

In this value system, the destruction of an old-growth forest by clearcutting, the flooding of a valley by a megadam, or the elimination of fish by drift-netting is treated as income generation rather than depletion of an asset. Voluntary services, friendship, sharing, co-operating, and caring, all acts that create a sense of community, do not contribute to the GDP. Nor does it factor in income distribution, unemployment, or the debt incurred to foreign countries. The GDP has no value for wise decisions made to ensure the long-term stability of communities or ecosystems.

Robert Kennedy, Jr., has said, "The GNP counts air pollution and cigarette advertising and ambulances to clear our highways of carnage. . . . Yet [it] does not allow for the health of our children, the quality of their education, or the joy of their play. . . . It measures neither our wit nor our courage; neither our wisdom nor our learning; neither our compassion nor our devotion to our country; it measures everything, in short, except that which makes life worthwhile."

An organization called Redefining Progress has issued a call for new measures of progress, which states: "Much of what we now consider economic growth, as measured by GDP, is really the fixing of blunders from the past and the borrowing of resources from the future." The organization proposes a new value called the Genuine Progress Indicator (GPI). The new indicator is an attempt to redress the deficits of the GDP by measuring the general well-being and sustainability of a nation. The techniques for calculating each component of the GPI are contained in Redefining Progress' book, *The Genuine Progress Indicator: Summary of Data and Methodology.*

In contrast to the GDP, the GPI contains adjustments for:

- Resource depletion — The loss of wetlands, farmland, and minerals (including oil) is a cost.

- Income distribution — "The GPI rises when the poor receive a larger percentage of national income, and falls when their share decreases."
- Housework and nonmarket transactions — Childcare, cooking, cleaning, and home repairs are GPI gains.
- Changes in leisure time — "The GPI treats an increase in leisure as a benefit and decrease in leisure as a cost."
- Unemployment and underemployment — These are costs.
- Pollution — This is a GPI cost.
- Long-term environmental damage — It is treated as a cost.
- Lifespan of consumer durables and infrastructure — This is calculated on the length of service rendered by an item rather than the money spent on its purchase.
- Defensive expenditures — The price of maintaining a level of service without increasing it is a cost in the GPI. "The amount of money spent on commuting, the medical and material costs of automobile accidents, and the money that households are forced to spend on personal pollution control devices such as water filters are examples."
- Sustainable investments — "If a nation allows its capital stock to decline, or if it finances its investments out of borrowed capital rather than savings, it is living beyond its means."

And what does Redefining Progress find in comparing the GDP and GPI? The GDP per capita in the U.S. rose steadily from a per person average of $7,865 in 1950 to $16,414 in 1992. The GPI reveals a different picture, rising from $5,663 in 1950 to a peak of $7,441 in 1969, then declining to $4,426 in 1992! By striving for continued economic growth, we have catastrophically lessened our quality of life, as indicated by the GPI.

Even a former president of the World Bank, Barber Conable, is aware that GDP values "represent an income that cannot be sustained." He says, "Current calculations ignore the degradation of the natural resource base and view the sales of nonrenewable resources entirely as income. A better way must be found to measure the prosperity and progress of mankind." I couldn't agree more.

11

CONSUMPTION:
BEYOND NEED

$\mathcal{N}$ow that the economy has become the dominant priority in our society, our lives are being shaped to serve its needs. Ironically, this subservience to economics impoverishes rather than enriches us. Built into this kind of economics is the necessity for each of us to be consumers. This obsession with consumption affects us, our values, and the way we live all around the world and diminishes the things that really matter — independence, self-reliance, community.

We in the industrialized nations are setting an example for the developing world. So long as we who are already obscene overconsumers demand more, there is no reason to expect poorer people to want any less. And the consequences of countries like China, India, Russia, and Indonesia attempting to emulate us will be ecologically disastrous.

FIFTY YEARS BACK AND TWENTY-FIVE YEARS AHEAD

A unique trait of our species, one that is critical for our survival, has been our ability to both reflect back on times past in order to understand how we got here and project our thoughts ahead into the future to see where we may be heading. Even though we are fixed in the present, our imagination enables us to roam across time and use that capacity to learn from the past and recognize options for the future.

A powerful thought exercise is to cast ourselves back in time and then ask what we would have wanted to aim for in the future. Imagine yourself back in 1945 as an example. The industrial world has just been pulled out of the Great Depression by war-driven economic growth. There are a little more than 2 billion people on Earth and most still live in small towns; the population of Greater Vancouver has just reached 400,000 and Toronto a million. Most of the planet's vast forests and oceans are still untouched and pristine. Food is free of pesticides. Asthma is a relatively rare respiratory problem. Television is in its infancy and technologies like oral contraceptives, satellites, transistors, computers, and compact discs are yet to come. There seems to be no limit to progress and the improvement of life for all people.

Would you then have wanted a society obsessed with consumption and driven by the blare of advertising? What would you have thought of a society in which people wore clothing and used products that displayed company logos so prominently that people become walking advertisements? Would you have felt that the cornucopia of consumer goods (25,000 items in department stores, more than 200 breakfast cereals) was a reasonable trade for the breakdown of neighbourhoods and families, the pollution of air and water, traffic congestion, and the disappearance of wilderness and species? Would you have accepted a world increasingly divided along lines of wealth, the ranks of the impoverished swelling as a diminishing proportion of humanity that was already obscenely rich continued to demand more?

These and many other things we accept today would have shocked and outraged people in 1945. By putting ourselves back in time, we can see that with foresight, we could have achieved a very different future. All we needed was the will to act. Today's problems might have been avoided or been solved far more easily and at far less cost had they been tackled when they were first anticipated or appeared.

For example, had the United States acted to stabilize its population at the 1945 level, the country would be completely self-sufficient in oil today! And there would have been many other positive repercussions in terms of natural resources, croplands, air and water quality, and old-growth forests.

Steps taken in 1945 to design an economy controlled by national governments and based on full employment, frugality, and product durability would have had vast social and ecological ramifications. These goals could have been achieved with far less upheaval or adjustment than is needed trying to reach them today. We must remember that this juggernaut called the global economy, which dictates so much of what our government and business leaders do today, is a very recent development.

When economists and politicians met in 1944 at Bretton Woods, New Hampshire, and established the World Bank and the IMF, they set in motion forces that would come to dominate our lives. Yet way back in the '30s, one of the major players at Bretton Woods, the economist John Maynard Keynes, had the prescience to warn that economies should remain profoundly national, not international, or they would be beyond government control.

Today, world-renowned scientists are telling us that multiple issues of population growth, overconsumption, poverty, pollution, climate change, and wilderness destruction increasingly impinge on our lives and render our political, economic, and social structures increasingly unstable and vulnerable to breakdown. If we cast ahead and assume that we continue with business as usual, scientists such as the Nobel prize winner Henry Kendall, the population dynamicist David Pimentel, and the modelling expert Donella Meadows foresee horrific outcomes within the lifetimes of our children.

Every day that goes by without serious attempts to address and act on our predicament will exacerbate the unpredictability and gravity of the problems in the future. And even where solutions are still possible, every day that passes without action ensures that the cost of attempting to resolve them will escalate.

Most people alive today will still be around in 2020. Will they curse us for having failed to act to avoid the problems they will face?

We know a catastrophe looms, but what does it take to act on it, and who is going to lead the way?

WE'RE ALL SLAVES TO THIS HABIT

I am a drug addict, and for twelve years I was a slave to it. It cost me thousands of dollars and no doubt affected my health and the well-being of my family. My addiction was to tobacco, and although I haven't smoked for more than twenty years I know that if I tried just one cigarette, I'd be hooked again. I know because I tried giving it up several times only to start again, each time with the rationalization that "only one won't hurt." From the occasional bummed cigarette in college, I had gradually worked up to a pack-a-day habit. From being a social smoker, I graduated to puffing alone with my breakfast coffee.

At some point my son began to torment me by snatching cigarettes out of my mouth and breaking them in two or putting whole packs under the tap. He kept it up, risking my angry response, until I finally realized he was terrified that I was harming myself. Because he loved me, he was willing to risk my wrath. For his sake, I had to give it up.

In many ways, my long nicotine addiction resembles our current obsession with consumption. Ever since the mighty economic engine created by the Second World War was forced to adjust to peace, advertising has been used to convince us that consumption brings happiness. We have been democratized into the all-inclusive class of "consumer," now a key component of the economy.

Like the tobacco plant, which has occupied a special place in many cultures for its medicinal properties and ceremonial role, consumption is vital in our lives. We work to be able to purchase to satisfy our physical and social requirements. But when consumption, like smoking, becomes an uncontrollable need, a reflex habit, it is transformed into something else. On rare occasions when I had to go for hours without a cigarette, I desperately yearned for a puff and the first drag was heavenly. But the pleasure was fleeting and was soon followed by a dull need for more, just like shopping. Store-hopping has become a social and recreational activity, and our addiction to it is perfect for business that wants a limitless market.

When I was a boy, my parents bought articles of clothing with a view to handing them down from child to child. They were proud when a coat served two or three children. But durable products pose a problem for business because the market is eventually saturated. And in the madness that passes as today's accepted economic wisdom, endless growth — an impossibility in a finite world — is considered essential for survival. One solution to dwindling markets was the introduction of disposable products sold with the promise of "convenience." When an item is used once and then thrown away, the market is endless.

Long-term balance and stability are achieved by reaching a steady state or equilibrium in nature, but are regarded as lethal in the economic realm. With society placing no value on sustainability of communities or ecosystems, the economy holds people to ransom. Governments inject funds into communities for short-term political gain more than long-term benefits to the community. Many communities have offered tax exemptions, free land, monopolies, etc. to transnational corporations, only to watch the companies move on when the benefits expire or better offers are received elsewhere.

Business leaders tell us that they make only "what the consumer demands." Nonsense. More than half our purchases in hardware, grocery, and department stores are spur-of-the-moment decisions, made when products have caught our attention and created a desire. I often discover something new, think, "Gee, what a great idea! I need one of those," and buy it. Who among us has demanded the 200 varieties of breakfast cereal that now vie for our attention? Wasteful packaging merely serves to entice us to buy what's inside, not serve our needs.

Only a few generations ago, when people lived with far less of everything, consumption beyond vital needs was a luxury. People worked and saved and savoured the anticipation of a purchase. Today, most consumption is for non-essential merchandise, which, like that first hit of nicotine, provides only a momentary kick, then leaves us wanting more.

Magazines inform us that more and more North Americans are seeking spiritual fulfilment. Our vaguely felt emptiness is a symptom of our isolation and disconnection from other people and other species. Disappearance of family, community, stability, security, and a spiritual sense of connection cannot be compensated by the accumulation of more trinkets, novelty, and titillation.

This economy, with its emphasis on endless production and consumption, has become one of the most destructive forces ever unleashed on the planet, and it has lured us into participation as overconsumers. Just as my son worried about my smoking, children today are alarmed that we are mortgaging their futures in our mistaken belief that we must have continued economic growth and ever more things to be happy. If our addictive assumptions and habits harm our children's futures, it's time to kick them.

A PORTRAIT OF A PIGGISH SOCIETY

A powerful frugality movement to make less and consume less is growing in North America. *Your Money or Your Life* by Joe Dominguez and Vicki Robin tells us how it can be done and what the benefits are. To some, making do with less may seem retrogressive, but studies indicate that 75 percent of American workers between twenty-five and forty-nine would like to see a return to a simpler society with less emphasis on material wealth.

Vicki Robin is the president of the New Road Map Foundation, which is trying to chart new paths to frugal living. In 1994 her foundation published a pamphlet, *All-Consuming Passion: Waking up from the American Dream,* which is filled with a series of stunning statistics that point to the contradictions in our beliefs and actions. Here are some of the non-metric numbers based on American studies.

Having more cannot be equated with greater happiness. In spite of a 50 percent increase in personal income between 1957 and 1991, the percentage of people who describe themselves as "very happy" did not change. In 1978, 41 percent of eighteen- to twenty-nine-year-olds thought they had a good chance of achieving "the good life"; by 1993, only 21 percent thought so.

People today are, on average, 450 percent richer than in 1900. Per capita consumption in the past twenty years rose by 45 percent, while the quality of life as measured by the Index of Social Health decreased by 51 percent.

Parents spend 40 percent less time with their children than they did in 1965. In part, that reflects the fact that employed people spend 163 hours more per year on the job than they did in 1969. Sixty-nine percent of Americans would like to "slow down and live a more relaxed life," while only 19 percent would like a "more exciting, faster-paced life."

The percentage of college freshmen who think it is essential to be well off financially was 44 percent in 1967 and 76 percent in 1987. In contrast, in 1967, 83 percent of college freshmen thought it was essential to develop a philosophy of life, while in 1987 only 39 percent did.

When we buy more things, we need more space in which to keep them. The median size of newly built houses rose from 1,100 square feet in 1949 to 1,385 in 1970 to 2,060 in 1993. Residential space per person increased from 312 square feet in 1950 to 742 in 1993. Ten million Americans own two or more homes; at least 300,000 are homeless.

Teenagers are exposed to 360,000 advertisements by the time they graduate from high school. The average American spends one entire year of his or her life watching TV commercials. As a consequence, 93 percent of teenage girls report store-hopping as their favourite activity. People can choose from more than 25,000 supermarket items and 11,092 magazines. Americans spend an average of six hours a week shopping and forty minutes a week playing with their children!

Increased consumption results from greater product variety and disposability. In 1981, two-thirds to three-quarters of houseware purchases were to replace items that had worn out; by 1987, less than half were. Each year, 180 million gallons of motor oil, the equivalent of sixteen *Exxon Valdez* spills, are sent to landfills or poured down drains. In 1989, Americans drank an average of 186 quarts of soft drinks and 149 quarts of tap water. It takes 2,200 calories of energy to produce a twelve-ounce can of diet soda, which provides less than one calorie of food energy.

North Americans have a disproportionate impact on the planet. Americans make up 5 percent of the world's population but use 30 percent of the world's resources and 25 percent of the fossil fuel consumed annually. The average American consumes as much energy as is used by 3 Japanese, 6 Mexicans, 14 Chinese, 38 Indians, 168 Bangladeshis, or 531 Ethiopians.

Eight percent of all people on Earth own a car; 89 percent of all American households own one or more cars. Since 1940, Americans alone have used up as large a share of the Earth's mineral resources as all previous generations of humans put together. A person in the United States causes one hundred times more damage to the global environment as a person in a poor country.

In the last 200 years, the United States has lost 50 percent of its wetlands, 90 percent of its northwestern old-growth forests, and 99 percent of its tall-grass prairie; up to 490 species of native plants and animals are extinct and another 9,000 are at risk. Every day, nine square miles of U.S. rural land are turned over to development. Each year, 1.3 million acres are blacktopped while one million acres of cropland are lost to erosion. In 1990, 78 percent of Americans believed a "major national effort" was needed to improve the environment.

These are just some of the statistics contained in the remarkable pamphlet. It provides a fascinating snapshot of a consumer society that has not delivered greater leisure and happiness. What people need are genuine choices that provide a high quality of life on less consumption.

BLEAK SIDE OF CHINA'S BONANZA

China's spectacular economic growth of more than 10 percent per year in the 1990s has fuelled an economic gold-rush. In 1994 Team Canada, a group of businesspeople led by Prime Minister Chrétien, blitzed China and returned home boasting of having negotiated new deals worth billions of dollars. But there's another side to China's "success," as Lester Brown reveals in "Who Will Feed China?" an article he wrote for *World Watch* magazine. "The country's capacity to produce food is projected to shrink due to the massive ongoing conversion of cropland to nonfarm uses."

Other countries have had similar experiences. For example, land that once grew grain but was shifted to other purposes with industrialization diminished farmland by 52 percent in Japan, 42 percent in South Korea, and 35 percent in Taiwan. As a result, Japan has had to import 77 percent of its grain, Taiwan 67 percent, and South Korea 64 percent. Japan is the world's largest importer of grain, at 28 million tons a year.

China's grain output rose spectacularly to surpass the U.S. at more than 300 million tons by 1984. But the benefits of the gains in production are blunted by the 14 million people still added to China's population annually. That will amount to an increase of 490 million people by 2030. Yet having more people to feed isn't the only issue.

Brown points out that if people have been poor all their lives, one of the first things they're likely to do with an increase in income is diversify their diet. They buy more expensive meat, milk, and eggs. But where will the food come from? In 1978, only 7 percent of China's grain was used for animal feed; by 1990 it was 20 percent. Already they have almost reached American levels of red-meat consumption. What will happen as China begins to consume more from the top end of the food chain?

Brown calculates that doubling egg consumption from 100 per person in 1990 to the government goal of 200 in 2000 will require an additional 24 million tons of grain to feed the additional chickens to lay the added eggs. The extra grain is about what Canada exports annually. If every adult Chinese decides to drink one more bottle of beer a year, it would mean another 370,000 tons of grain would be needed to make that beer.

China's grain-growing land is decreasing by one percent annually, down from 90.8 million hectares in 1990 to an estimated 87.4 million in 1994 because of industrial growth that requires more factories, railways, housing, and roads. In 1994 alone, 10,000 miles of new highways were built. The productivity of the remaining cropland is threatened by "soil erosion, waterlogging and salting of irrigation systems, air pollution and global warming."

Brown predicts that with grain production falling by at least 0.5 percent annually, the country's grain output will be decreased by at least 20 percent by 2030. That's a stunning shift from 1990, when the country produced 329 million tons of grain while consuming 335 million tons. Increased population alone will raise China's demand for grain from 335 million tons in 1990 to 479 million tons in 2030. "Even if China's booming economy produced NO gains in consumption of meat, eggs and beer, a 20 percent drop in grain production . . . would leave a shortfall of 216 million tons, a level that exceeds the world's entire 1993 grain exports of 200 million tons."

A small rise in per capita grain consumption, from about 300 kilograms at present to 350 kilograms in thirty-five years, will increase total demand to 568 million tons of grain, a deficit of 305 million tons! "If grain consumption per person were to rise to 400 kilograms, the current level in Taiwan, or one-half the U.S. level, total consumption would climb to a staggering 641 million tons and the import deficit would reach 378 million tons."

China's economic boom will provide ample income to pay for the needed grain imports. But what nation could fill its needs? The simple answer is none. Annual world grain exports since 1980 have averaged about 200 million tons, almost half of that coming from the United States. But the U.S. is also losing farmland, and its population will rise by 95 million people in the next forty years. More than one hundred countries already import grain from the U.S., and while their needs will certainly rise the amount of grain available for export is already committed.

"No country, or combination of countries, has the additional export potential to fill more than a small fraction of the potential food deficit forming in China. At the same time, huge deficits are projected for other parts of the world. Africa is expected to need 250 million tons of grain by 2030 — ten times current imports." Brown predicts China's appetite will create a ferocious competition for grossly inadequate supplies and send world grain prices skyrocketing. China's demand for food will create global scarcity.

Brown concludes: "In the booming economy of China, we will

see the inevitable collision between expanding human demand for food and the limits of some of the earth's most basic natural systems. . . . The shock waves from this collision will reverberate throughout the world economy with consequences that we can only now begin to foresee." A fuller account of the ecological impact of China's growth is contained in *Full House: Reassessing the Earth's Population Carrying Capacity* by Brown and Hal Kane.

I first visited China in 1976 and learned that with a population thirty times greater than Canada's, their total consumption of oil was equal to ours. I wrote at the time that if every Chinese adult aspired to owing a motor bike, the ecological consequences would be catastrophic. Today I am told that most adult Chinese want to own a car, and they are on a steep curve of increased personal consumption.

Government planning is predicated on the short-term political vision of its practitioners. Without the inciteful long-term perspective provided by Brown, we will miss the far-reaching implications of China's vaunted economic performance.

REMEMBER THE LAST SECRET PLAN?

People delight in speculating on conspiracies that suppress the real facts behind high-mileage cars, Kennedy's assassination, or flying saucers. I don't take conspiracies seriously because they make me feel helpless. But there are times when the failure of politicians and the media to pursue the dimensions and implications of the planet's environmental problems seems almost deliberate.

For example, only two weeks after the largest gathering of world leaders in history at the 1992 Earth Summit in Rio, leaders of the Group of Seven industrialized countries meeting in Munich didn't even mention the environment or the Earth Summit. Stark warnings about ecological degradation signed by leading scientists, including numerous Nobel laureates, were deemed "not newsworthy" and ignored by major TV networks and newspapers.

As a scientist, I am astonished that although the media love to blare the latest scientific "breakthrough" or scare, they ignore eminent scientists warning of impending dangers. There may not be a conspiracy, but the contradiction is pretty disturbing.

In a talk he gave to the Minnesota Investment Forum, Daniel Quinn, the author of the novel *Ishmael*, suggested that "During the Second World War, the people of Germany invested heavily in a secret plan. This plan was so secret that many Germans managed to keep it secret even from themselves. Except in the highest military and political circles, the plan was never discussed." He was referring, of course, to the genocidal program of race purification that ended in the Holocaust. Quinn suggests that the tacit or overt support of Hitler's plan by the German people bore an enormous cost: "They invested their consciences. They invested their place among the family of nations. They invested their self-respect."

When the war ended, "the German people lost their investment . . . they and their children and indeed their children's children. They're still paying off their losses for this dreadfully bad investment."

Quinn believes there is in the industrialized nations a contemporary counterpart to Germany's plan that is also never discussed openly. There are no overt lessons about this plan at home or at school, yet before they finish their formal schooling children not only know about it, they too are part of it. According to Quinn, "we're investing everything we have in it. We're investing our future in it, our children's future in it — for generations to come. . . . Our secret plan is this: we're going to go on consuming the world until there's no more to consume."

Quinn knows that some people are trying to act to save the environment, but he believes that we fail to confront the heart of the problem — our demand for more. "We're going to recycle, we're going to conserve — but we're also going to go on consuming until there's no more to consume. We don't know when it will all be gone. We don't want to know — just as the people of Germany didn't want to know what happened to their Jewish neighbours when the Gestapo carried them away. . . . One thing we do know, however: It won't happen in our lifetime." Quinn believes we must face up to the reality of what we are doing if we are to avoid the kind of revulsion and horror that people felt after learning what happened in Germany.

"If we continue to pursue our plan to consume the world until there's no more to consume, then there's going to come a day, sure as hell, when our children or their children's children are going to look back on us — on you and me — and say to themselves, 'My God, what kind of monsters WERE these people?' If you're like me and would like to avoid looking like a monster to your grandchildren, then I suggest you stop being silent about our plan to go on consuming the world until there simply isn't any more there to consume." The silence might not be a conspiracy, but it may be just as effective.

TWO REASONS TO COUNT OUR BLESSINGS

The holiday season is the time to sit back and reflect on the past year and consider what lies ahead. As I wade through the mob of last-minute Christmas shoppers, I am amazed at the array of dazzling consumer products begging to be bought. But this is a time to reaffirm the importance of family and friends and to "count our blessings," so it is also an appropriate moment to ask whether all of our material possessions make us happier and "better off."

For most of the year, we seem hell-bent on supporting the belief that economic growth and development are essential for our well-being and happiness. It is based on the faith that more and bigger are better.

I lived in London, Ontario, during the 1940s and 1950s, and I remember feeling proud when the city reached a population of 100,000 because we assumed that a bigger city meant we were more cultured and sophisticated. And that was only the beginning; London's population has since grown more than 300 percent!

Now I'm a Vancouverite, and we are proud of the spectacular geography and moderate climate of this unique Canadian city. In aspiring to make Vancouver a "world-class" city, a succession of mayors has encouraged greater growth and development. The city's pre-eminent architect, Arthur Erickson, once boasted that good architects could fit 14 million people into the city!

All across the country, villages, towns, and cities seem determined to increase their tax base and revenue by doing all they can to stimulate development and economic growth. Now that logging has cleared most of the forest, a major highway is planned for the centre of Vancouver Island to open it up to development. The dry climate and stunning setting of Kelowna and Penticton are creating a population boom. And so it goes.

One day, there could be Kelowna- or Penticton-sized cities all up and down Vancouver Island, while Kelowna and Penticton will surpass London's current size. London will reach Vancouver's size and Vancouver will surpass modern-day Toronto. Toronto will grow towards New York and New York may catch up to present-day Mexico City. After all, that's what progress is all about, isn't it?

If the communities to which we presently belong have features that make them good places to live, then we ought to ask what will happen to them when we approach bigger-city status. At each successive stage, the things that we treasure are inevitably destroyed or replaced by new problems — traffic jams, ugly strip malls, loss of community, environmental degradation, pollution, violence, garbage, slums, alienation, crime, etc. The current equation of greater size with economic benefit may mean quick profits for developers and entrepreneurs, but it ignores factors that ensure long-term social stability, local community, personal safety, and accessibility to jobs and recreation.

On a visit to Japan in 1994, I learned of two attempts to resist the notion that bigger is better. In 1972, when Okinawa reverted from U.S. military occupation to Japanese control, the village of Yomitan had reached 32,000 people. This qualified Yomitan to be reclassified as a town, but the inhabitants turned this down and chose to remain a village. In Japan, that was unheard of because villagers are thought to be backward, primitive, simple-minded, unsophisticated yokels or bumpkins. In going against the prevailing conventions, the Yomitan residents affirmed the importance of community values that disappear with growth and development.

Even in Tokyo, I encountered a hint of change. In Japan, the car is king, and neighbourhoods and pedestrians are expected to make way for it. The lowly bicycle is a far better way to navigate Tokyo's narrow, crowded, winding streets, yet city bureaucrats consider them a nuisance, an antiquated symbol of poverty that is even blamed for petty crime. People who bike to subway stations must park them illegally because there are no bicycle parking areas; they often return to find them impounded.

Kazuko Murata is an environmental journalist who has been elected to the council of Sumida borough, a crowded area that houses 300,000 in the heart of Tokyo. She campaigned to give the bicycle a higher priority by designating bike-parking sites at all subway stops and creating a system of one-way streets that inconvenience drivers but give more room to cyclists. The borough's bureaucrats fought her proposal, but, to their surprise, the residents of the district gave the plan overwhelming support and now Murata is spreading her ideas.

These are minor stories in a country, indeed a world, that is hell-bent on increasing economic growth and development. As symbols, however, they suggest that as we count our blessings, we can also think about ways to preserve them. Bigger isn't always better.

SOME THINGS HAVE A VALUE BEYOND PRICE

It looked like a piece of cheap, dime-store costume jewellery lying in the grass, but I picked it up and carried it over to the booth at the park entrance. As soon as I held out the brooch, a woman came running over and seized it with a squeal. "That's mine! Thank you so much." She then proceeded to hug every bit of air out of my chest. She had been frantic over the brooch's loss because, as she told me, it had belonged to her great-grandmother and had been passed down to her by her mother.

That piece of jewellery was priceless to its current possessor and I doubt that any amount of money could have made her part with it. Yet its value on the market could not have been more than a few dollars. The history, sentiment, and memories that gave that trinket worth to the woman could not be discerned in its physical properties. Its value was only in the woman's mind.

The human brain is unique in its capacity to put "value" on intangible things. We do that with many things that really matter to us. Before each one of our children was born, my wife and I saved everything from mementoes and friends' congratulatory cards to poems and notes that we wrote about our hopes and thoughts for the future of the child growing in my wife's body. And after each of their births, we saved hospital ID bracelets, the first lost baby teeth, drawings and scribbles. When the children reach adulthood, they will get albums containing some of the landmarks of their lives. And I know that if our home should ever catch fire, the first things I would try to save would be those albums, because to me they are irreplaceable and beyond price. Yet they would be worthless if I ever tried to sell them.

My first years of life were in a Vancouver community where most of our neighbours had lived for decades, many in houses that had belonged to their parents. Today, with land flipping and "starter homes," people occupy houses temporarily, sell them, and move on. A house has become mere property, an investment, a tax dodge, a quick profit; it's no longer a place in which part of our lives exists.

And yet we can form deep sentimental attachments to places rather quickly. My wife and I spent months searching for a bit of wilderness to which we could retreat for rest and renewal. After months of looking, we discovered a magical place that we knew instantly was "Tangwyn" (Blessed Peace).

Tangwyn is an intact piece of land with ocean bays, a creek, and many trees that are hundreds of years old. The real-estate agent missed our motives and confided that the property could be cut into three lots. "You could sell two and have the third for yourself free," he suggested. What he didn't understand was that we had fallen in love with it and wanted to hold it so that it could be passed on to our children intact. The ancient trees and the middens, and the arrowheads exposed on the eroding shore banks offer mute testimony to a long history of occupation, and it is a privilege to be another link in the chain.

Money has become such a preoccupation today that we measure all value in dollars and cents. But surely that woman's brooch, my children's albums, and Tangwyn inform us that there are many precious things whose value cannot be measured monetarily. The reasons we cherish them are very real and important, but they are, for lack of a better word, *spiritual* in nature. It's time to divert our excessive attention away from matters economic and acknowledge the reality and importance of those spiritual values.

The heart of the global ecocrisis today is the loss of any sense that the Earth and its animate and inanimate components are "sacred" gifts from the past and the rightful inheritance of all future generations. It is a terrible mistake to get caught up in the sham of trying to assign economic worth to things that are beyond anything economic.

Even if our species is able to survive the spasm of mass extinction that is now consuming the planet's biodiversity, we would be bereft of the companionship of other species, a loss that cannot be calculated in economic terms. I believe the revulsion one feels upon first seeing a large clearcut is a visceral recognition of a desecration: we know to our very core that this is not the way to treat the Earth.

In demanding that prices be assigned to forests, rivers, prairies, species, and atmosphere, political and business leaders deny the existence, let alone the importance, of matters spiritual. Yet those non-material values are what make life rich and hold the promise of love and happiness. In our current preoccupation with global markets, competitiveness and efficiency, maximizing profitability, and increased consumerism, we merely encourage the insatiable and unsustainable demands that are destroying our home, the planet.

A family heirloom, a child's album, Tangwyn — all give evidence of other values to counter our economic obsession.

THE THINGS IN LIFE THAT REALLY COUNT

In mid-August 1995, driving from the ferry dock at Quathiaski Cove to Heriot Bay on Quadra Island, we pass empty cars clumsily and erratically pulled off the road. Then we notice people plunged to their elbows in thorny vines. The blackberries are ripe! All through the islands in the Georgia Strait and the lower B.C. mainland, blackberries thrive, and few things match the sensuous pleasure of a squirt of tangy, sweet juice and pulp from a ripe, sun-warmed fruit. Bushes studded with plump, glistening berries prove irresistible, and even though we are frantic to reach the cottage we finally succumb, pull off the road, and wade in.

After reaching our place and satisfying our need to canoe, swim, and feast on clams and oysters, we visit our neighbours, Dan and Audrey Leclere. Though they are well into their seventies, they enthrall us with their knowledge of local lore and history. They have just gathered wild chanterelle mushrooms and traded them at the local store for peaches. Audrey has finished bottling the peaches and now is cooking apples to make jam. Audrey shows us a salmon soaking in brown sugar and salt that will be smoked tomorrow. Dan's sister says, "Audrey is so fast that she prepares four salmon for every one I do."

Dan tells us, "We just got back from a trip on the boat. Got our limit in ling cod, but they're getting smaller and harder to find." Dan and Audrey fished for a living for many years and still consistently catch fish all through the Discovery Islands.

"We were skunked seven times this year," Dan tells us sadly. "Finally got lucky on this trip. We caught a nice sixteen-pound spring salmon and a coho." Then he adds a shocker: "But now I feel guilty. Chinook and coho are going extinct. We shouldn't be catching them at all. I've decided to stop fishing for salmon any more. We should be paying more attention to herring. They've about disappeared, and if there's no herring there's no food." He knows more than any salmon management "expert," and Dan's warning scares me. As we leave, we are offered a basket of blackberries Audrey and Dan picked along the road.

When I was a boy, the year was marked by specific signposts. One of the earliest was asparagus; when they appeared, I would roam along the railway tracks gathering the delectable spears. Growing up in the farm country of Essex County in Southern Ontario, I have vivid memories of the delight I felt when cherries ripened, followed by strawberries, raspberries, tomatoes, melons, and peaches. As each fruit or vegetable made its appearance, our kitchen filled with the wonderful aromas of jams, preserves, or pickles. Even today, as foods mature through the seasons, I recapture that childhood expectation and excitement.

When I was a child, time seemed to creep along as I waited for some special treat like Halloween, a birthday, or Christmas. But all that waiting and anticipation heightened the joy when the event finally did arrive. Patience has little virtue these days because there's no need to wait any more. If we want something now, we can, thanks to modern technology, often gratify that demand instantly.

With the entire planet a source of products marketed by major corporations, we can choose from a mind-boggling assortment of consumer merchandise. A radio commercial invites us to "choose from 10,000 products under a single roof." And once the novelty of a new purchase fades, we can forage for more in malls and megastores.

Here on Quadra, freed from the demands of a telephone, television, and daily newspaper, I rearrange my city-formed priorities. It is sheer delight to see an eagle snatch a fish right in front of us, watch a river otter running off with one of our oysters, or snorkel among squid laying eggs just off our dock.

We gather seaweed, limpets, and periwinkles to cook on the beach. The taste is exquisite. Play with the children and simple meals gathered from the shores and the forest are so much more intense and satisfying here than in the city. We are "slowed down," so there is time to enjoy the simplicity of the daily routine and rituals, and there is delight in the most elementary discoveries or acts.

But why do we do this only on holiday? In cities, where most of us live, we are assaulted by noise, images, and pollution; in order to function, we have to clamp down on our senses and ignore much of the sensory input. Quadra shows how to open up more deeply to our surroundings.

What are our aspirations for fulfilment and happiness? Will they come through more economic growth and more and cheaper consumer goods? If we learn to take time, open our senses, and pay attention to our surroundings, we will find there are other rewards and we can live more lightly on the planet. For me, picking blackberries is a simple ritual that acknowledges the changing seasons and reconnects us with the Earth.

12

EXPONENTIAL GROWTH AND ITS CONSEQUENCES

Our species is undergoing not only an explosive growth in numbers but also an even steeper rise in technological power and consumptive demand. These factors have made us a spectacularly destructive predator whose activities ripple through every part of the biosphere.

Human expansion can be directly correlated with vanishing wilderness, loss of topsoil, species extinction, and toxic pollution. The decline of ocean fish and the increased concentration of greenhouse gases attest to the ubiquity of the impact of human numbers. The impact has been summed up in a chilling article in the Atlantic Monthly *entitled "A Special Moment in History" by Bill McKibben. Once exponential growth is under way, trying to slow or deflect it becomes analogous to trying to change directions on a supertanker using an outboard motor. The tremendous momentum resists change.*

The scientific evidence is all around us. Peter Vitousek, a Stanford University biologist, and his associates calculated the total amount of the planet's primary productivity, that is, the amount of sunlight captured by photosynthetic activity, used directly or indirectly by our species. His calculation includes not only plants consumed for food, but also plants killed by our toxic emissions, forests logged, grasslands paved over or grazed by domestic animals, and so on. He came up with the astonishing figure of 38.8 percent! So one species out of perhaps 10 million to 30 million is co-opting almost 40 percent of the Earth's primary productivity, and what we exploit is denied to other species. In another fifty years, our numbers could double once again. Will we then demand twice as much of the primary productivity of the world?

Suppose an immense alien creature came to Earth in a spacecraft from a distant galaxy and began to tear up the planet. Striding at the rate of a step a second, with each footstep crushing an acre of forest, belching poisonous gases into the atmosphere and excreting toxins onto the earth and into the water, the monster would fill us with fear and galvanize all of humanity into an all-out effort to vanquish it. The impact of that hypothetical alien mirrors the actual destruction being wreaked on Earth by us. Seen this way, it becomes obvious we need to be united as a species to stop the deadly assault.

STARK FACTS ON ECOLOGICAL FOOTPRINTS

The steep rise in human numbers and technology is having serious ecological repercussions that can't be stopped by merely tinkering with the social, economic, and political structures. We need to shift our priorities to find ways to live more lightly on the planet while ensuring that important human economic and social needs are not compromised.

One UBC professor, Bill Rees, and his associate, Mathis Wackernagel, confront us with stark facts that demand response. In *Our Ecological Footprint: Reducing Human Impact on the Earth*, they define our real needs: "Human life depends on nature's resource production, waste sinks and life-support services. Securing ecological stability is therefore a non-negotiable bottom line: nature's limited productivity is an ecological constraint within which humanity must live."

Rees uses a concept called the ecological footprint, which measures "a community's demand on the global carrying capacity and compares this with nature's available longterm carrying capacity. In other words, nature's productivity is compared with human demands. . . . In the long run, humanity cannot continue to consume more than nature produces. Human activities are bound to remain within the globe's ecological carrying capacity. To avoid the destruction of nature's productivity, humanity's ecological footprint must be reduced to the globe's carrying capacity."

Using this analysis, Rees's student Mathis Wackernagel explores in more detail the basic human needs that are provided by nature: "Energy is needed for heat and mobility, wood for housing and paper products, and we need quality food and clean water for healthy living . . . green plants convert sunlight, carbon dioxide, nutrients and water into plant matter, and all the food chains which support animal life — including our own — are based on this plant matter. Nature also absorbs our waste products, and provides life support services such as climate stability and protection from ultraviolet radiation. Further, nature is a source of joy and inspiration."

Sustainable futures depend on not using renewable resources more quickly than they can be restored and on not releasing more wastes than nature can absorb. "We know from the increasing loss of forests, soil erosion and contamination, fishery depletion, loss of species and the accumulation of greenhouse gases that our current overuse of nature is compromising our future well-being."

The Vancouver-based Task Force on Planning Healthy and Sustainable Communities developed methods to measure human consumption in terms of units of land needed to supply those services: "Appropriated Carrying Capacity or ecological footprint is the land that would be required on this planet to support our current lifestyle forever." Wackernagel says, "The ecological footprint of an average Canadian adds up to over 4.8 hectares or an area comparable to three city blocks." That includes 1.3 hectares for food, 1.0 for housing, 1.1 for transport, and 1.1 for consumer goods. Looked at another way, land use involves 2.9 hectares for energy, 1.1 for farmland, 0.6 for forest, 0.2 under pavement and buildings.

Wackernagel calculates the ecological footprints of different kinds of households: a single parent with child has annual home expenditures of $16,000 and requires 3.1 hectares; a student living alone needs $10,000 and 3.9 hectares; an average Canadian family

(2.72 people), $37,000 and 4.8 hectares; a professional couple with no children, $79,000 and 13.5 hectares.

The ecologically productive land available to each person on Earth has decreased from 5 hectares in 1900 to 3.6 hectares in 1950 to 1.7 hectares (0.3 arable) in 1990. Assuming no further soil degradation and current population growth, it will decline to 0.9 hectares by 2030! Land appropriated by richer countries has increased from one hectare per person in 1900 to two in 1950 to four to six in 1990. Wackernagel's shocking conclusion is that "If everyone on Earth lived like the average Canadian, we'd need at least THREE EARTHS to provide all the material and energy essentials we currently use."

He goes on: "The Lower Fraser Valley, the area east of Vancouver, contains 1.7 million people, or 4.25 people per hectare. If the average Canadian needs 4.8 hectares, then the Lower Fraser Valley needs an area 20 times what's actually available for food, forestry products and energy. . . . In other words, human settlements don't affect only the area where they're built."

Concentrating people in cities can, however, reduce the energy needed for transportation and housing. The challenge, says Wackernagel, is "to find a way to balance human consumption and nature's limited productivity in order to ensure that our communities are sustainable locally, regionally and globally. We don't have a choice about whether to do this, but we can choose how we do it. All of us are consumers of nature's productivity. We must work together to achieve a more sustainable way of living now in order to ensure that resources continue to be available not only for ourselves, but also for future generations."

Rees, Wackernagel, and their associates have provided us with a powerful tool to recognize the extent to which we are now exceeding the capacity of our surroundings to support us. If we expect that people in all countries have the right to aspire to our level of consumption, then clearly we are in for a major crisis. Sustainable living means coming into balance with the capacity of our surroundings to support us. The ecological footprint analysis provides a standard that should dictate our actions and politics for the future.

FATE OF THE FRASER: A TEST OF OUR RESOLVE

In nature, over long periods of time, populations of plants, animals, and micro-organisms in an ecosystem achieve a dynamic balance. There are always fluctuations in specific populations, but an entire system can be resilient and enduring.

Human beings have long had a deeper effect on ecosystems. Even with simple technologies, prehistoric people overexploited resources and extinguished species. The first people in Australia more than 40,000 years ago radically altered the flora and fauna of the continent by their practice of setting fires. The palaeolithic people who burst into the Americas are thought to have extinguished a number of large species as they migrated south. However, in diverse ecosystems around the world, people were able to exploit their surroundings without exceeding the local "carrying capacity."

That has all changed with our rapid growth in population, technological power, and consumption. But now that the economy has become a major preoccupation, ecological concerns have vanished from the government's agenda. It is a suicidal omission because no matter how sophisticated we may think we are, we remain dependent on nature's bounty. In our rush to keep the economy growing, we are depleting natural capital that rightly belongs to our children. Consider the Fraser River watershed in British Columbia.

The Fraser is one of the truly great rivers of the world, draining more than one quarter of B.C.'s total land mass. The Lower Fraser is known to support more than 300 species of birds, 45 mammals, 11 amphibians, and 5 reptiles as well as countless unidentified insects and micro-organisms. (Already, 132 plant and 10 bird species are classified as rare or extremely rare.) Twenty-one million hectares of forest surround the Fraser basin and provide a livelihood for more than 44,000 people. But a very conservative estimate is that the annual allowable cut (a volume of wood the forest department calculates can be cut on a sustainable basis by the forest industry) exceeds the sustainable level by at least 14 percent!

The Fraser is famous for its fish. The river supports five salmon species and fifty-seven other fish species, including the giant sturgeon.

Eleven fish species are considered rare, imperilled, or critically imperilled. Of B.C.'s total salmon catch, the Fraser contributes 66 percent of the sockeye, 60 percent pink, 16 percent chinook, 11 percent chum, and 8 percent coho, supplying work for 15,000 people.

For millennia, this great waterway was a corridor for the movement of wildlife and aboriginal people, a habitat for fish, birds, and mammals, and the watershed serving vast forests. So it has been a magnet for human beings. Today, 2.4 million people, more than two-thirds of B.C.'s population, use the waters of the Fraser daily.

Greater Vancouver is Canada's fastest growing urban centre. The human population is expected to reach 3 million by 2021, a 70 percent increase in thirty years, while the number of automobiles grew by 30 percent between 1986 and 1992, to nearly a million cars. Human activity has also transformed the river. Since 1900, 82 percent of the salt marshes of the Fraser estuary and 95 percent of the wetlands of the north arm have disappeared. Only two of fifty original free-flowing streams in Vancouver still exist. Since 1967, more than 36,000 hectares of farmland have been converted to urban use. Today there are few clues to tell us that Vancouver that rests on the delta of a mighty river. The great flood plain east of Vancouver, which was drained to create rich farmland, is being converted to immense housing developments, garish shopping malls, and industrial parks.

In 1995 the Outdoor Recreation Council of B.C., representing more than fifty recreation and conservation organizations, listed the Fraser as the province's most endangered river. At the same time, the Fraser Basin Management Board released its report, which sounded a major alarm and cited a litany of causes of the river's demise: logging operations that stir up sediment; pulp mills that release toxic effluent; dams and diversions of tributaries; landfills that leak into watersheds; gravel pits; industries; farms and golf courses that leak manure; insecticides, herbicides, and fertilizers; steel plants; paint factories; rafts of logs treated with chemical preservatives; emissions of cars, trucks, and buses; and one million cubic metres of untreated sewage (93 percent from the Lower Fraser) that is pumped daily into the estuary.

The report states that salvaging the river will require a major shift in attitude: "As our population grows and we continue to consume at unsustainable rates, we use up our natural capital and our range of choices diminishes. We will never 'catch up' by repairing our previous mistakes and reacting to today's demands. We need to look further into the system to make fundamental changes in how we choose to live in the basin."

The Fraser River is a symbol of ecosystems everywhere. Its fate will tell us whether we can change our attitudes and behaviour enough to live in harmony with the natural world that supports us.

A Scientist's Assessment of the State of the World

David Pimentel is a distinguished population biologist at Cornell University who has spent years studying the impact of human numbers and consumption on the long-term prospects for humanity. Recently, he authored a major article, "Natural Resources and an Optimum Human Population," for *Population and Environment.* The article attempts to set an ideal population for the United States based on maintaining a high standard of living while still protecting the environment and the country's renewable resources.

To understand the discussion, we must remember that the present population of the United States is 258 million and that is growing at 1.1 percent per year. For the rest of the world, the population is 5.6 billion and the growth rate 1.7 percent, while for China, the numbers are 1.2 billion and 1.4 percent. At the present rate, the population of the world will double in forty-one years; the U.S. population will double in sixty-three years. It is worth pointing out that every time the population doubles, the new total is greater than the sum of all people who have ever lived in the past.

But ecological impact is not just a matter of human numbers. As Pimentel points out, "Each American consumes about 23 times more goods and services than the average third world citizen . . . and 53 times more than a Chinese citizen." The U.S. level of consumption sets an impossible standard for the rest of the world because the planet cannot deliver this level to everyone. The American standard of living is made possible by the exploitation of resources from around the world, which, Pimentel says, is why the U.S. has the highest debt load in the world. According to Pimentel, the U.S. average standard of living began a decline during the last decade that will continue if its population continues to rise.

An indicator of the health of the environment is the availability of food. The total consumption of fish globally equals the total of all cows and chickens consumed, but most people in the world live primarily on grain. Only 29 percent of the planet's surface is land, of which 12 percent grows crops, 24 percent is pasture, and 31 percent is forests. A third of the land is unsuitable for agriculture, forest, or pasture.

The slender base of productive farmland that supports all of humanity is losing more than 10 million hectares a year through soil degradation. But because of the addition of more than 90 million people a year, another 5 million hectares of new land have to be brought under cultivation annually to feed them. That means 15 million hectares have to be found each year just to stay at the current level of production. Deforestation is the primary source of new land.

Worldwide, Pimentel says, "Soil erosion [is] the single most serious cause of soil loss and land degradation." In Africa, the rate of soil loss has accelerated twentyfold over the past three decades. Topsoil is constantly created by the contribution of organic material from living organisms. But today soil is being lost twenty to forty times faster than it can be replaced. Pimentel predicts a 15 percent to 30 percent depression of world food production over the next quarter century as a direct result of topsoil loss.

Pimentel also points to the disparity in food consumed. It takes 1,374 kilograms of agricultural products to feed an average American each year, compared with a mere 585 for a Chinese and a world average of 718.

Readily available freshwater is also a limited commodity that is being exploited to the maximum. Growth in human numbers will have a major impact because a 20 percent rise in world population will double the demand for water.

Economics has become an instrument of ecological destruction because it is based on human creativity and productiveness but fails to account for the innumerable services performed by nature. Pimentel documents the kind of irreplaceable functions provided by the planet's biodiversity:

- pollinating crops and wild plants (each year in the United States, bees both wild and domesticated pollinate $30 billion worth of crops);
- recycling manure and other organic wastes;
- degrading chemical pollutants;
- purifying water and soil; and
- acting as a reservoir of genetic diversity for agriculture and forestry.

Yet human activity now eliminates an estimated 150 species per day.

Even when it no longer pays to spray pesticides, we continue the practice. Despite a thirty-threefold increase in the use of synthetic pesticides in the U.S. since 1945, the loss of crops to pests continues to increase. Thus corn losses have quadrupled despite a thousandfold increase in the use of insecticides on corn.

Pimentel adamantly maintains that our rising use of energy cannot be sustained. A hundredfold increase in the use of fossil fuels in Chinese agriculture since 1945 is matched by an escalation in energy use of twenty to one thousand times in the same period in the U.S.

Reserves of fossil fuels are finite and estimated oil reserves have plummeted. Energy is an American weakness, with the U.S. importing more than half its oil. Oil is also a finite material, and the end of its role as a major source of energy is in sight. Pimentel calculates that if everyone on the planet lived the way we in North America do and global population continued to rise by 1.7 percent a year, all of the world's known deposits of fossil fuel would be exhausted in a mere twenty years.

Our dependence on fossil fuels is a very recent phenomenon. Only 150 years ago, with a population of a mere 23 million people, the United States relied on wood for 91 percent of its energy; today fossil fuels account for 93 percent of the nation's energy. Hydropower provides another 3.5 percent. Developing countries, meanwhile, exploit solar energy for a third of their needs.

Pimentel outlines an economy based on the sustainable use of energy, land, water, and biodiversity and a relatively high standard of living. It would require a massive shift to solar energy, which would be harvested on about 90 million hectares of non-agricultural and non-forest land. With high energy and resource efficiency and a major effort to reduce pollution and waste, Pimentel foresees a conserver society in which the U.S. population would optimally be about 200 million.

Globally, if a major effort was made to recover enough food for each person on 0.5 hectare and to conserve soil, Pimentel believes about 3 billion people could be sustained better if a renewable energy source was exploited globally, 1 to 2 billion people could live relatively prosperously around the world. Clearly his calculations mean the current population of 6 billion and the projected 10 billion by 2040 are catastrophic.

Pimentel recognizes that any serious attempt to lower the global population to 1 to 2 billion humans will cause tremendous social, economic, and political upheaval, but all of his calculations lead him to predict that the impending rise in human population to 10 to 12 billion will "condemn future humans to a lifetime of absolute poverty, suffering, starvation, disease and associated violent conflicts as individual pressures mount. The ultimate control of the human population will be imposed by nature."

Pimentel issues a dire warning that the present level of American prosperity and standard of living cannot be perpetuated without population control. But as is the case in Canada, U.S. policy is predicated on the belief that economic growth must be maintained at all costs, and one way to do that is with a constantly expanding population base.

Our quality of life is a direct reflection of the health of our surroundings. But at all levels of government, there has been a failure to recognize that simple fact. So instead of promoting conservation and efficiency while aiming for a reduced level of population and consumption, we increase our exploitation and degradation of the planet's productive ecosystems.

Canadians must heed Pimentel's urgent advice: "Starting to deal with the imbalance of the population-resource equation before it reaches a crisis level is the only way to avert a real tragedy for our children's children."

WHY WE MUST ACT ON GLOBAL WARMING

"So much for global warming," a friend remarked while discussing the frigid winter suffered in the East in 1994. With that dismissive comment, he had leaped from a single observation to a conclusion that is simply not warranted.

During the run of extremely hot summers of the late 1980s, concern about global warming reached a peak. But the fact that six of the hottest years on record occurred in the '80s did not constitute "proof" of global warming. That run of hot years could simply have been part of a normal pattern of fluctuations. Those hot years did not prove any more than one cold winter did. I reminded my friend that while the East was freezing, B.C. was experiencing record high temperatures. Global warming is about global, not regional, temperatures.

It is going to take a lot more data-collecting and hypothesizing to prove whether or not global warming really is a threat. So should we hold off doing anything, as many economists and businesspeople suggest, until the evidence is in? At a conference in Geneva in 1990, more than 700 atmospheric experts from all over the world agreed that we are putting unprecedented amounts of greenhouse gases into the upper atmosphere, and that all signs indicate the world has warmed over the past century.

Human beings are adding even more greenhouse gases like carbon dioxide and methane, as well as completely novel ones like CFCs, into the upper atmosphere than can be removed annually. It is a fact of physics that these molecules and others may act like the glass of a greenhouse, allowing sunlight to reach the surface of the planet and also reflecting heat back onto the Earth. This phenomenon is what has kept the planet at a temperature in which life flourishes. More of these molecules will increase the effect.

The long-term consequences of this excess in greenhouse gases are hard to predict. As the Earth heats up, it is acknowledged, there will be greater evaporation from the ocean surfaces. This will lead to greater cloud cover and, as that spreads over the Earth, sunlight will be blocked. That, some conclude, will lead to a cooling rather than a heating of the Earth, and that is a reasonable hypothesis.

Others suggest that with rising temperatures, there will be greater turbulence in the air as different parts of the planet heat up at different rates. Convection currents could sweep upward and create tall columns of clouds rather than flat horizontal sheets. That would expose even more clear sky, so the Earth would heat up even faster. This too is a valid possibility.

The fact is we don't know what will happen. By tweaking parameters and factors in complex computer models of the atmosphere, we can get predictions ranging from an impending ice age to catastrophic heating. In view of the range of possibilities, many scientists suggest that the highest priority is to give more research funds so evidence can be gathered to make better predictions. That suggestion is too self-serving, however, if it is then assumed that we can carry on with business as usual until the data are all in.

Human numbers and technology have expanded to a point where we are changing the biophysical features of the Earth. With little from the past to guide our actions, we are playing a crap game with the only home we have.

We have to learn to live within the mechanisms that keep a balance among the components of complex ecosystems. In many areas of human activity, that means cutting back and hoping that the regenerative powers of nature will redress our damage. That's what we're doing with CFC damage to the ozone layer and overfishing off the Atlantic Coast. We have to reduce logging of old-growth forests and change agricultural practices that degrade soil and poison the land. And we have to decrease greenhouse gas output because the atmospheric changes, whatever they are, will have massive consequences and must be minimized.

The shocking fact is that studies in Canada, the United States, Australia, and Sweden all reach the same conclusion: a significant reduction of the output of carbon dioxide, one of the main green-house gases, will enhance health and the environment while saving billions of dollars! Unfortunately, the costs of reduction must be paid immediately while the benefits accrue only years later, beyond the time frame of political vision. So there is little political incentive to do the best thing.

We have no choice but to act now to minimize the extremities of our uncertain future. But first, we've got to stop confusing a change in temperature with a statement on the climate.

POLITICIANS TOO COOL TO WARMING

On June 24, 1988, Jim Hansen, a leading climatologist at NASA's Goddard Institute for Space Studies, testified before a U.S. senate committee that, based on scientific evidence of atmosphere change and annual global temperatures, "We can state with about 99 percent certainty that current temperatures represent a real warming trend." He concluded, "It is time to stop waffling so much. . . . The evidence is pretty strong that the greenhouse effect is here."

A week later, at The Changing Atmosphere: Implications for Global Security, an international conference in Toronto, one Canadian scientist, Kenneth Hare, predicted "a revolutionary change in world climate, of a sort not rivalled in the history of civilization." He suggested, "If decision-makers are willing to listen to economists, they should be even readier to listen to us."

The conference itself concluded: "Humanity is conducting an unintended, uncontrolled, globally pervasive experiment whose ulti-mate consequences could be second only to a global nuclear war." Delegates called for a 50 percent reduction in CO_2, the main green-house gas, with a 20 percent cut in 1988 levels by 2005. The 20 percent target was reiterated in the Liberals' vaunted Red Book in the 1993 federal election.

In February 1990, fifty-two Nobel prize winners told U.S. presi-dent George Bush: "Global warming has emerged as the most serious environmental threat of the 21st century. . . . Only by taking action now can we insure that future generations will not be put at risk."

Those calling for immediate and serious action on global warming are leading scientists and scientific organizations of the world, not irresponsible alarmists.

So what has been the response of politicians? In 1989, the federal environment minister, Lucien Bouchard, told me in an interview that global warming "threatens the survival of our species" and warned that without immediate action, we faced "a catastrophe." When his successor, Jean Charest, produced a Green Plan in 1990, the goal on CO_2 emissions was merely to stabilize 1990 levels by the year 2000! That was the same target of the UN Framework on Climate Change, which Canada signed in 1992 at the Earth Summit in Rio.

Both Finance Minister Paul Martin and Sheila Copps sat on the all-party Standing Committee on Environment, which issued reports on global warming in 1990 (*No Time to Lose*) and 1993 (*Our Planet . . . Our Future*). The 1993 report warns that reducing global warming "will be difficult and time-consuming, but that is no reason for further delay."

The standing committee cited a poll indicating that individual Canadians accept personal responsibility for environmental protection, but also expect strong government leadership, especially at the federal level. Yet in 1995, a meeting of federal and provincial energy ministers signalled a shift of responsibility to the provinces. Instead of devising strong programs to reduce CO_2, the ministers offered vague platitudes and calls for voluntary action. If we are lucky, by the year 2000, Canada may keep its per capita *increase* at 13 percent!

Canadians are per capita the most profligate CO_2 producers in the industrialized world (only some Arab countries exceed us); cold climate is no excuse when a northern country like Sweden releases half as much. Government inaction on global warming becomes incomprehensible when its own studies indicated that reducing 1988 levels of CO_2 emissions in fifteen years was not only achievable but also would have resulted in a net savings of billions of dollars!

Do politicians really mean it when they warn us that the hazards of global warming are second only to nuclear war or that it threatens our species' very survival? We are gambling with the future of the only home we have, and now this reluctance to act is fuelling a call for mega-technological fixes.

UPDATE: In December 1996, the Intergovernmental Panel on Climate Change, a United Nations' panel of experts, after reviewing more than 20,000 scientific papers on weather and climate, concluded that global warming is occurring and that human activity is a significant contributing factor. When the "World Scientists' Call for Action at Kyoto" was released, Nobel prize–winning physicist Henry Kendall stated: "Let there be no doubt about the conclusions of the scientific community: the threat of global warming is very real and action is needed immediately. It is a grave error to believe we can continue to procrastinate. Scientists do not believe this and no one else should either."

Despite the overwhelming scientific evidence supporting the need to seriously reduce greenhouse gas emissions, delegations at Kyoto from the JUSCANZ nations (Japan, the United States, Canada, Australia, New Zealand) fought against the imposition of any reductions in current output. The final treaty was a travesty — 6 percent reduction below 1990 levels by 2008 to 2112 with no defined methods of enforcement and so many loopholes that industrialized countries will be able to increase greenhouse gas output and still claim to have met the target.

On July 8, 1998, meteorologists announced that following the hottest year ever recorded, every month of the first six months of this year were the hottest on record.

WHY A WARMER WORLD WON'T BE A BETTER ONE

In an article in *Ambio*, the Nobel laureate Henry Kendall and the population-dynamics expert David Pimentel point out that humanity is exceeding the Earth's capacity to support us all.

The community of Earth's diverse living things cleanse, alter, and regenerate air, water, and soil. Yet now we "either use, coopt or destroy 40 percent of the estimated 100 billion tons of organic matter produced annually by the terrestrial ecosystem." In this way, we drive many other organisms who are keeping the planet habitable to extinction. Ozone depletion also has frightening repercussions, in that "of some 200 species studied, two-thirds show sensitivity to ozone damage."

And global warming, say the authors, "will be catastrophic for agriculture, changing rainfall patterns, drying some areas such as the central area of North America and increasing climatic variability. There will be effects on the growth of plants as well as collateral effects on plant pathogens and insect pests. Whole ecosystems may undergo major change."

This isn't just hypothetical or speculative. The hottest year on record so far, 1998, was "accompanied by a mid-continent drought which resulted in a 30% decrease in grain yield, dropping U.S. production below consumption for the first time in some 300 years. Similarly, Canadian production dropped about 37%."

Sustainable food production can be increased with better genetic strains and more efficient use of resources, but all have limits. To minimize global warming, fossil-fuel emissions must be cut drastically and forests must be preserved so they can remove carbon dioxide. Improving life for all people while reducing emissions will require a staggering "three- or fourfold increase in effective energy services."

Kendall and Pimentel consider three different scenarios in a warming world to the year 2050:

- Business as Usual (BAU) — Population rises to 10 billion; soil erosion, salinization, and waterlogging increase; no increase in aid for developing countries; no action to reduce global warming and ozone depletion.
- Pessimistic — Most dire predictions realized; high global temperature rise; high ultraviolet radiation; population growth to nearly 13 billion and worsening debt.
- Optimistic — Adoption of heroic efforts and major technological achievements; population stabilizes at 7.8 billion; energy-intensive agriculture is expanded; soil and water conservation

improves; developed countries increase financial aid and technology; food is more equitably distributed and diets shift from animal to plant protein in developed nations.

The results of each projection:

- BAU — Grainland declines from 718 million hectares in 1980 to 620 hectares in 2050. There are 0.06 hectares per capita for grain production, less than a quarter of what was available in 1991. Food production in the developing world will be depressed by between 15 and 30 percent over the next twenty-five years; topsoil erosion will reduce rain-fed cropland by a daunting 29 percent. The result will be an average per capita loss in grain production in Africa, China, India, and other Asian nations of more than 25 percent.
- Pessimistic — This will lead to a further 15 percent decrease in grain production from BAU. Per capita production will be down by 40 percent despite a 30 percent rise above 1991 levels. For most of humanity, this means malnutrition and hunger.
- Optimistic — This scenario is based on almost doubling grain production by heroic efforts to increase irrigation and fertilizer use. Food production and environmental protection will have to be given the highest priority while the cost and technological innovation would be carried by the industrialized world for the developing nations. If all people in the industrialized countries become vegetarians, food production is *tripled*, and the amount of energy expended to develop the world's agriculture is increased fifty to a hundred times, then Kendall and Pimentel conclude 7.8 billion people might be adequately fed by the middle of the next century. But they add with understatement, "This would appear to be unrealistic."

Kendall and Pimentel conclude with a stark warning and stiff challenge: "The human race now appears to be getting close to the limits of global food productive capacity based on present technologies. Substantial damage already has been done to the biological and physical systems that we depend on for food production. . . . A major reordering of world priorities is a prerequisite for meeting the problems we now face."

These are not the rantings of zealots announcing the end is nigh, they come from eminent scientists. Considering the media coverage given the death of Princess Diana and the sexual escapades of U.S. president Bill Clinton, surely Kendall and Pimentel deserve more attention than they've received.

13

INFORMATION: A SHATTERED WORLD

he hype surrounding the millennial shift is fuelled by the spectacular growth in the information business. The continued doubling of the storage capacity of silicon chips every two years renders computers obsolete in months, creating an illusion that knowledge is expanding just as rapidly. The capacity to deliver visual images via CD-ROM, satellite feeds, and cable now takes humanity around the world.

The Net, cable television, interactive TV, virtual reality, and electronic shopping all encourage speculation about the imminent demise of books, libraries, shopping malls, and workplaces.

But people are beginning to question the vaunted claims for the information superhighway and the coming Information Age. In the past, people knew that they and the many parts of their surroundings were profoundly interlinked. Increasingly, we are disconnected from history, culture, or context, so those connections have been obscured, and we are blinded to the way our actions ripple out and ramify in the real world. We need to examine the nature of this infoglut critically to gather insights into its weaknesses and dangers.

LIVE BY THE BOX, PERISH BY THE BOX

The futurist being interviewed on the radio talk show ecstatically extolled the benefits of the coming electronic revolution. After discussing the wonders of shopping, playing games, ordering movies, and checking the stock market, all from home through a computer and a television set, he gushed, "It sure beats having to put up with grumpy 'clerks, crowds, bad weather and traffic jams." The tone of his remarks seemed to suggest that reality like weather and other human beings is a nuisance compared with the kind of controlled world we can now access through our TVs.

The electronic revolution is being touted as offering a cornucopia of limitless variety of titillation and experience. The marriage of computer and telecommunication gives us "virtual reality," which, its proponents boast, is even better than the real thing. After all, one can enjoy the gut-wrenching thrills and excitement of hand-to-hand combat, the raunchiest sex, a car race or aerial dogfight, all without any of the attendant risks.

Television is already the most pervasive and powerful medium of communication and information today, and it brings us more and more of our history lessons, values, priorities, and knowledge about the world. And the medium does provide astounding images few of us can ever experience in person — a view of war from the tip of a Patriot missile, close-up glimpses of Mars from a space vehicle, an intimate portrait of a patient's intestinal polyps, daily blow-by-blow skirmishes within a dysfunctional family.

Advances in the technological side of television have been breathtaking. They can be seen in their most impressive state on every broadcast of a sports event or in computer-animated commercials. From a viewer's perspective, television is better than reality; it's faster, more intimate, and clearer than real life. As we rush towards a 500-channel universe, we are told that it also has unlimited educative potential — but education about what?

Not long ago, the television set was referred to as the "boob tube," a pejorative expression that reflected the perceived lack of intellectual content of its transmissions. Not any more. The television set will be the central component of the universe of virtual reality and the much-touted information highway. All but forgotten are those nettlesome questions about the real lessons being acquired from this electronic world by the viewing audience.

In real life, nature is exquisitely complex and diverse, but for television it has to be jazzed up because the pace of the natural world is too slow for the viewer conditioned to a constant stream of changing images. Consider what goes into a typical nature program. A wildlife photographer may spend months patiently waiting for a shot of a lifetime, one seldom seen by another human being. Incredible shots, such as those of a large mammal giving birth, avoiding a predator, finding food, or playing, are edited together to make a fast-paced program chock-full of great sequences. They can't help being powerfully moving and evocative. Yet the final impression is often more like "Animals Do the Darnedest Things" than a genuine insight into their daily routines. Don't visit the Amazon rainforest or an Arctic island if you expect to see the riot of colour, shape, and movement portrayed in nature programs on television. Shows like that aren't a reflection of reality, they are creations.

By substituting television pictures for the real thing, we are profoundly distanced from it. And through living with the artifice of electronic images, we find it easier to think human technology and control are supreme, the sheer inventiveness of our species having allowed us to escape the constraints of our biology. It is such thinking that enables economists to reach the absurd conclusion that since 97 percent of the American economy is not directly dependent on climate, global warming will have little impact on the economy and the cost of any preventive measures will far outweigh the benefits.

Humanity's greatest need today is a restored sense of connection, interdependence, and love for other species. That can come about only by our experiencing directly with our bodies the vastness of the world around us and out there. We have to feel the heat and cold, smell the aromas and stink, savour the taste and the texture of real living things. We need to appreciate the ebb and flow of real time on geological, evolutionary, and biological scales, not the fragmented, disconnected, sped-up images that assault our senses through the box.

Most urban dwellers today feel uncomfortable, even frightened, by the unfamiliar surroundings of the real world that is our home. The futurist was dead wrong. The titillation of virtual reality and information superhighways is superficial and fleeting and renders us even more susceptible to the dangerous conceit that we no longer need nature.

ARE THESE TWO REPORTERS ON THE SAME PLANET?

The media thrive on novelty. While daily newspapers struggle for readers, tabloids flourish with lurid stories from outer and inner space. As competition for viewers intensifies with the proliferation of television channels, TV stories become shorter, kinkier, more violent, and more sensational than ever. All the while, our threshold for shock and violence rises.

Demand for increased titillation has changed the nature of documentary reporting. When I began television reporting in 1962, three- to four-minute interviews with articulate, thoughtful scientists were not at all unusual. Today they might get half a minute. Stories are shorter, punchier, faster, and slicker, but they are also shallower and less detailed in historical and social context. In-depth reporting gives way to the exploitative and anecdotal. It's not surprising then that Paul Bernardo, Lorena Bobbit, and Tonya Harding received coverage far in excess of their global significance.

During the 1970s and 1980s, as public awareness grew over the ramifications of our lifestyles and technology on the planet, we were constantly shocked and surprised by the unexpected interconnections and consequences. Who would have believed that DDT sprayed on fields to kill insects would end up causing thinner egg shells for birds, or that the heavy industries of Pennsylvania would affect trees in Quebec? The stories were alarming and the media reports reflected it.

But it was inevitable that sooner or later, stories that once sparked shock and outrage would induce yawns. Nothing is more stale than yesterday's newspaper. Peter Desbarais, dean of journalism at the University of Western Ontario, told *Maclean's,* "I tend to resist articles announcing some new environmental threat. I feel that I've heard it all before." He's right. Virtually all environmental problems can be traced to the same causative factors of rapidly growing human numbers, overconsumption, and excessive technological power. But while murders, wars, business failures, political crises, or sports finals are eventually resolved, the solutions to environmental problems are seldom simple and easy, they are complicated and require long-term attention. That doesn't make for good press.

The stories that do emerge often question the credibility of the environmental issues themselves. A spate of books, articles, and television programs have disputed the reality of the claimed hazards of global warming, overpopulation, deforestation, ozone depletion, and so on. Other stories are built around ever more frightening possibilities.

An article in the *Atlantic Monthly* by Robert D. Kaplan has galvanized both fear and denial. Entitled "The Coming Anarchy," the report paints a horrifying picture of the future for humanity. Kaplan suggests that the terrible consequences of the conjunction between exploding human population and surrounding environmental degradation are already visible in Africa and Southeast Asia. As society is destabilized by an epidemic of AIDS, government control evaporates, national borders crumble beneath the pressure of environmental refugees, and local populations revert to tribalism to settle old scores or defend against fleeing masses and marauding bands of stateless nomads.

Kaplan believes that as ecosystems collapse, this scenario could sweep the planet, first in the Eastern bloc countries and then the industrialized nations. It is a frightening scenario built on a serious attempt to project the aftermath of ecological destruction. And it has generated a great deal of discussion and controversy.

Marcus Gee pronounces Kaplan's vision "dead wrong" in a major article in the *Globe and Mail* headlined "Apocalypse Deferred." Assailing "doomsayers" from Thomas Malthus to Paul Ehrlich and the Club of Rome, Gee counters with the statistics favoured by believers in the limitless benefits and potential of economic growth. Citing the spectacular improvement in human health, levels of education and literacy, availability of food, and length of life even in the developing world, Gee pronounces the fivefold increase in the world economy since 1950 as the cause of this good news. He does concede that "immense problems remain, from ethnic nationalism to tropical deforestation to malnutrition to cropland loss," but concludes that Kaplan has exaggerated many of the crises and thus missed the "broad pattern of progress."

Are these two reporters on the same planet? How could they come to such different conclusions? And what is the reader to conclude?

Kaplan believes what he saw in Africa and Southeast Asia was the beginning of a global pattern of disintegration of social, political, and economic infrastructures under the impact of ecological degradation, population pressure, and disease.

In contrast, Gee focuses on statistics of the decline in child mortality and the rise in longevity, food production, and adult literacy in the developing countries to reach a very different conclusion — things have never been better! Economic indicators, such as a rise in gross world product and total exports, indicate, he says, "remarkable sustained and dramatic progress . . . life for the majority of the world's citizens is getting steadily better in almost every category."

Kaplan's frightening picture is built on a recognition that the planet is finite and that degradation of ecosystems by the demands of population and consumption has vast social, political, and economic ramifications. Gee's conclusions rest heavily on economic indicators. He points out the annual 3.9 percent rise in the global economy, and the more than doubling of the gross output per person, that has occurred for the past thirty years. World trade has done even better, growing by 6 percent annually between 1960 and 1990, as tariffs have declined from 40 percent of a product's price in 1947 to 5 percent today. Yet all this time, the gulf between rich and poor countries has increased.

Gee skips lightly over such facts as Third World debt and the daily toll of 22,000 child deaths of easily preventable diseases, and even admits the real threats of loss of topsoil, pollution of the air, loss of forests, and contamination of water. Nevertheless, he concludes there is little evidence that they are serious enough to halt or even reverse human progress. He even suggests the preposterous notion that global warming and ozone depletion "may cancel each other out."

Gee's outlook rests on a tiny minority of scientists who have faith in the boundless potential of science and technology to transcend the physical constraints of air, water, and soil so that a much larger population can be sustained. His final proof? The concomitant rise in living standards and population. But the relationship between changes in living standard and population growth is a correlation, not proof of a causal connection.

Gee quotes the "American scholar" Mark Perlman: "The growth in numbers over the millennia from a few thousands or millions of humans living at low subsistence, to billions living well above subsistence, is a most positive assurance that the problem of sustenance has eased rather than grown more difficult over the years." Even the World Bank, which is not an organization known for its sensitivity to the sustainability of ecosystems or local cultures, is quoted as stating "the food crisis of the early seventies will be the last in history."

Gee relies heavily on Julian Simon, once an economic adviser to Ronald Reagan. Simon's position was revealed when I once interviewed him and asked him about the population crisis. He retorted: "What crisis?" and went on to say there have never been as many people so well off, and there will never be a limit to population because more people means more Einsteins to keep making life better. But neither Simon nor Perlman is a scientist.

If we inherit a bank account with a thousand dollars that earns 5 percent interest annually, we could withdraw fifty dollars or less each year forever. However, suppose we start to increase our withdrawals, say up to sixty dollars, then seventy dollars, and more each year. For many years, the account would yield cash. But it would be foolish to conclude that we could keep drawing more from the account indefinitely. Yet that is what the Gees, Simons, and Perlmans believe. As the Atlantic ground-fishery shows, we are using up the ecological capital of the planet (biodiversity, air, water, soil) rather than living off the interest. It is a dangerous deception to believe that the human-created artifice called economics can keep the indicators rising as the life-support systems of the planet continue to decline.

The value system that pervades most of the popular media not only perpetuates the delusion of infinite expansibility of resources and the economy, but also creates blinders that filter out the urgency and credibility of warnings that an environmental crisis confronts us.

LUDDITES KNEW WHAT THE THREATS WERE

A 1995 cover story in *Newsweek* stated that technological innovation is creating "a social and political revolution." It declared that these changes are "outstripping our capacity to cope, antiquating our laws, transforming our mores, reshuffling our economy, reordering our priorities, redefining our workplaces, putting our Constitution to the fire, shifting our concept of reality." Yet the revolutionary changes are seldom challenged, let alone resisted.

But one who is resisting is the writer Kirkpatrick Sale. He is inspired by the eighteenth-century Luddites, a group that opposed the increased mechanization that was threatening their communities. The Luddites lost their battle, but Sale believes their spirit persists in the form of environmentalism, aboriginal movements, and activists fighting against nuclear power, clearcutting, animal experiments, and toxic waste. Sale says we must learn from the experience of the original Luddites. He lists their lessons as follows:

1. "Technologies are never neutral and some are hurtful." That's because "tools come with a prior history built in. . . . A conquering violent culture . . . is bound to produce conquering, violent tools." For example, after the Second World War, when American weapons industries went into agriculture, "It was a war on the land. . . . It could be no other way. If a nation like this beats its swords into plowshares, they will still be violent and deadly tools."
2. "Industrialism is always a cataclysmic process, destroying the past, roiling the present, making the future uncertain. . . . [It is the] nature of the industrial ethos to value growth and pro-

duction, speed and novelty, power and manipulation." Sale believes that because industry's priorities are materialistic and economic rather than social or civic, its effects are invariably disruptive of society.

"The familiar evils — incoherent metropolises, spreading slums, crime and prostitution, inflation, corruption, pollution, cancer and heart disease, stress, anomie, alcoholism — almost always follow." Yet governments continue to keep the economy expanding as if the resultant social problems are unrelated.

3. "Only a people serving an apprenticeship to nature can be trusted with machines." Without a profound understanding of our embeddedness in the natural world, Sale says, we become blind to the ecological consequences of what we do. Perhaps the most dangerous repercussion is the loss of a "sense of the human as a species and the individual as an animal, needing certain basic physical elements for successful survival, including land and air, decent food and shelter, intact communities and nurturing families. . . . An economy without any kind of ecological grounding will be as disregardful of the human members as of the nonhuman."

4. "The nation-state, synergistically intertwined with industrialism, will always come to its aid and defense, making revolt futile and reform ineffectual." Sale points out that in 1812–13, 14,000 soldiers (a force seven times larger than any other sent out to protect peace in England) were called out to put down the Luddite revolt. Since then, the alliance of industry and government has simply expanded across the political spectrum. "Not one fully industrialized nation in the world has had a successful rebellion against it."

5. "Resistance to the industrial system, based on some grasp of moral principles and rooted in some sense of moral revulsion, is not only possible but necessary." The most important legacy of the Luddites is that they resisted out of a deeply held sense of right and wrong. Even against enormous odds, they felt they had no choice but to make a stand and resist.

6. "Politically, resistance to industrialism must force the viability

of industrial society into public consciousness and debate." This means we must look beyond the media hype of such innovations as the information highway, genetic engineering, and space travel and ask, "what price it all comes to and who is paying for it. What purpose does this machine serve? What problem . . . needs this solution? . . . Who [are] the principal beneficiaries? . . . Who are the winners, who the losers? Will this invention concentrate or disperse power, encourage or discourage self-worth? Can society at large afford it? Can the biosphere?"

7. "Philosophically, resistance to industrialism must be embedded in an analysis . . . that is morally informed, carefully articulated and widely shared." It already exists in such writers as Lewis Mumford, E. F. Schumacher, Thomas Berry, Jerry Mander, and Chellis Glendinning, and "in the lessons and models of the Amish and the Iroquois; in the wisdom of tribal elders and the legacy of tribal experience everywhere."

Sale believes we must realize we are embedded in the biosphere and are not the centre of the universe. Globalism must be replaced by an emphasis on strong local communities. "Principles of conservation, stability, self-sufficiency and cooperation" must replace the "exploitation and degradation of the earth." I couldn't agree more.

IN CONTEXT, EVEN A SUN LOOKS GREEN

Delegates to the Earth Summit in Rio in 1992 declared that, from that point forward, economics and the environment must be inseparably linked. Yet today we are being told that the economy comes before anything else. And since most of us live in cities, it's often hard to recognize how much we need the environment.

The media serve bits of information lacking any framework of history, time, or place. But if we read context and detail into news stories, even a newspaper like the *Vancouver Sun* resembles an environmental publication. Try this. Take any paper at random and rummage through the stories with a view to setting them in a broader context. Here's what I found in the November 3, 1995, *Vancouver Sun*.

Pages of ads announce bargains, sales, and specials, but ought to remind us that rampant overconsumption in industrialized nations is the greatest cause of environmental degradation. The business section touts the benefits of maximal economic growth, free trade, and currency speculation. But these claims should be balanced by including the "costs" of destabilization to local communities and ecosystems.

People with deep roots in a place should cherish and protect the land but are often sidetracked by politics and economics. Several seemingly unrelated reports were really about a sense of place. Unspoken but implicit in post-referendum reports (page A1) is the tremendous attachment Québécois have to their part of Canada.

The First Nations, on the other hand, from Canada ("Mercredi Warns against Exclusion," A4) to New Zealand ("Maoris Angered by Failed Treaty Mar Queen's Visit to New Zealand," A24) believe the land has been theirs since the beginning of time. In Sri Lanka war rages over the land ("Refugee Flood Feared as Tigers Routed: Sri Lankan Army Set to Take Tamil Enclave," A1), while Okinawans fret over foreign occupation ("Three American Servicemen Charged in Assault That Aggravated Okinawans' Deep Resentment," A11). Terrorists try to gain land in Algeria ("French Police Foil Bomb Attack, Arrest Suspected Terrorists," A1), Bosnia ("U.S. Wants Bosnian Serb Leaders Ousted in Quest for Lasting Peace," A11), and Israel ("Suicide Bombers Injure 11 Israelis," A11).

Human competition for land and space also pushes animals such as bears and tigers towards extinction, a plight worsened by human demand for their organs to treat sexual and medical disorders. Traffickers in animal parts receive only a token punishment ("Fine Too Light, Bear Watch Group Claims," A2).

Whales are symbolic of all endangered species, yet even though commercial whaling has been banned since 1986, Japan continues the practice under the guise of research ("Japanese Plan to Catch 400 Minke Whales," A12).

Nuclear power exemplifies the unanticipated and uncontrollable costs of technological innovation ("Chernobyl Closure Undecided," A11), yet France continues to test weapons in the face of massive global protests. Australian PM Paul Keating has criticized Britain's tepid stance ("Major's Nuclear Stand Assailed," A11).

Toxic pollution is now widespread ("Key Fishery Off Louisiana, Texas Threatened by Influx of Man-made Nutrients from Mississippi River: 'Dead Zone' Expanding in Gulf, Scientists Say," A12). Pollution undoubtedly affects people too. In a village of 120 people in Zhizhong county, thirty-two are dwarfs who appeared suddenly where there were none sixty years ago ("Water Taint in China Suspected for Unusual Number of Dwarfs," A20).

Models of climate change predict extreme, unpredictable fluctuations in weather patterns, and they are happening ("Typhoon Flattens 15,000 Homes as Floods, Winds Rake Philippines," A14). The most effective counter to global warming has now been demonstrated to be forests ("Scientists Prove Rain Forests Absorb Tonne of Carbon Dioxide per Hectare," A12).

Neither the United States nor Canada has a department of population, even though rising human numbers have enormous economic, social, and ecological consequences. We seem unable to deal with population growth politically ("U.S. Pro-Choice Supporters Alarmed After Congress Bans Type of Late-term Abortion," A13).

A new form of haemorrhagic fever was reported near Achuapa, where more than 2,000 people were stricken ("Mystery 'Cursed Fever' Claims 18 in Nicaragua," A24). On August 19, cyanide was spilled into two rivers when a dam broke, yet people affected are afraid to testify ("Guyanese Public Snubs Spill Probe," A24).

Many more headlines underscore the environment's role in our lives. "Lower Mainland Residents Going Green, Survey Shows" (B1). "Aircare Tests to Cost More" (B4). "Canadian Companies Run Toxic Mines, Chileans Say" (B4). "Trek to Beautiful Lakes Has Become Rite of Autumn" (C11). "Cassiar Timber Area Set for Threefold Expansion" (D1). "Yellow Pages Publishers on Edge, B.C. Forestry Union Leader Says" (D1). "Hydro Blames Low Water Flow, Rising Interest for Low Income" (D2).

The media keep telling us the environment is no longer an issue of concern or priority, yet, read properly, every issue of the *Vancouver Sun* is filled with stories of ecological significance.

A BEACON OF AUTHORITY IN THE INFOSTORM

These days we are assaulted by vast amounts of data and information made readily accessible through the electronic and print media and computer networks. Much of it, though, is infojunk, not worth wasting time on or at least not worth remembering. But when we're overwhelmed by infoglut, how can we decide what is credible and worth paying attention to? The quandary is worsened by the fact that the media have created an audience with a short attention span and hooked it on sex, violence, and the sensational.

Fortunately, there is a bright beacon of authority on global environmental issues, the Worldwatch Institute (WWI). The organization maintains its credibility by refusing to accept any money from government or corporate sources, relying instead on revenues from charitable foundations and publication royalties. All of the organization's publications are carefully written to be accessible to the concerned citizen and are also extensively footnoted and exhaustively referenced. Around the world, WWI publications generate an average of forty articles a day, every day of the year!

The WWI is the inspiration of its founder and president, Lester Brown, described by the *Washington Post* as "one of the world's most influential thinkers." Brown is an expert on food. He was a farmer and studied agriculture and agricultural economics in university. He also has an international perspective, acquired while working in India and in the federal department of agriculture.

The WWI was established in 1974 to analyse global environmental issues, and it now has an enormous impact around the world. Ten years after starting WWI, Brown began publishing an annual *State of the World* book, the best up-to-date report on issues of social, environmental, and economic concern. Although often grim, the book contains concrete steps that can be taken to change the deteriorating conditions. *State of the World* is so highly regarded that, in the United States alone, it is used in more than one thousand college and university courses! The annual report is now translated into twenty-seven editions in all of the world's major languages.

Information is the institute's major product, and this can be seen in the many books authored or edited by Brown and his associates. They cover topics ranging from population growth to overconsumption, food, water, soil, and energy. The WWI has also published dozens of monographs that focus on specific topics like soil erosion, indigenous people, forestry, and fisheries. In 1988, WWI began to publish a popular bimonthly magazine, *World Watch*.

In 1992, the WWI started producing *Vital Signs*, an annual compilation of dozens of up-to-date key indicators of the state of our economic, social, and ecological health. In *Vital Signs*, one can quickly acquire a sense of the direction we are going by scanning the trends in many areas.

The indicators provide revealing snapshots of what is happening on the globe. For example, the 1994 edition reports, "Some 520 species of insects and mites are now resistant to one or more of the pesticides that are widely used to control them. Some 17 species are now immune to virtually all pesticides used against them. . . . This situation is analogous to . . . more and more species of disease-causing microorganisms becoming resistant to antibiotics."

The data on AIDS are stark. It "is still spreading rapidly in most of the world — indeed, still gaining momentum in many regions. In some urban regions of Africa, 30 percent of all adults now test positive for HIV. . . . Last year, more than a million HIV-positive infants were born in Africa."

Many of the indicators inform us of the finite nature of resources and warn that we are hitting the ceiling on many. For example, in the oceanic fisheries, "for the fourth year in a row, the fish harvest has been static, changing little from the preceding year. Falling water tables and spreading water scarcity are bringing us face to face with the limits of the hydrological cycle. Water scarcity is beginning to shape the evolution of the global farm economy, altering production patterns and diets. . . . In some countries, farmers are no longer able to raise the productivity of their land. In Japan, rice yields have not increased at all for a decade despite a powerful economic incentive. . . . Life expectancy, still rising in most of the world, is dropping in some countries. The largest to register a decline is Russia."

As nations around the world continue to press for economic growth while depleting their ecological capital, the Worldwatch Institute will carry on issuing the facts, analyses, and prescriptions, a welcome relief from the infobabble.

14

POLITICS:
FROM OLD-FASHIONED
TO GREEN

*O*ur great faith in democracy is based on the assumption that the people we elect will represent us and, after much information-gathering and thought, make decisions that are best for us. But political priorities are set by a different agenda. Instead of reflecting our interests, they reflect the interests of the politicians' or the parties' backers, of the people with the greatest access to the elected representatives, and of each politician's personal education, values, and general awareness. Here and there are examples of politicians from Canada to Japan to Australia who, upon election, exhibit a deep understanding of ecological matters and a willingness to stand on matters of principle. And if it can happen in a country like Japan, with its high premium on conformity, it can happen anywhere.

FOREST'S FATE SEALED BY PROFIT MOTIVE

If we are ever to avoid repeating environmental problems, we have to learn from mistakes already made. A new book, *The Last Great Forest: Japanese Multinationals and Alberta's Northern Forests* by Larry Pratt and Ian Urquhart, examines the history and forces that have sealed the fate of Alberta's great boreal forest.

The northern mixed-wood forest occupies more than 40 percent of the land, covering most of the province north of Edmonton. The principal tree species are white spruce, lodgepole pine, poplar, aspen, and balsam. Aspen makes up 32 percent of the forest and was long regarded as a "weed" with "no utility or economic value" and therefore "not worth conserving."

Provincial forestry philosophy was summed up in a department of lands and forests document: "Timber and other products of the forest are a crop. This is the underlying thought of all forest management or conservation work." The Alberta Forest Service looked at the forest as "an underutilized resource that needed development."

Peter Lougheed had the good fortune of being in office during the Arab oil embargo, which sent oil prices skyrocketing. Alberta boomed and its Heritage Fund grew. But after 1981, falling oil prices and high interest rates caused a decline in new investment, a rise in unemployment, and business failures. The province's economy rested on a narrow resource base of oil and agriculture.

In 1979–80 there was a sudden increase in the demand for wood pulp to make paper. This so-called chip shock caused the price of softwood chips to double, making Alberta forests into an economic opportunity, but Lougheed ignored it. In 1985 Alberta's new premier, Don Getty, pinpointed forestry, tourism, and technology/research for development even though, according to Pratt and Urquhart, "There was no economic plan; there was not even a coherent rationale for the areas chosen."

In 1986 world oil prices fell from $27 (U.S.) to below $10 per barrel, causing the loss of up to 50,000 jobs and $10 billion in revenue in the petroleum industry. Pratt and Urquhart say Getty aggressively pursued foreign investors, with a view to turning over "the long-term economic and environmental management of the great northern forests of Alberta to the biggest transnational firms in exchange for jobs, stability and the development of some value-added industry."

In the end, Pratt and Urquhart report, "a handful of transnational companies acquired immense timber hinterlands in northern Alberta at the expense of the many existing forest companies and sawmills that account for most of the employment in that sector and now have very limited prospects of growth."

Getty ignored the pleas for help of small, already established sawmill owners, independent loggers and contractors, and Native communities. According to Pratt and Urquhart, one of the small independents said, "The province was always looking for industry. The big timber quotas went to the big companies and they didn't have to pay anything for them. It was the small companies that had to pay."

Alberta's environmental movement was in its infancy, and the province was renowned for being gung-ho for development. But suddenly, confronted with the prospect of immense pulp mills emitting large quantities of dioxins and furans into the water and air, grass-roots organizations sprang up and demanded environmental accountability. At the same time, aboriginal people such as the Lubicon recognized the threat government commitments posed to their lands and raised wide support for their claims.

It was a battle of environmentalist and Native Davids against industry and government Goliaths. Pratt and Urquhart document government and industry deception, secrecy, and insensitivity while local groups and Natives fought to make the consequences of logging vast areas a major issue. In spite of widespread public apprehension and almost no scientific base of knowledge about the composition and basic biology of boreal forests, water, and soil, the government went ahead.

In less than two years, Pratt and Urquhart write, "The Getty Cabinet approved construction of five new pulp and newsprint mills and the expansion of two existing kraft mills and allocated virtually the entire boreal forestry resource." Yet "the Alberta government had no knowledge as to the likely environmental impact of these multiple developments on these systems."

This book makes very clear that industries are driven by the need to maximize profit for investors and they have no commitment to sustaining local communities or ecosystems. Moreover, political agendas are inevitably short term, opportunistic, secretive, and unprincipled. Until society as a whole recognizes that fundamental biological, social, and spiritual needs must never be compromised, we will never achieve the protection of ecological bottom lines.

The Last Great Forest provides insights relevant to most of the environmental problems we face in this country today.

UPDATE: The boreal forest spans Canada and Eurasia and is the largest remaining intact forest on the planet. Vast as it is, the boreal is now coming under increasing attack as countries like Russia permit extensive logging contracts while Canada is caught up trying to keep feeding the massive mills that were built at great public expense. In Alberta, the Lubicon fought against the logging of their traditional territory by the Japanese company Daishowa and gained support of a group called Friends of the Lubicon, who brought the issue to the public by urging companies to boycott paper products made by Daishowa. They succeeded in persuading more than fifty companies not to use Daishowa paper. Daishowa retaliated by suing Friends of the Lubicon, first to stop them from continuing the boycott campaign and then to recover lost revenue (claimed to be more than $12 million). In March 1998, the court rejected Daishowa's suit. On May 19, 1998, Daishowa announced it would not log on Lubicon territory. Meanwhile, the boreal forest continues to be liquidated.

Until the 1970s, Canada's boreal forest was a net carbon sink, that is, it absorbed more CO_2 than it emitted. However, it is now a net carbon emitter, producing 45 megatonnes a year.

A fifth of the boreal forest's biomass has now been lost in Canada. The loss is especially striking in Alberta where less than 9 percent of the province's woodlands remain in a pristine state. Between 1975 and 1993, the annual area logged increased by 125 percent. A 1998 report on Alberta's forests concluded that the rates of human depredation in the province "almost match and exceed those reported from Amazonia from 1975 to 1988."

WHAT MIKE HARCOURT FAILS TO GRASP

My family spends each Canada Day weekend in the Okanagan picking and gorging on cherries. We return to Vancouver on the Coquihalla highway, the extravagant monument built by the then premier, Bill Bennett, for Expo '86. Large clearcuts gash the cover of trees that have been the hallmark of "Beautiful British Columbia" all along the route. The lovely Coquihalla River, which runs along the valley bottom, has been forced into acquiescence by culverts, rockfill, and bulldozed trees. This year (1994) we stopped just outside the town of Hope and came across a sign prohibiting fishing in an attempt to save the steelhead run. Once numbering more than one thousand fish annually, now a mere one hundred return, the sign informed us.

A few days later, two news stories on CBC Radio caught my attention. The first reported that the summer run of Coquihalla steelhead had been officially declared "endangered" because over the past two years fewer than fifty had returned. The second story announced that Premier Mike Harcourt was on his way to California in an attempt to head off a boycott of B.C. forest products by telling businesspeople about B.C.'s progressive new forestry policies. The new regulations limited the size of clearcut areas to forty hectares, still a large opening in a forest, while increasing the width of the protected area along the riparian zone of rivers and streams. The two stories highlight our inability to grapple with the roots of the environmental dilemma.

Selective breeding by farmers over the past ten millennia has created the impressive array of domesticated plants and animals we use today. Their utility and productivity in modern agriculture depend upon rigidly controlled environmental conditions. In British Columbia, the great forests and runs of fish have been treated as if they are farm crops. Fast-growing individuals of a species are selected and then released or replanted in a decimated area in large numbers. Yet one of the great surprises of modern genetics research has been the discovery that individuals within a species are not freely interchangeable or equivalent.

The fish and trees that are such a critical part of B.C.'s history and economy are "wild" organisms and have evolved over long periods of time in balance with the rhythms and demands of their specific surroundings. While the same species of economically important fish and trees may be found in many different watersheds and valleys, each population is genetically unique, a reflection of its evolutionary history and the specific conditions of its local habitat.

Steelhead and trees are not merely "resources" or "economic opportunities," they are communities of living, interacting creatures. Human scientists and managers know very little of the basic features of the biophysical landscape that have made these populations so abundant. It does not demean such experts to point out their ignorance; indeed, it is because we understand so little of the vast and multilayered world out there that most scientists have gone into research in the first place.

The Coquihalla steelhead population is biologically unique and is on the verge of extinction. When and if it disappears, an irreplaceable record of evolution and adaptation will vanish forever. Of course, scientists can freeze cells and preserve DNA sequences of individual fish, but they will never refill the hundreds of river systems with the "races" of steelhead or salmon that have disappeared.

The Coquihalla steelhead leave the ocean to run a gauntlet of salmon-fishing fleets and pollution in the Fraser River, only to reach a spawning habitat that has been massively disrupted by road construction. That population will not be protected by merely restricting fishing at the top end of the run. We've already seen how the same simple-minded approach to complex biological populations and unwillingness to regulate the totality of human depredation has created havoc in the Atlantic ground-fishery.

It is true that Premier Mike Harcourt's forest policies represent an improvement over the legacy of his predecessors, but that wasn't difficult to do. For decades, the forest industry defended the escalating volume of trees cut while denying the accusations of critics that it was not sustainable. Now the industry and government admit the criticisms were valid but claim to have turned over a new leaf and changed their ways. However, decades of irresponsible stewardship and overharvesting cannot be overcome by a mere invocation of responsible stewardship.

Harcourt, like most politicians, does not understand what ecological carrying capacity really means nor the dependence of the economy on the health of the environment. He would be more credible if he recognized that nature cannot be forced to conform to human demands; we know too little to manage populations of wild organisms, and the fate of any population — human or nonhuman — is inextricably linked to other organisms and the physical state of air, water, and soil. Now if we acknowledged that, that would be a great reason to celebrate Canada Day.

UPDATE: Mike Harcourt resigned in 1996 after a controversy arose over misuse of funds by the NDP. He is now a professor at the University of British Columbia in the Sustainable Development Research Institute. Harcourt left a legacy of new parks and forest legislation that was unparalleled in the province. His successor, Glen Clark, has turned back the clock, returning to the bad practices of the past — shipping of raw logs overseas, reducing stumpage fees, and relaxing the rules of the Forest Practices Code — all with a view to helping an ailing forest industry, but all likely to ensure the continued depletion of B.C.'s great wilderness and the dependent creatures who live in it.

WHAT CLINTON AND CHRÉTIEN NEED TO KNOW

On October 16, 1995, in Washington, D.C., hundreds of thousands of African-American men gathered in front of the Capitol building in search of a renewed sense of worth, family, and community. The Million Man March completely masked the arrival in Washington of eight Yukon Gwich'in people. The group included seventy-three-year-old Edith Josie; Chief Robert Bruce; the Council of Yukon First Nation's environmental co-ordinator, Norma Kassi; and four youth, the youngest being nine-year-old Paul Kevin Josie. They had come to plead with politicians to abandon plans that could destroy the Gwich'in way of life.

In 1995, for the first time in decades, Republicans led both the Senate and the House of Representatives. The new crop of politicians was poised to throw out three decades of environmental legislation and open up public lands and forests, even national parks, to the private sector. It was done by stealth; amendments and riders attached to vital bills slid by without public debate.

At a press conference on September 22, Secretary of the Interior Bruce Babbitt directed his anger at the problem: "The lobbyists are really in control of this place. They're all over. The money changers are swarming through the temples of democracy in the nation's capital." Babbitt said, "The lobbyists have invented a process here of short-circuiting the normal legislative process."

Congress intended to privatize the national parks and to allow mining, logging, and development in them. A major focus of this attack was the Arctic National Wildlife Refuge, a vast coastal plain along the Beaufort Sea that extends from the northeast corner of Alaska to the Yukon. The refuge's annual migration of more than 150,000 caribou is a wildlife spectacle that is often called America's Serengeti. The huge herd moves more than 600 kilometres from its wintering grounds in Canada to the Alaska plains to calve.

In 1987, in recognition of the significance of the caribou both globally and to the Gwich'in people, the United States and Canada signed the Porcupine Caribou Herd Conservation Agreement. The area is also an important habitat for polar bears, which are covered in the Agreement on the Conservation of Polar Bears, signed by five circumpolar nations in 1973. More than 300,000 snow geese feed in the refuge on their way south and there are resident musk oxen, wolves, grizzlies, and a host of other bird and mammal species.

The biologist George Schaller has said it is "one of the last true large wilderness areas left on earth, an area unspoiled, its biological systems intact. Our civilization will be measured by what we leave behind. The Refuge was established not for economic value, but as a statement of our nation's vision."

But with Alaskan oil running low, the industry was tantalized by the strip of Arctic refuge along the Beaufort. This despite the fact that the most optimistic estimates for the Arctic refuge calculate it would add 0.4 percent to world oil reserves and service only a fraction of one percent of the national debt. If the U.S. used only Arctic refuge oil, the estimated reserves would last for ninety days! The interior department estimates that oil drilling on the plain will decrease caribou populations by 40 percent and musk oxen by 25 to 50 percent.

As Babbitt said, "This Congress has chosen to deal with that issue in the dark of the night. Rather than risking a public debate through the normal processes . . . this Congress has chosen to put that quietly into the reconciliation bill, thereby opening up the Wildlife Refuge to drilling."

To a reporter's suggestion that Congress was merely carrying out what people elected it to do, Babbitt scoffed: "It's nonsense. These issues were not debated in the last election cycle. The environment and our natural resources were not a part of the election campaign mix."

Polls consistently indicate that while Americans are concerned about the economy, the deficit, and over-regulation, they want to keep strong environmental legislation. A large majority is against oil drilling in the Arctic refuge. The challenge is to expose the implications of what is being done "in the dark of the night."

All Canadians, not just the Gwich'in of Old Crow, have a stake in protecting the Porcupine Herd, which is acknowledged in a formal agreement for joint management by the two nations. Babbitt warmly praises Canadian co-operation and protection of the area, but we have to demand that the U.S. live up to its signed commitments.

That tiny band of Yukon Gwich'in was fighting for its survival as a group of people whose culture and lives are built around caribou. Their fight is our fight, a battle for the preservation of an irreplaceable heritage for all future generations. Bill Clinton, Jean Chrétien, and Sheila Copps need to know that we want to keep oil drilling out of the Arctic refuge forever.

UPDATE: A recent U.S. Geological Survey has determined that the oil reserves on the Arctic refuge are greater than previously thought. But the deposits are spread apart in small pools that make them less cost-effective to exploit. So pressure to allow drilling has decreased and Clinton is upholding the bill that restricts drilling. However, there is no formal legislation, only an agreement of understanding between the two countries not to proceed. The future of the caribou herd is far from assured.

THE BUZZSAW OF "PROGRESS" HITS SARAWAK

Politics is a dominant force in our society. The values and actions of our elected representatives lead us into the future. We think this is the only way things can be, but there are societies with very different ways of governing themselves and they clash with what we are used to.

Having been adopted by the Eagle clan of the Haida people, I attend the annual assembly of the Haida nation in Haida Gwaii (Queen Charlotte Islands). At the end of the meetings, we all take part in a wonderful feast. Tables are heaped with homemade bannock, cakes, and pies, along with clams, crab, herring roe, salmon, and halibut caught in local waters. After eating, guests are showered with gifts and treated to songs and dances.

Here, culture, history, and community are rooted in the abundance of the forests and surrounding waters that define "home" and "belonging." The Haida bring to mind a remarkable speech delivered in 1993 before the United Nations by Anderson Mutang Urud, a Kelabit from Sarawak in Malaysia. His words were rich with ideas and insight for all of us.

While Sarawak is less than 2 percent the size of Brazil, it produces almost half of the world's tropical timber. Even if the rate of logging is cut in half immediately, Mutang says all primary forest in Sarawak would be gone by the year 2000. And as the forest is cleared, there is a domino effect: "Fish, wild animals, sago palms, rattan and medicinal plants disappear. The trees which bear the fruit which feeds the wild pigs are cut down for timber. The pigs disappear, and with them vanishes the main supply of meat for our peoples. . . . Trees and vines with poisonous barks are felled, and find their way into the streams, killing all the fish. Mud from the eroded lands pollutes the rivers, bringing us diseases and destroying our source of drinking water."

Like Canadians, Malaysians have shown little respect for the sacred burial sites of the indigenous people: "The logging companies bulldoze through them, with no regard for our feelings. . . . When we complain about their destruction, they sometimes offer us a small sum of money as compensation, but this is an insult to us. How can we accept money that is traded for the bodies of our ancestors?"

There is a fundamental clash between value systems. Progress and development are the words government uses to justify the logging activity. To this, Mutang says: "For us, their so-called progress means only starvation, dependence, helplessness, the destruction of our culture and demoralization of our people."

Like those of British Columbia, the forestry practices of Sarawak are aimed at maximizing profit with little regard for sustaining communities or conserving the forests. Mutang sees this as the ruse it is: "The government says it is creating jobs for our people. But these jobs will disappear along with the forest. In ten years, the jobs will be gone; and the forest which has sustained us for thousands of years will be gone with them."

The real problem is that Western notions of progress tear apart ways of life that support communities and families: "My father, my grandfather did not have to ask the government for jobs. They were never unemployed. They lived from the land and from the forest. . . . we were never hungry or in need. These company jobs take men away from their families for months at a time. They are breaking apart the vital links which have held our families and our communities together for generations. These jobs bring our people into a consumer economy for which they are not prepared. . . . The Penan, the Kelabit, and the other indigenous peoples view the forest as our home. When we see a thief enter our home, we try to defend what is ours." Since 1987, there have been peaceful blockades to which the government has responded by arresting and imprisoning scores of people. Mutang himself has been tried in absentia and will be arrested if he ever returns.

Mutang relates: "A high government official once told me that in order to have development, someone must make a sacrifice. I replied, why should it be us who must make this sacrifice? We have already become poor and marginalized . . . while companies get rich from our forests, we are condemned to live in poverty. Now there is nothing left for us to sacrifice except our lives.

"In our race to modernize, we must respect the ancient cultures and traditions of our indigenous peoples. We must not blindly follow that model of progress invented by European civilization. We may envy the industrialized world for its wealth; but we must not forget that this wealth was bought at a very high price. The rich world suffers from so much stress, pollution, violence, poverty, and spiritual emptiness. The wealth of indigenous communities lies not in money or commodities, but in community, tradition, and a sense of belonging to a special place. . . . The world is rushing toward a single culture. We should pause and reflect on the beauty of diversity."

Mutang's appeal on behalf of his people is relevant here in Canada. In Haida Gwaii, the land and waters are still rich with life that gives an opportunity to define progress differently and follow a different path.

UPDATE: Environmentalists have long criticized Malaysia and the government of Sarawak for logging practices that are both unsustainable and destructive of the forest home of the Penan people. Malaysia showed little concern in the face of global condemnation. Now, in quick succession, we have learned of a massive cloud of smoke that hung over Indonesia and Malaysia for weeks in 1997, while in 1998, reports have revealed that drought-induced fires have been burning uncontrollably in Sarawak. Pictures of suffering orangutans have replaced the images of the Penan as symbols of victimhood of avaricious forest destruction.

A NEW KIND OF LOCAL POLITICS

Economic issues have dominated our lives in the 1990s. The economy seemed to be the only issue in the last federal election and has remained the main preoccupation of governments at the federal and provincial levels on all sides of the political spectrum. During the recession of the 1990s, financial support for environmental groups has plummeted while environmental issues have all but disappeared from the media.

So is it all over now as the public turns to more pressing preoccupations? Not at all. People are worried about the economy, of course, but I still sense among the general public a continuing and deep concern about the environment and about their children's future. They know things must change and they are willing to pay for it and make personal adjustments. But people want a concrete vision of where we are heading and a realistic strategy to achieve it. Consider Australia, a country very similar in many ways to Canada.

Sydney in New South Wales is one of the most stunning cities on this planet. But it has many of the familiar urban problems: streets littered with refuse and pet droppings, terrible traffic jams, storm sewers carrying toxic chemicals into water systems, and harbour bottoms laced with heavy metals. As a result, in 1994, Leichhardt, a municipality in the inner core of Sydney, elected a mayor, Larry Hand, who ran on a green platform.

Hand and his council have already passed legislation mandating solar water heating and the provision of shade in all new buildings and major renovations. In future, the council proposes to ban all use of rainforest timber, to legislate mandatory sterilization of all pet cats, and to levy fines against people who fail to sort their garbage. Mayor Hand advocates "a green vision and local action plan for the development of an ecologically, socially and economically sustainable environment." His goal is "the restoration of a healthy natural environment."

The New South Wales Environment Protection Authority (EPA) recently completed an exhaustive poll of 1,115 rural and urban dwellers. Each was interviewed in person for an average of forty minutes. The results indicate that politicians lag far behind voters when it comes to environmental matters. When asked to list their main concerns in descending order of priority, the interviewees ranked their top concern as unemployment, followed by education, health, crime, and the environment. But when asked what they thought would be the main priority ten years from now, they moved the environment well ahead of the other four!

Four of every five interviewees said they had changed their behaviour over the past five years for environmental reasons. Among the changes were recycling, purchase of household products on the basis of their environmental friendliness, conservation of water, and trying to convince someone else to be more "green." More than 80 percent agreed with the statement "There is a lot I, as an individual, can do to help protect the environment."

In terms of specific issues that concerned them, Sydney voters listed ocean and beach pollution, followed by freshwater and air pollution, and then waste management and disposal. Almost half agreed that "we are doing too little, too late, to protect the environment." The EPA concluded that there is a huge base of public support for environmental action.

One of the most interesting questions was what sources of information people considered most reliable. National and local environmental groups were first and second choices. Third were the municipal councils, and schools were fourth. Scientists and technical experts ranked only fifth, government departments eighth, churches eleventh, and business and industry twelfth and dead last.

Chris Harris of Greenpeace Australia believes that there is a deep public understanding of the ecological crisis but that environmental groups "haven't adequately found ways to communicate to the public how they can recognize what people can do individually. There's a gap between people's knowledge of the problems and their knowledge of what they can do."

My own personal experiences in Australia and Canada corroborate the EPA poll. Politicians and media pundits make a big mistake in downplaying the environment. The challenge for environmentalists is to show the inseparable linkage between the environment and the economy and begin to formulate an alternative vision of a future that will be truly sustainable. I suspect local councils like Leichhardt are going to lead the way.

UPDATE: This story reveals the place where there is a real opportunity for change: local government. In Australia's Newcastle, the Green Party holds the balance of power on the city council. As a result, the city has the most progressive environmental and social program that I've ever encountered. In addition to rejecting a proposed massive development of prime beach area, the council is committed to reducing garbage output by more than 50 percent by the end of the century.

In Canada, as the federal and provincial governments continue to jettison or download fiscal responsibilities, municipalities are put under tremendous financial pressure. As a result, the 20 percent club, cities committed to reducing CO_2 by 20 percent by 2005, is already reporting that such reductions are possible and that millions of dollars can be saved while creating new jobs.

A GREEN JAPANESE POLITICIAN

The public's low opinion of politicians is reinforced by the paucity of examples of legislators putting their jobs on the line for a principle. And has there ever been a politician who, having gained political office for high ideals and with no hint of scandal, has passed the office on to others at the height of power? I met such a person in Japan, of all places. His name is Kiichiro Tomino and he could well be an inspiration for us in Canada.

Tomino is fifty years old and lives in Zushi, a city of 68,000 people, many of whom commute to work in Tokyo. His family has lived in this region for more than 300 years! Tomino's great love was astronomy, but when his father died he quit his Ph.D. studies and returned to Zushi to take over the family business.

Adjacent to the city is the Ikego forest, a 290-hectare tract that was expropriated and used for munitions storage and military training during the Second World War. After the war, Ikego was left alone and reverted to a rich wilderness that was much loved by the people. But in 1982, the Japanese government announced plans to reclaim the forest in order to construct a housing complex for U.S. Navy personnel. Tomino was galvanized to oppose the development, and was joined by housewives, elders, environmentalists, and anti-war activists.

The group collected 46,000 signatures opposing the development. But the mayor and council favoured construction and ignored the opposition. Three housewives were sent to Washington to plead with Defense Secretary Caspar Weinberger. He turned them down. So in 1984, the group decided to run a housewife for mayor. She backed out at the last minute and Tomino reluctantly replaced her, handily beating the incumbent mayor of twelve years.

But Tomino was faced with a pro-construction majority on council. In 1986, the pro-construction group forced the recall of Tomino, who ran again and won. Meanwhile, Tomino's group collected enough signatures to force the recall of the entire council. In the ensuing election, twelve antis and fourteen pros were elected. When one of the pros died, another anti was elected to deadlock the council at thirteen to thirteen.

In the mayoral election in 1988, Tomino won easily, and in the 1990 election of councillors, fifteen antis and eleven pros were elected. A third term is the time when a politician's work matures to fruition, yet in 1992 Tomino passed on a third term so a housewife could run. She won, along with six other women councillors, for the second highest ratio of women in a Japanese government. Although the housing development hasn't been built, the pro-constructionists continue to try to thwart grass-roots opposition through backroom deals. But the story is the best kind of example of grass-roots democracy at work.

When I asked Tomino what he is most proud of having accomplished during his terms as mayor, he answered without hesitation: "That I remained a citizen and didn't become an official. What that means is that I did my politics with common sense. When I negotiated with the central government, I always believed the citizens were the most important. I always worked with citizens to make policy." He added, "Japanese think that laws can't be bypassed, but we showed that the mayor and citizens could."

Tomino praises women as the key element in the anti-construction movement and as responsible for his success. When I asked him whether he can generalize about differences between women and men in politics, he answered: "Yes — women don't lie. Men easily resort to lies and believe that's a natural part of politics."

Tomino never forgot that he was a part of the grass-roots. He instituted a monthly news report to keep citizens informed about the goings-on in city hall. He established a number of citizens' committees that anyone interested could join.

Tomino set up a public-service company that now hires seventy elders to work at jobs like controlling traffic for school children, working in libraries, and driving school buses. They are paid more than the minimum wage and are proud to serve their community.

Tomino is a remarkable Japanese. He is enthusiastic, upbeat, optimistic, and positive. He believes passionately in the power of the grass-roots. "To understand what's happening in Japan, don't look to the central government. It's dead. It's all happening at the local level. Right now it's invisible, but in five years, you'll begin to see it." His story is a powerful model of how to involve the grass-roots to bring about change.

15

SCIENCE AND TECHNOLOGY: LIMITS, BENEFITS, AND COSTS

The most powerful force shaping our world today is science as applied by the military, industry, and medicine. Consider the impact of nuclear power, DDT, and antibiotics, just three of dozens of powerful technologies that science has unleashed in the past century.

Until fairly recently, in most areas of research, a scientist could not make a lot of money. Science was a leisurely, curiosity-driven activity. But after the Second World War, discoveries in chemistry, physics, and more recently, biology, became the generating force for ideas that attracted investors and speculators. Money changed the nature of the scientific enterprise. The time frame was suddenly shortened; there was greater emphasis on competition, secrecy, and patents.

As science exploded, especially after Sputnik *was launched in 1957, prospective science students were put under increased pressure to take more courses in specialized subjects. Courses like history, philosophy, literature, and religion were jettisoned so students could become more highly specialized and focused. As a consequence, scientists today are less prone to question their own area, to reflect on its strengths and weaknesses, and to consider the ramifications of discoveries on society and the environment.*

Even as some scientists try to point out the level of ignorance about the world around us, governments everywhere are cutting back on basic research in the guise of fiscal responsibility. Yet basic knowledge, especially in biology, is most desperately needed. For without an understanding about how the world functions, we will have no idea how new technologies might affect us.

SCIENCE'S REAL LESSON IS HUMILITY ABOUT HOW LITTLE WE KNOW

The Nobel prize-winning scientist François Jacob once wrote that the human brain has an innate need for order. If we perceived the world "out there" as our senses register it, the world would seem totally chaotic. With our in-built curiosity and ability to observe and learn, we can make sense of our milieu by recognizing patterns and regularities and fitting them into a framework invented by the mind. Those rhythms and cycles of nature give a comforting context that human beings have been able to exploit.

Throughout history, that need and ability to create order has generated what anthropologists call a world-view. A world-view contains all of a society's accumulated insights, speculation, beliefs, and wisdom. It is all-inclusive. In such a construct, nothing exists in isolation. Everything — past, present, and future — is part of an uninterrupted continuum. Each rock, stream, and tree, every star, cloud, and bird, is part of a single interacting and interdependent whole. World-views are profoundly rooted to a locale on the planet and suffused with an understanding of the human place within it.

Science has shattered world-views with a fundamentally different way of viewing one's surroundings. By focusing on a single aspect of nature — isolating it and controlling everything impinging on it — scientists acquire knowledge about that fragment. But in searching for principles that are universal and timeless, scientists disconnect the object of study in time and space, yielding a fractured picture of our environs.

Today, science's value is perceived to be the revelation of insights that permit the domination and control of nature. It is a dangerously mistaken notion. Early in this century, physicists recognized that individual components of nature interact with each other to create properties that cannot be anticipated from their behaviour in isolation. Thus, information gained from studying each part of the natural world does not add up to a complete picture. So in biology, baboons studied in a zoo, for example, provide little insight into their normal behaviour in the wild.

Even if acquired scientific knowledge could be pieced together like a jigsaw puzzle, our database is so minuscule that only a liar or fool would claim to possess enough information to "manage" nature or natural resources.

The most important and intriguing part of science is to ask questions. Scientists try to organize the bits and pieces of knowledge they have into a framework that allows the formulation of a question that can then be tested experimentally. That's how science progresses, and most of the time, the answers obtained cause models and hypotheses to be radically altered or even discarded. Most of what scientists do reveals that our current ideas are naive or incorrect. That is not a denigration of science, it is the very way that science advances.

But it also means that scientific models of the world are so simplified that they bear little resemblance to reality. The models are merely a means of focusing the thrust of experiments or the collection of data. It is a grotesque misapplication of research when these simplifications of complex ecosystems are used as the basis and justification for their "scientific management."

This is the heart of the absurdity of claims that old-growth forests, wild fish like salmon and northern cod, and populations of caribou and moose can be managed. It is also the reason that claims that one species or another is to blame for a natural disaster are ridiculous. Such a deflection of attention from the central role our species plays in creating ecological problems results in killing wolves in the Yukon to increase ungulate populations and slaughtering seals on the East and West coasts to expand fish stocks.

By extirpating a major predator in a food chain, populations of prey can be affected. But it is an ephemeral effect, an illusion that the population change reflects understanding and control. In the same way, it is a mockery to equate a tree plantation that grows after massive clearcutting with a "forest." A forest is a community of micro-organisms, plants, and animals, most of which are not even identified, *and* air, water, and soil that support them.

Science is one of our species' great achievements. But the tiny window it opens into our surroundings merely serves to emphasize the scale of our ignorance. We can celebrate the breathtaking insights we acquire while recognizing that this fractured image of the world does not encompass the complexity and interconnectedness of the real thing.

NOBEL PRIZES ALSO REFLECT OUR IGNORANCE

Each year, the Nobel Prizes are announced, but the research they are awarded for is far too arcane for the public to understand and soon disappears from view. In 1995, though, the awards had special significance for environmentalists.

The Nobel Peace Prize was given to a remarkable physicist, Joseph Rotblat. He quit working on the atomic bomb for the Manhattan Project out of repugnance and has devoted much of his life to warning of its dangers. Although the nuclear arms race between the two superpowers has ended, Rotblat's prize served to remind us that France continues to pursue its own nuclear agenda despite widespread condemnation. Rotblat's outspokenness contrasts with the silence of Canadian political and scientific leaders on France's outrageous nuclear testing.

The Nobel Prize in Chemistry went to three scientists who discovered the vulnerability of the ozone layer to human-created molecules. In 1970 Paul Crutzen observed that airborne nitrogen oxides could break down ozone. Then, in 1974, Sherwood Rowland and Mario Molina found that chlorofluorocarbons (CFCs), which were valued for their chemical inertness, could be split apart by sunlight to liberate chlorine, which is highly reactive and breaks down ozone. Their report generated vigorous denials from the chemical industry, although the public responded by reducing the use of

CFC-containing aerosols in the 1970s.

But it took the discovery of a "hole" in the ozone layer over Antarctica in 1984 to induce serious discussions on how to reduce CFC production. Few environmental issues are as clear as the CFC–ozone connection, yet CFC production will not be completely eliminated globally until the next century. Meanwhile, the World Meteorological Organization reported that 1995's thinning of ozone over Antarctica was more extensive and was occurring faster than ever.

I take great vicarious delight in the award of the Nobel Prize in Medicine to my fellow geneticists, indeed, fellow fruit-fly researchers. Their test animal, *Drosophila melanogaster*, has contributed as much to our understanding of heredity as any other organism, including ourselves. Press reports of the prize-winners' work skimped on details and stressed the possible implications for understanding "some birth defects and miscarriages." But the studies deserve more explanation. All three geneticists were intrigued by the long-standing biological puzzle of how a nondescript blob, the fertilized egg, transforms itself into a complex organism made up of many different cell and tissue types that all act together in one functional fly or human.

The California Institute of Technology's Ed Lewis is an elder statesman in an esoteric field called chromosome mechanics, whose practitioners skilfully move genes from one location to another among the chromosomes. As a wunderkind back in the 1940s, Lewis demonstrated that genes are not the smallest unit in heredity but could be dissected into parts. He went on to show there are different kinds of genetic subunits that regulate the activity of other gene parts. In other words, there are switches that can turn genes on and off at different times in various parts of the body. Lewis demonstrated that the major architectural landmarks of a fly's body — head, thorax, abdomen — are determined by special blocks of genes.

Princeton's Eric Wieschaus and the Max Planck Institute's Christiane Nuesslein-Volhard combined traditional genetics and embryology with molecular methods. Using mutations that act only through the female to affect the survival of the eggs, Wieschaus and Nuesslein-Volhard found that genes acting in the mother's ovaries predetermine top and bottom, head and tail, as well as the destiny of cells to become gonads, muscles, and so on.

These elegant experiments demonstrate once again the power of scientists to frame questions, design experiments, and analyze data to penetrate nature's mysteries. The great strength of science is in description, and we have far too little of it.

With these insights, geneticists can do spectacular things such as raising flies with twelve legs instead of two, or with eyes growing on different parts of the body or a leg growing from the mouth! Nevertheless, after the billions of dollars spent on fruit-fly research, we still don't know how they are able to survive Canadian winters, how an egg is transformed through larval, pupal, and adult stages or how this species interacts with other species.

Drosophila melanogaster is just one of tens of thousands of fruit-fly species, each unique and special in its own way. We have no idea what role drosophilids play in nature, and they are only a minor group among all insects, which are the most abundant and significant group of animals on Earth.

As we destroy coral reefs, forests, and wetlands, we lose any possibility of even identifying what organisms there are, let alone how they interact to create a vibrant, productive community. The Nobel Prizes celebrate what we have learned and remind us how much more there is to discover.

A HUMBLING MESSAGE OF ANTS AND MEN

Harvard's Edward O. Wilson is a world-renowned authority on the variety of living organisms occupying the planet, an expertise based on a lifetime consumed with collecting and studying ants. Wilson's latest book, *Naturalist*, is an autobiography that informs us of how the wonders of the natural world became the formative focus of his childhood and persist as the source of his creativity and environmental activism. He emphasizes that nature has been the well-spring of our biological and social origins, provides the biophysical underpinnings of our lives, and inspires us with wonder and endless mysteries to ponder.

Wilson's story raises questions about our rush to lure students into science by stocking schools with expensive, glitzy interactive CD-ROMs and computers. The hi-tech machines carry an implicit worship of human technology and ingenuity, at whose altar much of the global environment has been sacrificed.

Wilson grew up in the Deep South during the Depression, a shy child whose parents divorced when he was seven. Yet his lost family life was compensated by the education he received in the swamps of Alabama and the coastal beaches of Florida. The very first memory he recounts is of a scyphozoan, a giant jellyfish, in the Gulf of Mexico. Like that of many scientists, Wilson's research career grew out of his childhood fascination with nature. "A child comes to the edge of deep water with a mind prepared for wonder. He is like a primitive adult of long ago, an acquisitive early Homo. . . . [H]e is given a compelling image that will serve in later life as a talisman, transmitting a powerful energy that directs the growth of experience and knowledge. He will add complicated details and context from his culture as he grows older. But the core image stays intact."

These days, acclaimed educational TV programs like *Sesame Street* perpetuate an accelerating information and sensory assault that precludes time for reflection or contemplation. Time is priceless. As Wilson writes: "Adults forget the depths of languor into which the adolescent mind descends with ease. They are prone to undervalue the mental growth that occurs during daydreaming and aimless wandering. When I focused on the ponds and swamp lying before me, I abandoned all sense of time. Net in hand, khaki collecting satchel hung by a strap from my shoulder, I surveilled the edges of the ponds, poked shrubs and grass clumps, and occasionally waded out into shallow stretches of open water to stir the muddy bottom. Often I just sat for long periods scanning the pond edges and vegetation for the hint of a scaly coil, a telltale ripple on the water's surface, the sound of an out-of-sight splash."

Sadly, opportunities to duplicate that kind of childhood experience have become increasingly rare as wilderness vanishes and more and more children grow up surrounded by a human-created environment of concrete, tarmac, and television. But even in the most developed urban areas, there is an opportunity to experience wild creatures. All we have to do is focus on the realm of the small: "They are everywhere, dark and ruddy specks that zigzag across the ground and down holes, milligram-weight inhabitants of an alien civilization who hide their daily rounds from our eyes. For over 50 million years, ants have been overwhelmingly dominant insects everywhere on the land outside the polar and alpine ice fields. By my estimate, between 1 and 10 million billion individuals are alive at any moment, all of them together weighing, to the nearest order of magnitude, as much as the totality of human beings."

Then Wilson offers this humbling thought: "If we were to vanish today, the land environment would return to the fertile balance that existed before the human population explosion. . . . But if the ants were to disappear, tens of thousands of other plant and animal species would perish also, simplifying and weakening the land ecosystem almost everywhere."

After a life spent revelling in the abundance and variety of Earth's life forms, Wilson has an urgent message: "We are bound to the rest of life in our ecology, our physiology, and even our spirit. . . . When the century began, people still thought of the planet as infinite in its bounty. The highest mountains were still unclimbed, the ocean depths never visited, and vast wildernesses stretched across the equatorial continents. . . . In one lifetime, exploding human populations have reduced wildernesses to threatened nature reserves. Ecosystems and species are vanishing at the fastest rate in 65 million years. Troubled by what we have wrought, we have begun to turn in our role from local conqueror to global steward. . . . [O]ur perception of the natural world as something distinct from human existence has thus also changed fundamentally."

Wilson has observed catastrophic changes in tropical forests since his first field trips to the forests of Cuba and New Guinea in the 1950s. Escalating human numbers, consumption, and pollution have altered the planet, and to Wilson, the most harmful consequence is a steep decline in biodiversity. Life's rich multiplicity constantly cleanses air and water, replenishes the soil, and recreates biological abundance. Once a species disappears, it can never be recreated. On the other hand: "If diversity is sustained in wild ecosystems, the biosphere can be recovered and used by future generations to any degree desired and with benefits literally beyond measure. To the extent it is diminished, humanity will be poorer for all generations to come."

Wilson points out that the most frightening aspect of the current extinction crisis is the enormity of our ignorance of what we are losing. While only about 1.4 million species have been named by scientists, the actual number in existence may lie between 10 and 100 million. There are only 69,000 known species of fungi out of an estimated 1.6 million. Arthropods (which include insects), the most abundant group of species, have at least 8 or 10 million members in tropical rainforests alone. There are also probably millions of invertebrates that live on and beneath at the bottom of deep ocean trenches.

But of all organisms, the ones we know least may be bacteria, of which a mere 4,000 species are recognized worldwide. Wilson cites a study carried out in Norway that found between 4,000 and 5,000 species among some 10 billion individuals in a gram of forest soil. Almost all of the species had never been identified before. When the biologists looked at soil taken from a nearby estuary, they discovered another 4,000 to 5,000 species; most of them were different from the forest sample and were also new to science.

By comparing the estimated rate of species loss today with the changes observed in the fossil record, Wilson concludes: "The number of species on Earth is being reduced by a rate of 1,000 to 10,000 times higher than existed in prehuman times." The annual loss of about 1.8 percent of tropical rainforest, home to more than half of all species on Earth, extinguishes or endangers perhaps 0.5 percent of species. Wilson calculates that if there are 10 million species in these habitats, more than 50,000 species may vanish each year. This is a very conservative estimate that ignores the effects of pollution and of competing exotic species in different parts of the world.

Species relationships that evolved over millions of years are being wiped out in a geological blink of an eye. Wilson predicts, "Unchecked, 20 percent or more of the earth's species will disappear or be consigned to early extinction during the next thirty years. From

prehistory to the present time, humanity has probably already eliminated 10 or even 20 percent of the species."

Extinction is a part of the evolutionary process. In the past,
there have been episodes of mega-extinction, the most recent of
which wiped out the dinosaurs. Wilson points out that there have
been five major extinction spasms over the past 550 million years. On
average, it took about 10 million years for evolution to restore
the species abundance and diversity lost in each episode. So the
catastrophic loss of a species taking place in a single lifetime will
never be made up during our species' existence.

I have heard it suggested that since human beings are a part of
nature, whatever we do must also be regarded as "natural." It therefore doesn't matter if we instigate a wave of extinction. Wilson
replies: "The vast material wealth offered by biodiversity is at risk.
Wild species are an untapped source of new pharmaceuticals, crops,
fibers, pulp, petroleum substitutes, and agents for the restoration of
soil and water. This argument is demonstrably true . . . but it contains
a dangerous practical flaw when relied upon exclusively. If species are
to be judged by their potential material value, they can be priced,
traded off against other sources of wealth, and — when the price is
right — discarded. Yet who can judge the ultimate value of any
particular species to humanity?"

I was a guest at a meditation session for cancer patients who
had ridden a roller-coaster of hope and despair after chemotherapy,
radiation, and surgery. Many spoke of "truly living" for the first
time. Almost all made reference to the importance of "being in
nature," whether walking in a woods, strolling a beach, or resting on
a farm or at the cottage.

Watch children respond to a wasp or butterfly. Infants seem
drawn to an insect's movement and colour, often reaching out to
touch it. They exhibit neither fear nor disgust, only fascination. Yet
by kindergarten, this enchantment with nature somehow gives way to
revulsion as many children recoil in fear or loathing at the sight of a
beetle or fly.

Edward O. Wilson believes nature's attraction for cancer
patients and infants is a natural inclination. He has coined the term

biophilia (based on the Greek words for "life" and "love") to describe what he believes is a genetically programmed psychological need humans have for other beings. In his book *Biophilia: The Human Bond with Other Species*, he defines biophilia as "the innate tendency to focus on life and life-like processes." It leads to an "emotional affiliation of human beings to other living things. . . . Multiple strands of emotional response are woven into symbols composing a large part of culture."

Wilson suggests the origin of biophilia lies in our evolutionary history, which "began hundreds of thousands or millions of years ago with the origin of the genus *Homo*. For more than 99 percent of human history, people have lived in hunter-gatherer bands totally and intimately involved with other organisms. . . . They depended on an exact knowledge of crucial aspects of natural history. . . . The brain evolved in a biocentric world, not a machine-regulated world. It would be therefore quite extraordinary to find that all learning rules related to that world have been erased in a few thousand years."

Wilson's ideas echo those of the late microbiologist René Dubos: "We are shaped by the Earth. The characteristics of the environment in which we develop condition our biological and mental being and the quality of our life."

But today most people in industrialized countries live in urban environments in which the rich tapestry of other living things has been drastically reduced. Wilson believes that the "biophilic learning rules are not replaced by modern versions equally well adapted to artifacts. Instead, they persist from generation to generation, atrophied and fitfully manifested in the artificial new environments into which technology has catapulted humanity. For the indefinite future, more children and adults will continue, as they do now, to visit zoos than attend all major sports combined."

The notion of biophilia provides a conceptual framework through which human behaviour can be examined and evolutionary mechanisms suggested. *The Biophilia Hypothesis* edited by Wilson and Stephen R. Kellert, compiles articles examining biophilia and its implications. The papers add up to strong support for the theory. For example, the architecture professor Roger S. Ulrich reports that "a consistent finding in well over 100 studies of recreation experiences in wilderness and urban natural areas has been that stress mitigation is one of the most important verbally expressed perceived benefits."

Yale professor Kellert says, "The biophilia hypothesis proclaims a human dependence on nature that extends far beyond the simple issues of material and physical sustenance to encompass as well the human craving for aesthetic, intellectual, cognitive and even spiritual meaning and satisfaction . . . a scientific claim of a human need . . . deep and intimate association with the natural environment. . . . The degradation of this human dependence on nature brings the increased likelihood of a deprived and diminished existence. . . . Much of the human search for a coherent and fulfilling existence is intimately dependent upon our relationship to nature."

To Kellert, our need for nature makes evolutionary sense: "Discovery and exploration of living diversity undoubtedly facilitated the acquisition of increased knowledge and understanding of the natural world, and such information almost certainly conferred distinctive advantages in the course of human evolution."

In the end, Wilson believes biophilia adds a spiritual dimension: "The more we know of other forms of life, the more we enjoy and respect ourselves. . . . Humanity is exalted not because we are so far above other living creatures but because knowing them well elevates the very concept of life."

MOTHERHOOD AT FIFTY-NINE FLOUTS NATURAL LAW

A portent for 1994 was the announcement that, thanks to a regimen of hormone treatment, in vitro fertilization, and embryo transfer, a fifty-nine-year-old post-menopausal woman in Italy had given birth to twins. Public response to the "achievement" appears to be split between those who applaud the feat as an advance freeing us from the constraints of nature and others who look on it as hubris and technological excess. Reproductive technologies, when coupled with powerful techniques to alter genetic make-up, create completely novel social consequences and regulatory headaches.

The most pervasive factor shaping twentieth-century life is technology, a legacy of the human curiosity and inventiveness that have been the major survival attributes of our species. But where our perception and creativity once meant the difference between life and death, today they often end up being used (as in the case of the fifty-nine-year-old mother) to serve human desires.

The questionable repercussions of modern technology are not just to be found in the medical sciences. From dam construction to forest clearing to nuclear power and the chemicals industry, our innovations have consequences that reverberate far beyond the immediate sphere of application. The challenge for us is to guess what those implications might be and where we might acknowledge limits.

Budding scientists today must specialize early and are not, as a rule, well grounded in subjects outside their area of expertise. Nor do they subscribe to a code of ethics that might guide their actions. Today the thrust of much of scientific inventiveness is not the elimination of poverty, oppression, hunger, or real physical suffering. Instead, new technologies are seen as the means of returning profit to investors or stimulating the economy. The overriding assumption seems to be that if it can be done, it must be done. Public input is therefore essential to add other perspectives and to develop guidelines regulating future innovation.

Our new-found technological prowess forces nature into submission, thereby conferring a temporary illusion of control. But again and again, after applying technology for a specific goal, we have discovered vastly complex ramifications that couldn't have been anticipated.

Nature itself can provide guideposts if we learn to respect it as the repository of a long history of evolution and the embodiment of a kind of wisdom. Aboriginal people often give thanks for the wind, the clouds, the mountains, the rivers and lakes, and other living organisms who are our "kin." Implicit in this attitude is an acknowledgement that, as clever and sophisticated as humans are, the forces on the planet and the cosmos that impinge on our lives remain far beyond our comprehension.

For billions of years, Earth and the life that arose on it have changed and interacted in unimaginable ways. Our generation is a brief moment in this long continuum. If we have genuine respect for this complex community of organisms that interact with each other and their surroundings, then we can draw lessons from their basic biology and interconnections that define natural limits or boundaries. Menopause is one of these natural limits.

The lack of respect for nature's boundaries emanates from an unwarranted sense of power and control, and it creates endless unanticipated effects. It makes me wonder what kind of human beings we become when the most sophisticated tools and concepts of science are used to satisfy our trivial wants instead of the more profound. Does our society tolerate inequities that enable a post-menopausal woman to gratify her decision to have a child while tens of thousands of people with healthy, normal minds and bodies lack the resources and support to rise above hunger and poverty? Are such experiments really worth the risk involved in escaping the constraints built into us by the long history of evolution?

A GROWING ANGST ABOUT ESTROGEN

Species evolve by mutational tinkering with the genetic apparatus, shuffling of genes into new combinations, and natural selection. Given the vast expanse of evolutionary time, the genetically controlled metabolic reactions that life uses to transform air, water, and food into itself are exquisitely co-ordinated. A chart of all the known chemical reactions in a cell occupies half an office wall and reveals the ways individual or sets of reactions are regulated.

One control mechanism is hormones, molecules that travel between cells and function as chemical messengers by informing their targets to crank up or shut down specific reactions. Their role is precisely determined and even a minuscule number of hormone molecules may play a large role in a cell's fate.

We are probably most familiar with hormones involved with sex, the dominant male hormone being testosterone, and in females, estrogen. They play a vital role during pregnancy, in regulating both the complex changes in the mother's body and the development and differentiation of gender and reproductive organs in the fetus.

As precise as the response of the cell's metabolism to hormones may be, it is not absolutely infallible. A hormone's role may be determined by its size, shape, and reactivity, properties that can be mimicked by other molecules, often called analogues. That is what chemists exploited to create birth-control pills. The synthesized analogue resembles estrogen enough to act like the hormone in cells, but it has also been chemically modified to make it resistant to gastric juices so that it can be taken orally. That means a hormone analogue can persist in the body and pass out in urine.

During the 1970s, when the Pill had become a major form of contraception, I half jokingly asked a physiologist how much synthetic estrogen could end up in the sewers. Doing a very rough calculation, he estimated an annual output of tonnes in Canada alone. In jest, I let my voice rise to a falsetto and suggested there might not be a population problem in the future.

But what seemed like science fiction may now be science fact. British media reports about estrogen pollution in drinking water have triggered near panic among residents living along the Thames River in London. Hermaphroditic fish are being caught in the Thames, particularly where urban sewage flows in. In some cases, more than 40 percent of the catches are hermaphrodites. A higher incidence of male sterility in humans has also been noted in the same region.

An estimated 3 million women who live near the river regularly take the Pill, which means up to 800 million pills a year ultimately pass into the river and end up in the drinking water. Waterworks officials respond that a man would have to drink an Olympic-sized swimming pool full of water to get enough of the estrogen to be affected. The fact is, no one knows what effects exposure to small but persistent amounts of estrogen analogues will have.

The Danish endocrinologist Niels Skakkebaek reported in 1992 that sperm counts in men in twenty-one countries, including the U.S., have dropped an average of 50 percent since 1938. Over the same period, testicular cancer has tripled. Skakkebaek speculates that the observed changes result from exposure of males to estrogen-like compounds while fetuses or as infants from their mothers' milk.

Even more alarming are other molecules that behave as analogues and have become equally ubiquitous. They include pesticides such as DDT (which continues to be sold in vast quantities to poor countries like Brazil), PCBs, polycarbonate plastic (found in such items as baby bottles and water jugs), and organochlorine derivatives from bleaching paper.

Accumulating circumstantial evidence hints that estrogen analogues all about us are affecting our reproductive systems. The International Joint Commission on the Great Lakes has reported increased numbers of hermaphrodites in fish and the birds that eat them, and recently speculated that PCBs and DDT in Lake Ontario may be causing increased incidences of small penis size and undescended testes in boys. Prior to 1921, there were only twenty cases of endometriosis, a painful inflammation of the uterine lining, reported in the entire world, but today 5 million women in the U.S. alone have the problem! Endometriosis is a prominent cause of infertility and is increasing in frequency while appearing in younger women.

Accidental spills of pesticides have affected the sex organs of wildlife, while exposures of pregnant women to estrogen mimics have affected the sex organs of their sons. There are even suggestive correlations of breast cancer with higher levels of pesticide products in women's tissues.

Our insights into the marvellous ways that our cells function allow us to exploit this knowledge. But they should also heighten our awareness that in our chemical-laden surroundings, aberrations in other creatures may well be a canary's warning.

A TECHNICAL SOLUTION THAT SANK

With sudden speed, human beings have levelled immense tracts of ancient forests, covered the land with concrete and asphalt, poisoned the Great Lakes, vastly reduced the range and numbers of other life forms, and changed the chemistry of the atmosphere. Although many of these damaging effects could be controlled by governments, politicians rarely act to minimize the potential harm of these changes.

When politicians are confronted by environmental problems

demanding major remedial action, they often have two choices. They can make a decision that is wise in the long run but guaranteed to create an immediate storm of protest, or they can do nothing on the chance that nothing catastrophic will happen soon. History shows they always gamble. It would be political suicide to do otherwise, especially when any benefits would be realized only many years later. That's why northern cod are commercially extinct and why, in 1995, politicians refused to act on commitments to reduce CO_2 emissions to levels that Canada had agreed to at the Earth Summit in 1992.

Businesspeople and economists often argue that unless we are absolutely sure an environmental hazard is real, it is foolhardy to act. Yet we invest billions in the armed services and gigantic economic initiatives to protect us from hazards that are far less certain. With global warming, we're playing dice with one of the underpinnings of our survival.

The future is already far less certain because the atmosphere, water, soil, and biological diversity that were once so reliable have been destabilized by human activity. Many scientists who know the global ecological perils are very real, and are worsening, believe that, "human nature" being what it is, people will respond only when we slam into physical limits and begin to see bodies.

Consequently, some argue, since the atmosphere is already being changed inadvertently and since people aren't going to make the necessary response, we have no choice but to use technology to try to correct the problems at hand. Geo-engineering is suggested as a way to neutralize the effects of rising greenhouse gases.

The proposed mega-solutions are neither sophisticated nor profound. In fact, they are sophomorically simple and imbued with hubris: if the Earth is warming up, then cut down the amount of heat reaching the Earth. How? Launch huge shields into space to cast a shadow on the Earth, or spread a layer of particles in the upper atmosphere to reflect sunlight back out into space.

Alternatively, if too much CO_2 is building up, find a way to remove the molecule from the air. During the 1980s, scientists observed that even though there was plenty of nitrogen and phosphorus in certain parts of the oceans, the phytoplankton that absorb CO_2

couldn't use it up because the water was iron-poor. When iron was added to flasks of such water, the plant cells multiplied explosively, increasing up to ten times their number.

So, it was suggested, if millions of square kilometres of the ocean around Antarctica were dosed with iron, huge phytoplankton blooms would absorb CO_2 into their cells and, on dying, would carry the carbon down to the ocean floor in their carcasses.

Now any ecologist would have warned that it's one thing to make an observation in a flask and a totally different thing to manipulate an infinitely more complex real world. Still, the idea appealed to some and it was finally tried in the fall of 1993. In an iron-poor area of the Pacific, 500 kilometres south of the Galápagos Islands, 480 kilograms of iron sulfate were spread over 8 square kilometres, increasing iron concentration a hundredfold. Over three days, phytoplankton concentration doubled. But instead of increasing to ten times the density, both the growth rate and the iron levels returned to normal in four days. Scientists then learned that iron aggregated in a previously unknown way and sank to the bottom; creatures that eat phytoplankton also multiplied rapidly and soon ate up the excess.

It is true that science and technology have advanced at an astonishing rate in the second half of this century. But while scientists are very good at description, they are far less capable at prescription. The reason is that the real world in which we attempt to carry out our ideas is far more complex than our fragments of insight can encompass, and we can't possibly anticipate all of the consequences.

We are too ignorant of the biological and physical components of the Earth and how they interconnect to even consider such simple-minded notions as geo-engineering the planet. Technology cannot endlessly repair damages created by technology in the first place. The only real control we have is over human activity. It is a dereliction of responsibility to cling to the false hope of technological solutions and therefore fail to curb our own actions.

It will not be a sacrifice or entail a reduction in quality of life for those of us in industrialized countries to reduce our consumption of frivolous goods or walk instead of driving on short trips. It will be good for us and it will signal our personal commitment to a change in direction.

HYDROGEN FUEL PROVING PRACTICAL

Modern society is characterized by the consumption of vast amounts of energy. But this consumption comes with environmental costs. The automobile engine contributes to ground-level air pollution and higher up to the greenhouse effect. Electricity is indispensable in modern life, yet contributes to global warming through coal-burning stations, carries risks of nuclear accidents, or causes massive ecological destruction by dams. But for most people, giving up the family car or using far less electricity is not a realistic option.

Now it appears there can be an improved environmental future that still includes electricity and cars. The secret factor is hydrogen. Hydrogen has long been touted as a potential fuel, but one with finicky volatility. Now that that volatility has been tamed, it offers an exciting source of electricity without combustion.

The technology was first invented in 1839 and was used in the 1960s as a one-time-only power source for the *Gemini* and *Apollo* space programs. When hydrogen is pushed onto a special polymer membrane, the atomic nucleus passes through, leaving behind its electron. The electron is captured and put to work as electricity while the hydrogen nucleus emerges on the other side of the membrane to combine with oxygen and form water. Thus, while electricity is generated, the only waste products are heat and pure water. It sounds almost too good to be true.

In 1983, Dr. Geoffrey Ballard, a Vancouver entrepreneur, began to develop the "proton-exchange membrane" to exploit hydrogen's energy potential. Like the first clunky computers that presaged today's PCs, Ballard's early fuel cells were bulky and heavy but soon progressed. Between 1988 and 1993, the power output per given density and volume increased 500 percent, and by 1998, it exceeded 50 kilowatts. In other words, more and more power was being packed into the same space in the way greater numbers of transistors have been crammed onto a silicon wafer. The implications are immense.

In 1992, a transit bus was outfitted with a 125 horsepower Ballard fuel cell; it can carry twenty passengers for 160 kilometres on a tank of hydrogen. In 1995, a sixty-passenger bus had an increased range of 400 kilometres, and in 1998, a seventy-five-passenger bus, while falling short of a predicted 560 kilometre range, more than met the transit system's needs. Since the end of '93, a Mercedes-Benz car powered by a Ballard fuel cell has been driven thousands of kilometres without a breakdown. There are now two more Mercedes running on those fuel cells. The company now predicts a fuel cell for commercial use in cars by 2004, for bus and power generators by 2001 and 2002, respectively, and a new portable unit by 2001.

Development of the hydrogen fuel cell has been stimulated by legislation in the United States. In 1990, the Clean Air Act reduced the volume of allowable emission of pollutants while regulating pollution sources such as vehicles. The same year, California legislated that by 1998, 2 percent of the cars sold in the state by each manufacturer must have no exhaust pollutants. By 2003, 10 percent must have zero emission. Since California represents 10 percent of all U.S. vehicle sales, this mandate has had a major impact on the auto industry. In 1994, the District of Columbia and twelve northeastern states, which represent 30 percent of the vehicle market, requested the same automobile standards as California. In addition, the Energy Policy Act of 1992 set energy-efficiency standards for industrial equipment. Taken together, this legislation has pressured industries to find better ways to meet the rigid standards.

The Ballard hydrogen fuel cell represents a massive decrease in total pollution per unit of energy and has zero pollution emission. It is portable, made of cheap, durable material, and easily mass produced. Hydrogen power is more reliable than solar energy and avoids heavy batteries and recharging time. There are few moving parts in the engine to break down. Hydrogen itself is readily available from a variety of sources, including natural gas and the electrolysis of water.

The bus powered by Ballard's cells demonstrates the immediate practicality of the technology; all indications are they will also work in trains and cars in the near future. Ballard already has hydrogen fuel cells producing thirty kilowatts of electricity (enough to provide the daily electrical needs of seven homes). The company plans to sell units starting at 250 kilowatts and going up to a megawatt. Small, reliable power plants would be ideal for remote communities and would decrease our dependence on huge, centralized electrical stations. Hydrogen fuel cells could substitute for nuclear-power units in submarines that already pose a pollution hazard in the world's oceans.

This is one of those rare stories in Canada, a home-grown technology with enormous environmental benefits. Ballard Power has been well-supported by government and leads the world in this field. It is also a corporate success. Daimler and Ford have invested one billion dollars in Ballard Power Systems and own 20 percent and 15 percent, respectively, of the company's stock. The stock market value of the company is $3.7 billion with 82 million shares trading.

Now the challenge is to transform government and industry rhetoric about global competitiveness into reality. In the long run, we still have to change our dependence on energy and transportation, but hydrogen fuel technology can buy us time to make the transition.

A MODEL FOR HEALING THE PLANET

When my father-in-law developed heart disease, the frightened family gathered to discuss the best way to ensure his health and survival. He talked to several doctors, read extensively, and changed his lifestyle. The family all took a course in CPR (cardiopulmonary resuscitation) just in case.

Like my father-in-law, the planet is exhibiting increasingly troubling signs of stress. Many of us are alarmed and have been trying to find the best strategy for action. The famed American environmentalist David Brower has called for a program of CPR for the planet. Brower's CPR stands for conservation, protection, and restoration. He told me that he believes restoration must be our major priority in the years to come, and I agree.

But how? The tiny fragmented insights science gains about the natural world don't allow us to manage our surroundings. Extinction, of course, is irreversible. And even heroic measures to keep an endangered species going don't stand much of a chance without profound changes in human behaviour and genuine protection of its habitat.

The thin layer of biological complexity that covers the planet ensures the productivity and cleanliness of the soil, air, and water. Only time and nature safeguard these life-supporting elements and keep them intact. Remarkably, if we pull back and decrease or halt our assault on a given environment, nature can be unbelievably forgiving and resilient. We've seen it in the recovery of Lake Erie, increased vegetation around Sudbury, and the return of fish to the Thames River in England.

Even though we don't possess the ability to recreate the likes of what once existed, there are things we can do to stimulate the natural process of regeneration. First we must rein in our destructive activity and then provide conditions that might encourage the return and regrowth of life. We can liberate land and creeks from rubbish, concrete, or asphalt, cultivate specific vegetation, and even reintroduce plant or animal species that were once present. But mainly we must give the Earth's restorative powers time to act. There is a project that could be an inspirational model for beginning to heal the planet.

Tasmania is a fabled island south of the Australian continent. In the remote mountain heartland of Tasmania's wilderness was Lake Pedder. Only 9.7 square kilometres in area, the lake was surrounded by high sand dunes and featured a long beach with a unique pattern of sand ripples. The lake was famous for its exquisite beauty, and the pink colour of the beach sand, and was the centrepiece of Lake Pedder National Park, established in 1955.

Yet in 1967, the Tasmanian government approved a proposal of the Hydro Electric Commission to build a series of dams that would flood Lake Pedder. The premier, Eric Reece, admitted there would be "some modification" to the Lake Pedder National Park.

An uproar followed, and in 1972 the world's first Green Party, the United Tasmania Group, formed to oppose the flooding. A massive Save Lake Pedder campaign attracted national support, but in the absence of legislation enabling the federal government to override the state the dams went ahead and were built.

Even as the flooding began in 1972, a small group vowed to

keep alive the hopes of taking the dam down and restoring Lake Pedder. In 1992, I received a letter asking for support to examine the feasibility of taking two of the dams down so that Lake Pedder could be refilled. The David Suzuki Foundation funded a study that demonstrated that economically, geologically, and biologically, it is feasible to try to restore the lake.

The Lake Pedder dam generates 60 megawatts and Tasmania has a surplus of 130 megawatts. In 1994, the International Union for the Conservation of Nature called on the Australian government to back the restoration of Lake Pedder "as a symbol of hope that humanity can recover some of the global heritage lost over the last century." The Australian government has set up an official enquiry into the future of Lake Pedder. Australia, host of the Olympics in the year 2000, would be a shining symbol of a new direction for an ecological millennium if it also restored Lake Pedder.

UPDATE: The feasibility study demonstrated that with energy conservation and increased efficiency, there was no need for the electricity generated by Pedder Dam, so it could be taken down without economic repercussions. All indications in terms of engineering and ecology suggest that it is feasible to remove the dam and that a great deal of the original ecosystem could return. In spite of the study, the Tasmanian government rejected the proposal.

The campaign to remove Pedder Dam continues. Around the world, megadams continue to be regarded as a symbol of "economic progress" and are being constructed in Latin America, Indonesia, India, and China. At the same time, in North America, proposals to remove dams are based on the recognition that their ecological repercussions are considerable. As a symbol of environmental awareness, dam removal has attracted much public interest.

16

WHO NEEDS NATURE? WE DO!

$\mathcal{T}$*he longer we live in the human-dominated surroundings of large cities, our need for novelty and titillation is increasingly satisfied by a variety of manufactured products, electronic games, and television. But the real source of inspiration and endless surprise and delight is nature.*

An ecosystem is a complex community of exquisitely intercon-nected, diverse organisms that are finely tuned to live in balance with the physical supports of the air, water, soil, and climate of the area. Honed by billions of years of evolution, nature has the resilience to survive the vast environmental upheavals that have occurred throughout time.

Nature works. We don't know how. But if we continue to treat it with so little respect, we will lose any opportunity to find out its secrets.

THE THRILL OF SEEING ANTS FOR WHAT THEY ARE

Watch a child's face while she's poking around in a tidal pool, peering under a rotten log, or netting tadpoles in a pond. The joy of surprise and discovery is instantly visible. When my daughter Severn was three or four, she asked me how worms are able to move through the ground. I told her they simply eat soil at the front end and poo it out the back. "Oh," she responded, "so dirt is worm-food?" And I could see a smile of delight at this new thought.

Charles Darwin shared Severn's fascination with worms. When he heard someone had estimated that there were 53,767 worms per acre, Darwin is reported to have "figured the worm population swallowed and brought up ten tons of earth each year on each acre of land. Earthworms therefore were . . . constantly turning it inside out. They were burying old Roman ruins. They were causing the monoliths of Stonehenge to subside and topple." Darwin concluded: "Worms have played a more important part in the history of the world than most persons would at first suppose."

One of the pleasures of science journalism is something that clicks on a light, suddenly providing an entirely new perspective on things around us. For example, in the '70s, the biologist Lynn Margulis suggested that structures called organelles, found within cells of complex organisms, are actually the evolutionary remnants of bacterial parasites.

She pointed out that organelles are able to reproduce within a cell and even possess DNA and distinct hereditary traits. So, Margulis proposed, organelles were once free-living organisms that invaded cells and were eventually integrated into the host. In giving up their independence, these bacterial relics received nourishment and protection from the host cell. Looking in the mirror now, I see a reflection of a community of organisms inhabiting trillions of cells aggregated as me.

In an interview for *The Nature of Things*, I once asked Harvard University's eminent biologist Edward O. Wilson why ants are so successful. His entire career has been spent studying these ubiquitous insects, and he became animated with enthusiasm as he answered. "There are only a few tens of thousands of species of ants, compared with millions of other non-social insects, but they dominate the world. Their secret is super-organism. A colony of ants is more than just an aggregate of insects that are living together. One ant is no ant. Two ants and you begin to get something entirely new. Put a million together with the workers divided into different castes, each doing a different function — cutting the leaves, looking after the queen, taking care of the young, digging the nest out and so on — and you've got an organism weighing about ten kilograms, about the size of a dog, and dominating an area the size of a house.

"The nest involves moving about 40,000 pounds of soil and sends out great columns of workers like the pseudopods of an amoeba, reaching out and gathering leaves and so on. This is a very potent entity. It can protect itself against predators. It can control the environment, the climate of the nest. When I encounter one of these big nests of leaf-cutter ants, I step back and let my eyes go slightly out of focus. And what you see then is this giant, amoeboid creature in front of you." It was a thrilling description that made me think about ants in a very different way.

In 1972, scientists in Michigan made the astounding announcement that the network of mycelia, thread-like extensions of fungi found in the ground, could be derived from one individual, not an aggregate of different organisms. They reported a single organism that extended throughout sixteen hectares! Not long after, biologists in Washington reported a fungus covering 607 hectares!

This fall I was filming in a grove of quaking aspen, the lovely white-barked trees whose leaves shimmer at the slightest puff of air. I learned that what I thought was a group of individual trees was, in fact, a single organism! Like a strawberry plant that can spread asexually by sending out runners that send down roots and sprout leaves, quaking aspen multiply vegetatively. From one tree, shoots may grow up from a root thirty metres away.

The aspen is another kind of super-organism that can exploit a diverse landscape — parts may grow in moist soil and share the water with other portions perhaps growing in mineral-rich soil higher up. In Utah, a single aspen plant made up of 47,000 tree trunks was discovered. It covers an area of forty-three hectares and is estimated to weigh almost 6 million kilograms.

We know so little about the varieties of species that exist and the specific attributes of individual organisms that we have endless opportunities for discovery. It is an exciting prospect to anticipate the delicious surprises that await us.

THE CASE FOR KEEPING WILD TIGERS

Conservationists predict that members of one of Earth's most magnificent species, India's Bengal tiger, may disappear completely from the wild within five years. The tiger is high on the food chain, so its disappearance would not be as ecologically disruptive as the loss of insects or fungi, for example. So one may wonder what it matters if one more species, especially a large carnivore that has long been feared as a "man-eater," disappears?

If the tiger goes from the wild, we will suffer spiritually. Tigers are part of the rich mythology and folklore of humankind, a symbol of our love-fear relationship with nature. Its beauty, size, ferocity, and power inspire awe and terror simultaneously, reminding us of our own frailty and vulnerability. Like beluga whales, marbled murrelets, and spotted owls, tigers are an "indicator" species whose fate informs us whether we are capable of sharing the planet with others.

In preparing programs on wildlife, I am constantly shocked at the speed and scale of loss. Years ago, I stood in the Delta marsh south of Lake Winnipeg during the fall migration of waterfowl. The sky was filled with a cacophony of calls and dozens of chevrons of geese at one time. It was thrilling to know that wild creatures still act out their genetic destiny as they have for millennia.

But those waterfowl migrating up the central North American flyway were a mere vestige of the past. A century ago, I was told, the birds literally filled the sky from horizon to horizon on their great flights along the continent. I was also amazed to learn that grizzly bears were not always confined to West Coast mountains — they once populated foothills and prairie grasslands all the way to Ontario and down to Texas and California! They were prairie animals living on the great herds of bison that were also exterminated.

Elders who have lived their entire lives along the East and West coasts, across the Prairies, or above the Arctic Circle recount depressingly parallel stories of decline in abundance and variety of living things. Their memories encompass a sweep of time that is often lost as time shrinks and the pace of life speeds up.

Farley Mowat's classic book *Sea of Slaughter* is a lament for the decimation of walruses, whales, and seabirds, and the confinement of the survivors to a fraction of their former range. Mowat's book anticipated the collapse of the northern cod, which has been catastrophic for Newfoundlanders.

In cities, gleaming displays of vegetables, fruit, and meat in supermarkets create an illusion that the Earth's abundance is endless. It's easy for urban dwellers to believe this fantasy of a world without limits when we are immersed in a human-created landscape and few of us get to experience seasonal rites of nature any more. But because our reference point is the urban setting and what we experience, we don't see the impoverishment of nature over the past two centuries.

Imagine what uplifting opportunities we have lost. Imagine the sight of tens of millions of bison moving across the Prairies. The plant intake and fecal output of those giant herbivores created the prairie grasslands, supporting the countless plants, insects, fungi, and birds that evolved along with them.

And passenger pigeons! Eyewitness accounts tell of day after day of darkness as billions of birds flew by. It is said forests rang with the cracking of branches collapsing under the weight of the resting birds. Night hunters, who slaughtered them to ship to Europe, slithered on guano-coated forest floors. The elimination of passenger pigeons in a mere blink of evolutionary time must have had catastrophic ecological reverberations.

In our total preoccupation with exploitation and consumption, we have become impoverished spiritually. The ultimate source of our solace, inspiration, companionship, and sense of place has always been nature. As we tear at the web of living things of which we are a part, we not only threaten our own biophysical needs, we eliminate our evolutionary relatives and fellow Earth beings. We live in a terribly degraded and empty world in which the companionship of our evolutionary kin is replaced by clever toys from the industrial juggernaut to keep us distracted.

The fact that my grandchildren will grow up in a world in which tigers exist only in zoos, books, and videos pains my soul.

WHY WE GROW INSENSITIVE TO DANGERS

A child's exuberant exploration of the world is a magical opportunity for a parent to relive his or her own childhood. The joy and enthusiasm of my daughters' discoveries immediately revive my own memories of catching a luna moth, noticing parasites on a beetle, or discovering a kildare's nest with eggs. When my children were very young, I usually had to call them over to show them what and how to observe. But these days my teenage daughters, Severn and Sarika, are often the first to yell, "Come over here and see what I've found," or "What do you think this is?"

Age has taken its toll on my senses of smell, sight, and sound and the girls are in better physical condition, so they're usually in front. But there's something else that explains why I'm slower to notice things. I'm preoccupied with my work and simply not as receptive to my surroundings as I once was.

In a crowded room, it's impressive to note our ability to focus on specific signals coming into our sense organs. It's possible to engage in an intense discussion with a single person even though there is a background din of many other conversations. Somehow we can filter out extraneous noise or ambience that we're not interested in. Youngsters amaze me with their claims to being able to concentrate on homework with the TV and stereo blaring out.

An Alaskan fur trapper once visited New York City for the first time. Walking along Times Square, he remarked, "I hear a cricket." His companion scoffed at the idea that a cricket could be heard amidst the cacophony of the city. The Alaskan took out a coin and flipped it into the air. Several passersby heard the coin land and glanced down to the spot, proving that we are sensitive to what we are conditioned to detect.

There is also a desensitizing phenomenon called habituation. When a sense organ is stimulated, it sends an electrical signal via neurons and it registers on our consciousness. But if the stimulus persists, the intensity of signals the neurons send to our brains gradually diminishes. Thus, a loud noise or sharp odour may be quite noticable at first, but when it persists we aren't as aware of it after a while.

Most of us are urban dwellers living in an environment awash with stimuli. Whenever I'm filming in a city, I'm shocked to realize how noisy our surroundings can be. We often have to wait for long intervals until a plane passes overhead, a beeping truck backs up, or people talking pass out of range of the microphone. Yet most of the time we are oblivious to the sounds. We are so habituated that we hardly notice. Perhaps that explains the way a frightening problem like ozone depletion, global warming, or toxic pollution seems to become less urgent over time even though it hasn't been dealt with.

Habituation and our ability to concentrate by screening out incoming information may protect us from being overwhelmed by the dimensions of the global ecocrisis. Our lives revolve around recognizing the latest hit song, TV, or movie star, seeing a puck enter the net, or paying attention to Dow Jones averages. We are sensitive to clothing styles, cars, stores, or advertisements that dominate our physical surroundings.

If we were more sensitive to the condition of the planet's physical features, like the air, climate, plants, or animals, we might be climbing the barricades to protest the fact that sunny days that were always a reason to celebrate now threaten us with cancer; Lake Ontario fish are no longer consumable; ancient forests, wetlands, and prairies are disappearing at a horrifying rate; etc.

Jeff Gibbs, the founder of the Environmental Youth Alliance, was a city boy who went on a kayaking trip to the Queen Charlotte Islands as a teenager. In a bay surrounded by a forest, he was suddenly overwhelmed by the vastness and power of nature. "I suddenly realized that humans had nothing to do with these incredible forests," he told me. "They have always been there and can go on without any input from us." This epiphany impelled Jeff into a career of environmental activism. Many people who are leaders in the environmental movement relate similar experiences that changed their lives.

In spite of my concerns for the state of the Earth, I know I've also become insensitive to my surroundings. The real reason that my daughters are able to spot things so much faster than me is that I'm not focused the way they are. My mind may literally be thousands of miles away or worried about some looming deadline. It takes a deliberate effort to shut off the filtering mechanisms of the "civilized" world in order to allow the senses to inform us about the state of our surroundings.

As our lives become increasingly dominated by the artifice of shopping malls and the electronic media, we need all the more the opportunity to experience the natural world. It is vital to plan nature into our urban surroundings, where most of us live and where today's children will spend their entire lives. It's time to rediscover the "real" world.

LESSONS FROM HUMANITY'S BIRTHPLACE

FROM MASAI MARA, KENYA — By comparing DNA from different sources, scientists have concluded that the common ancestor of all of humanity may have lived along the Rift Valley of Africa, one of Earth's landmarks that is visible to astronauts in space.

Here in the cradle of humanity at the north end of the fabled Serengeti Plain, we get a hint of what the conditions may have been like when those first human creatures made their appearance. Descending from the trees and walking upright, they shared a vast expanse of grassland with herds of grazing and gambolling animals beyond count.

In Masai Mara, as in the Galápagos Islands, the animals haven't learned to fear our species. Large gatherings of wildebeest graze along with Grant's and Thompson's gazelles, zebras, and topi. We encounter giraffes, elephants, and lions along the road's edge. The Mara River is filled with hippos bellowing and blowing while immense crocodiles lie motionless on the banks.

For the bird lover, this is truly a paradise, as flocks of dignified crested cranes glide by, plovers leap screaming at our intrusion, and even starlings are spectacular. There are frogs, lizards, and snakes to satisfy the most demanding herpetology buff.

As a long-time lover of insects, I am enthralled at their variety here, from praying mantids to walking sticks, grasshoppers as big as mice, and scarab beetles rolling balls of dung. (When I was a child, I avidly captured and killed insects for my collection, but how times have changed. My daughters share my passion for insects, but adamantly refuse to kill them just for display. Now pictures have replaced boxes of pinned specimens.)

For city dwellers from industrialized countries, the Serengeti's diversity and abundance of wildlife are a stunning contrast with our barren urban habitat. But coming from such an impoverished environment, we have no basis for judgement about the state of life here on the plain. To get a fuller perspective, we read written records of early adventurers and talk to elders, men and women who have lived here for their entire lives. They inform us that the make-up and numbers of animals have been profoundly altered in this century and that in spite of greater awareness, national parks, and ecotourism, the change continues.

Only a few decades ago, one of the truly charismatic mammals in the world, the rhinoceros, numbered in the tens of thousands. Today in Masai Mara, there are fewer than twenty, and African children now take for granted a profoundly restricted range and number of their animals. Cheetahs, chimpanzees, and leopards that once flourished across large parts of the continent are currently confined to tiny areas in parks, reserves, and private game farms.

When Ed Sadd, the owner of Bushbuck Camp where we are staying, came to Nairobi in 1978, Kenya's population was 12 million people. Today there are 28 million! With one of the highest birth rates in Africa, Kenya's population will double again in a mere 17.5 years. This puts enormous pressure on the habitat of the wild animals. It is simply not enough to set aside tracts of wilderness for animals when exploding numbers of people need income, land, wood, and food.

Like millions of others from industrialized countries, I am here as a tourist. "Ecotourism" is much touted as a way for countries in the South to preserve wilderness while generating much needed income. But tourism is not benign, it too is "consumptive." Here on the Mara, the impact of tourism is readily apparent.

It has rained heavily and the ground is saturated with water, so the four-wheel-drive vehicles quickly cut criss-crossing tracks and ruts across the plains. Trucks and vans frequently bog down, their spinning wheels cutting deep trenches through the grass.

We have chosen to stay put in one camp and take time seeking and observing specific species, but most tourists stay in this area for only two or three days, so their drivers whip across the grass to maximize the number of animals sighted.

The drivers watch other vehicles closely. We come upon a male lion mating with two females and soon there are eight other cars surrounding the animals and parked within a few metres of them. It is a thrilling experience to have such an intimate view of nature, and yet the snickering and giggling of the tourists and our close proximity make it seem like the animals are performing for our titillation.

There are few places on Earth that have the number and diversity of animals that still live here in Kenya and Tanzania. But they face unprecedented challenges of pressure from human beings. Can we learn to share their space so they can flourish?

Ecotourism is certainly preferred to extensive logging, damming, or otherwise developing wilderness. But ecotourism is invasive and consumptive. Ultimately, we will have to learn to revel in knowing that wildlife exists free and beyond our presence.

STUDY GIVES BIODIVERSITY A BIG BOOST

For years, environmentalists have sounded the alarm over the threat of species extinction. Whooping cranes, whales, spotted owls, and marbled murrelets have been at the centre of debate over the fate of the biological make-up of all life on Earth.

The explosive rise in human numbers and consumption has accelerated the rate of species extinction. Our use of space for housing, food, materials, and energy has put enormous pressure on wild places and organisms. Complex ecosystems are transformed into biological deserts by our dams, farms, and housing developments. In imposing human power and priorities on our surroundings, we radically reduce biological diversity on the planet.

By our actions, we have shown little regard for the value of biological diversity, yet heterogeneity is a characteristic of populations of living organisms. It is found at the level of DNA within a species. This genetic variability has been assumed to be responsible for the evolutionary persistence of a species by conferring resilience and flexibility. That's why there is concern for the fate of species like bison and tigers, which have been reduced to a small number of survivors. With a reduced genetic base, they are more vulnerable to a new threat such as predation, disease, or environmental change.

Biologists have long theorized that biodiversity confers flexibility on species and ecosystems, enabling them to survive different assaults and bounce back from disasters. On the other hand, it has been suggested that maintaining maximal species and ecosystem diversity isn't that urgent because many species are similar. This idea implies that what really matters is representation of species within major groupings because related species are ecologically redundant. In a time of explosive disputes over the fate of the Great Whale River and the Clayoquot forest, these opposing suggestions have serious repercussions.

In a paper entitled "Biodiversity and Stability in Grasslands," published in the prestigious scientific journal *Nature*, the ecologists David Tilman and John Downing have accumulated strong evidence for a biological role of biodiversity. In a twelve-year study, they counted between one and twenty-six different species in 207 Prairie test plots, each measuring three metres by three metres. For each plot, they determined the biological productivity by the weight of vegetation.

In 1987–88, the study region underwent a severe drought and the researchers found that the productivity of the plots correlated strongly with the number of plant species. Vegetation shrank to about half of the pre-drought average in plots with the most species, and all the way to about an eighth in the most species-poor plots.

Equally significant was the observation that the resilience of the plots after the drought was also correlated with the biodiversity. Thus, by 1992, the species-rich plots had returned to pre-drought levels of productivity, while the species-poor land still hadn't achieved those levels. The authors conclude, "This study implies that the preservation of biodiversity is essential for the maintenance of stable productivity in ecosystems."

Tilman says, "Biodiversity of an ecosystem has a major impact on its stability and functioning. This work leaves little doubt that biodiversity matters and that habitats with more species withstand stress better and recover faster. . . . The more species you have, the more likely some will be resistant to drought or other stress. We should preserve biodiversity because it's nature's insurance policy against catastrophes. . . . By sustaining biodiversity, we help sustain ourselves." Downing adds: "Instead of eliminating species from our forests, wetlands, roadsides, lake shores, power-lines, parks and lawns, we should be preserving them."

Based on his work, Downing warns: "Today humans are greatly reducing biodiversity, not just in the tropics but right here in North America. More than 12 percent of plant species in the U.S. are already listed as rare or endangered, and in Canada, more than 1 percent of known species are threatened. Some countries may lose as many as 30 percent of their plant species over the next two decades. This loss of species has serious long-term implications for life on Earth. It makes the environment more susceptible to insects, disease, fire, drought, abnormally hot or cold weather, floods, acidification and other stresses."

Right now, as an example, rising temperature from global warming wreaks havoc in marine and terrestrial populations. Forests may have to move one thousand kilometres a century to stay within a tolerable temperature range. Forests can and do move, but normally at a tenth of that rate. Only biodiversity offers the hope of harbouring the right combinations that can adapt to climate change. Unfortunately, most of that diversity resides in ecosystems that seem irresistible for human exploitation and development, which end up reducing variety.

And now, humanity itself is being monocultured at an alarming rate. Media and advertising spread the perspectives and values of a single culture dominated by economics worldwide. Free trade, global competition, and uniform mass products of transnational corporations are blanketing the world with a notion of progress and development that has proved highly destructive of local communities and ecosystems. At this very moment, we need an infusion of other views, especially the attitudes and knowledge base of ancient, indigenous cultures.

But governments around the world seem determined to pull us into tighter globalization and diminished diversity, even though current ideas of progress, wealth, and development are not enhancing the quality of life for the vast majority of people. It is in the diversity of local communities and local ecosystems that we will find the solutions for stability and a sustainable future. With concrete scientific evidence for the value of biodiversity, the question is, Does our society take science seriously?

WHY THE BRAVEST POSITION IS BIOCENTRISM

We learn to see the world through the lenses of the individual beliefs and values that we have acquired from personal experience, family, and society. People often share a commonality of truths and values that are so widely accepted that they are seldom questioned.

We can't help seeing our surroundings through the perceptual filters of our preconceptions, yet the media continue to hold out an ideal of journalism that is "objective" and "balanced." But any journalist's personal values are bound to influence the "facts" selected and the way they are juxtaposed and arranged to create a story. The best way to strive for balance is to have many journalists presenting a wide array of world-views.

Understandably, people in media are preoccupied with human affairs — wars, budget deficits, sports, and entertainment. Even environmental stories are usually built around the human costs and benefits for health, aesthetics, jobs, or the economy.

When wilderness habitats are invaded and species threatened with extinction, their preservation is often justified by their potential utility for human beings. Thus it is pointed out that perhaps a quarter of the active ingredients of all medicines are natural compounds extracted from living organisms. When species disappear, a vast repertoire of potentially useful materials is also lost. It is also argued that wilderness may generate revenues through ecotourism or provide spiritual solace.

Everything we use in our homes and workplaces — electricity, metal, wood, plastic, food — comes from the Earth. Our economic system is based on our need for them and their scarcity or abundance. Consequently, the future of old-growth forests, coral reefs, or watersheds often rests on the merits of economic returns from protection or exploitation.

An "anthropocentric" ecological ethic recognizes that environmental protection is ultimately in our self-interest because, as biological beings, we depend on the integrity of our surroundings for our very survival.

There is an alternative perspective called biocentrism, which Bill Devall, co-author of *Deep Ecology*, defines as "a worldview emphasizing that Nature has intrinsic value, that is, value for itself rather than only aesthetic, commodity or recreational value for humans; that humans have the capacity for broader identification with Nature as part of our ecological self; and that compassionate understanding is the basis for communication with Nature as well as with other human beings." This is the central belief that underlies deep ecology.

Critics often accuse deep ecologists of being misanthropes, caring more for other species than for our own fellow human beings. I've heard it said derisively: "They want to protect trees and the spotted owl and don't care if people are thrown out of work." To such criticism, the U.S. poet Gary Snyder responds: "A properly radical environmentalist position is in no way anti-human. We grasp the pain of the human condition in its full complexity, and add the awareness of how desperately endangered certain key species and habitats have become. . . . The critical argument now within environmental circles is between those who operate from a human-centred resource management mentality and those whose values reflect an awareness of the integrity of the whole of nature. The latter position, that of deep ecology, is politically livelier, more courageous, more convivial, riskier and more scientific."

When we acknowledge our dependence on the same biophysical factors — air, water, soil, biodiversity — that support all other life forms, the responsibility for "managing" all of it becomes a terrible burden. In fact, it's an impossible task because, in spite of the impressive sophistication and progress in science and technology, we have nowhere near enough information to understand, let alone predict and control, the behaviour of complex systems like watersheds, forests, oceans, or the atmosphere.

Amid the barrage of information from the print and electronic media, we must recognize the inherent biases that often flow from our anthropocentrism. For example, in all of the discussion about the catastrophic loss of northern cod or the fate of the old-growth forest of Clayoquot Sound, all of the "stakeholders" in the fishing, logging, tourism, and Native communities seem to accept that the underlying economic and political institutions are beyond question or change, even though they may well be the very cause of the crisis.

By looking at the world through biocentric lenses, we may recognize the roots of our destructive path. The landscape may be uncomfortable and strange, but we can't afford to dismiss the problems viewed from this perspective as a lack of balance or simple bias.

REFLECTIONS WHILE BACKPACKING

On Thanksgiving weekend in 1995, my family passed up turkey and all the trimmings to backpack up the Stein Valley near Lytton, B.C. For more than a decade, a rancorous battle has pitted the logging community against people of the First Nations and environmentalists over the fate of this valley, the last intact watershed in southwestern B.C. To date, the logging road has been kept out.

Exactly five years earlier we had made the same trip, so we were anxious to see whether much had changed. To our joy, nothing had been perceptibly altered in the interim. The river was full of pink salmon, nicknamed "humpies" for the big lump on the back of the hook-nosed males. These animals had fought their way past obstacles of hooks, nets, pollution, and human development. And here they were gathered in pools to rest, battered and spotted with white patches of fungus that would devour their carcasses. Driven by the imperative to reach the spawning beds before their genetically programmed deaths, they still clung to life and possessed the power to leap barriers in the river.

Within a few hundred metres of the trailhead is a rock wall

covered with ancient pictographs that reminded us that this was a sacred valley for the aboriginal people whose descendants still live in the territory. The steep stone faces of the valley are pocked with caves, some of which are burial sites. During the annual Stein Festival, held to celebrate this watershed, Native people often referred to the place in reverential terms as a temple, a sacred place, a sanctuary.

Puffing up the Devil's Staircase, I tried to ignore the pain of cramped muscles by concentrating on other things. I remembered when I was flown up this valley eight years earlier with a guide who pointed out cedar groves that supplied bark, grizzly feeding areas, and the site of an ancient battle between warring tribes. The helicopter pilot chimed in to say that a week before, when he had flown a party of forest industry and government officials up the same valley, all they had talked about was "cubic metres of wood, jobs, and profit." Two parties looking at the same ecosystem yet seeing radically different things.

I think of the president and CEO of a major forest company, whose letter to local mayors had described environmentalists as "anti-everything." Environmentalists are often dismissed as too "depressing," "pessimistic," or the "messengers of doom and gloom." They are castigated as "radicals" or "eco-terrorists." Nothing could be further from the truth. What is truly depressing are the people who so lack understanding that all they can do is mindlessly push for what has clearly failed: more economic growth regardless of the social and ecological costs.

Environmentalists are the true conservatives — they want to save, protect, and slow down the pace of life. People who want to rush into wilderness areas like the Stein that have never been studied or inventoried and trash them without regard to whether they can be sustained or restored are the real radicals and eco-terrorists. I reflect on the words of the B.C. biologist Bristol Foster, who described the struggles to protect areas like the Stein: "In saving wilderness, every victory could be temporary, every defeat is permanent."

Environmentalists are not against everything, they are for the most important things on this planet, things that keep us alive and wealthy. They are for clean air, clean water, clean soil, and a diversity of creatures all over the world. Environmentalists work for local communities that are sustainable, for economies in which full employment, security, and spiritual needs are paramount. And as they work to protect wilderness areas, they celebrate the wondrous variety of life forms that share the planet with us.

On arriving at the start of the trail, we found eight parked vehicles, yet in three days of hiking we didn't see a sign of litter or human debris. For those three days, my wheezing from a newly acquired bronchitis disappeared in the clear air. As we drank the pure, frigid water from the river, it was like a sacrament. There was an overwhelming sense that the salmon, the dazzling fall leaves of the alder, the autumn mists sliding over the mountains confirmed the timelessness of nature's rhythms, which are so easily forgotten in urban areas. By being there, we were giving thanks for this special place and other special places on the planet.

LESSONS TAUGHT BY NATURE

"Look at that insect," the grandmother said, pointing at the beetle lying motionless on the sidewalk. "Oh, its battery must be dead!" responded the boy.

This story was related to me in Japan in 1994. Apocryphal or not, it was meant to illustrate how disconnected from nature modern people have become. To the boy, even an insect is merely an object manufactured by humans.

I thought of that anecdote while lying on a dock on the shores of Smoke Lake in Algonquin Park. The reason we have become so reckless with the ecological birthright of our children must be the illusion that we are in total command of our surroundings. Here in Algonquin, we have an opportunity to see that nature is complex beyond our understanding.

The brilliant panoply of stars overhead at night is a startling contrast to the limited display visible in any large city on a "clear" night. Gazing at the spectacular starscape above me, I wondered whether urban children responded to their first sight of an Algonquin night sky with awe or fear. I suspected a bit of both.

Our perceptions and values are formed by our experiences and surroundings. For example, Prairie people have told me of their great love of the big sky and the distant horizon, which makes them feel claustrophobic in Vancouver, hemmed in by mountains that seem to push them into the ocean. For most people today, the human-created environment of cities shapes priorities and the way we see the world. Here in Algonquin, we have to recognize that there is a different rhythm, driven by the seasons, the climate, the forest, and the animals, over which humans have no control at all.

"Tonight is 'wolf night' in Algonquin," someone said, to explain the people who had gathered to howl into the forest. The haunting reply of a wolf confirmed an inter-species communication and sent squeals of delight through the crowd. This is quite a change in attitude from that reflected in fairy-tales where vicious wolves try to make a meal of Little Red Riding Hood or the three little pigs.

This summer I have been able to spend time relaxing on Quadra Island and rafting down the Babine River in British Columbia, travelling in the Arctic around Baffin Island and Greenland, and now holidaying in Algonquin, the jewel of Ontario's park system. Taken together, these places give an overwhelming sense of the awesome beauty of this part of the planet. But these islands of wilderness are decreasing in number and size under the relentless pressure of human beings. Too many of us want too much to be sustained indefinitely by the productive capacity of even the most distant ecosystems. Communities of organisms with whom we are discovering a spiritual kinship — grizzlies, walruses, wolves — are threatened by our need for "development" and "resources."

The degradation of natural systems has become inevitable because of an economic system that is fatally flawed by its species chauvinism. Economists appraise everything in the world on the basis of perceived utility for human beings alone — if we can use it, it has a value; if we can't, it's worthless. That might work if implicit in such a system was an understanding that our survival and quality of life depend on what we extract from the Earth — air, water, soil, biodiversity. Unfortunately, that isn't how it works. Economists have traditionally defined those things — the very things that keep us alive — as externalities to the system they've invented! And therein is the basis of our destructiveness.

And nowhere in such a system is there any acknowledgement of the importance and reality of spiritual values. The immense expanse we call Canada includes some of the most dazzling and biologically rich places on this planet. The chortle of a loon, which has inspired generations of Canadian artists and writers, brings me back to a reality too easily forgotten in cities. Loons and moose remind me how important it is to me to be able to share this Earth with other species. They inform us that we must temper our impulse to exploit and profit because there are forces and phenomena that lie beyond our scientific understanding.

Away from Ontario's wilderness gem at Algonquin, we travelled to northern British Columbia. Rafting the Babine River along a 160-kilometre arc above Smithers, we are transported back in time. For three days, the only hint of the existence of other people is the whisper of a far-off jet. Away from the familiar urban setting, we live by a different rhythm and rules and see through different eyes. There is much to think about and time to do it.

"Daddy, is it safe to drink the water?" my daughter asks, reminding me how much our world has changed since camping in my childhood, when we drank from rivers and lakes without a worry. Her whoop of delight when I answer yes reassures me that the simple joy of being in a pristine environment persists.

Hundreds of eagles precede us in a steady relay. Drifting by rock strata pointing straight up, we can only speculate at the forces that caused these geological upheavals. And everywhere we wonder at trees that have somehow found a roothold on rock cliffs or whole forests growing out of thin topsoil coating solid stone.

From where we start just below Babine Lake to our finish at the Kispiox River, the water drops almost 500 metres, creating both spectacular scenery and a navigational challenge. On the way, we meet the early arrivals of the sockeye-salmon run. They leap past one of the hundreds of obstacles on the way to spawning channels almost a thousand kilometres from the sea. And all along the route, fewer and fewer evade the deadly string of predators depending on them.

We sight twelve grizzly bears, perhaps 10 percent of the population in this watershed, and watch three of them fishing in a narrow canyon. Wild and free, large animals like grizzlies need a lot of room to move. As powerful as they are, they are extremely wary of humans and almost always vanish with a shout. But as the relentless pressure of human activity encroaches on their homes, bears can't just move away or squeeze in tighter. I wonder how much room we will leave for these magnificent animals, for whom this is ancestral land.

At each camp site, the children are respectful but unafraid. They know the bears will give us a wide berth if we are careful and make enough noise to let them know we're here. River guides tell stories of urban dwellers for whom this kind of wilderness is terrifying because it is beyond human understanding and predictability. Yet it is exhilarating and somehow reassuring to discover forces of nature still intact and beyond our comprehension and domination.

For four days, the forest around is intact, untouched by road or logging, but at the junction with the Skeena River we sight the first patches of clearcuts. A massive fire in 1978 on Cutoff Mountain gave forest companies an excuse to "salvage" the burned trees by clearcutting. Those companies often argue that fires and outbreaks of insects and disease are the natural analogues of clearcuts, but after such logging there's nothing left to salvage. The unlogged parts of the Cutoff burn have much more vegetation and regrowth. Standing or fallen dead trees continue to hold the thin soil and nourish a host of organisms, including small trees.

Along the Skeena, fresh clearings far exceeding the legal limit of fifty hectares appear on both sides of the river. Forest companies boast that for every tree cut, two or three more are planted, as if a few seedlings crudely stuck in the ground are an equal exchange for trees hundreds of years old. A mature tree bears hundreds of cones, each producing hundreds of seeds. Of tens of thousands of seeds, perhaps a few hundred will actually sprout and begin to grow, while only a few dozen may reach small treehood. Of them, a handful may reach full maturity. Every merchantable tree, then, is a survivor of tens of thousands of mini experiments, not two or three seedlings.

The forests, fish, and bears here, as in most parts of the planet, are threatened by the relentless demands of human numbers, consumption, and economics. Those calling for the preservation of areas like the Babine River basin are called "greedy" because only a few hundred people may actually experience it annually. But when such an area is developed, an exquisitely balanced and complex ecosystem thousands of years in the making vanishes in a geological blink of an eye.

Human beings have needs that are more than just physical and social; we are spiritual animals. I believe we have a built-in need to experience wilderness and nature, a craving that can be fulfilled partially by knowing that there are such cathedrals to nourish the soul. In trashing wilderness areas that only time and nature create, we diminish ourselves with the loss of an integral component of our spiritual make-up.

When we began the trip at the head of the Babine River, we put our rafts in at a weir built by the federal government. Sockeye salmon completing their long journey from the sea up the Skeena River and then the Babine are stopped by that weir so scientists can determine the number and make-up of the run and regulate the number of fish in the spawning beds.

Driven by the powerful urges of their genes, the fish gather restlessly behind the barrier until they find a series of slots through which they swim only to be trapped in metal cages. At regular intervals, summer students open a horizontal slit so the fish can slither by and be counted and classed as mature or "jacks" (immature males).

Impounded in the metal cage, the fish frantically leap into the air, repeatedly smashing themselves against the metal sides. It was a horrifying reminder of a giant dam on the Parana River in South America. Many of the fish in the Parana migrate up and down the river, foraging for food or spawning beds. So a fish "elevator" was installed to carry the fish from one side of the dam to the other. Fish attempting to escape the elevator made the same sickening clank of flesh on metal as the desperate animals on the Babine. The elevator is a cruel and ridiculous technological solution to fulfill the natural instincts of fish. And here in Canada, in the name of science, experts were treating fish in a similarly unnecessary and destructive way.

Tourist rafting on the Babine has increased the human traffic considerably. This summer (1994), two or three hundred people will probably make the trip. Since there are very few sites along the rugged banks that can comfortably accommodate tents and rafts, there is increasing pressure on them. There is also concern that, though wild, animals could become habituated to humans by rooting through any refuse or even digging up latrines.

Our rafting guides went to impressive lengths to minimize our impact. There wasn't a sign of human detritus like packaging, bottle tops, or cans on the entire trip. Every bit of food that was brought in was consumed, carried back out unused, or burned and the ashes spread on the river. Only small branches of dead driftwood were collected and used for firewood so they could be burned completely and the ashes dispersed. Most surprising was the collection of all human feces so it could be transported away from the river. Of course we did have an impact on the ecosystem, but every effort was made to minimize it.

It was a privilege to enter territory where the wild creatures — eagles, salmon, and bears — so clearly belonged. Without even being aware of it, we showed our respect by our own behaviour. When we encountered grizzly bears fishing, we waited and watched quietly until they had finished and left before we continued on our way.

At the Skeena River, we encountered our first evidence of clearcut logging on both sides of the river. Along the riverbanks, a fringe of trees was left all the way up to the tops of the banks. But the sky was visible through the highest trees and the narrow strip of trees became an insult, an inadequate illusion of a real forest. There was a striking contrast between the river banks along the Babine and those on the Skeena. Slides where rock and dirt had come away and dropped towards the river carrying trees with them were not at all noticeable on the Babine — in fact, I didn't see any. But once we hit the logged area, slide after slide was obvious along the banks, many of them recent.

It may be true that the bottoms of natural slides are places where some of the largest trees in a wild forest can be found. When thin soil piles up at a slide's bottom, it can be an exceptionally fertile area for future trees. But along a river, the soil slides right off the hills and into the water, while the gashes remaining are inhospitable challenges for any future trees. So even where trees are left for cosmetic purposes, clearcut logging nearby has visible effects.

In the wild, the interconnectedness of living systems becomes obvious. The salmon and steelhead runs up the Skeena and Babine are famous and important for sport, commercial, and Native food fisheries. But they are also intimately connected to biophysical and meteorological rhythms that are disrupted by large-scale clearcutting. And the populations of bear, eagles, and micro-organisms are intertwined with the fate of salmon. An experience of the wild uplifts the human spirit and also makes us rethink some of our assumptions and beliefs.

WHERE SMALL REALLY IS BEAUTIFUL

FROM PANGNIRTUNG, NORTHWEST TERRITORIES — The white domes of the radar station stand out sharply against the grey rock of the mountain top. At the head of Mercy Bay on the east coast of Baffin Island, the structures were once part of the DEW (Distant Early Warning) Line designed to pick up the first sign of missiles from the Soviet Union. Upgraded into the NWS (North Warning System) to detect evasive, low-flying cruise missiles, the station is no longer occupied. Computers now fire information via satellite to a NORAD centre in North Bay. Ironically, we came here on a Russian ship, the *Alla Tarasova*, and the Russian crew took us ashore without meeting any resistance.

The ship has been transporting about ninety tourists per trip to visit Inuit communities from Cape Dorset to Pangnirtung on Baffin Island and their Danish counterparts on Greenland. By experiencing the unique wildlife and cultural communities of the Arctic, we are seeing the world from a very different perspective.

Aboard the *Alla Tarasova*, it's hard to believe that for decades, the crew were our enemies as the two superpowers were locked in a terrifying buildup of nuclear weapons. It was appropriately called MAD (Mutual Assured Destruction), the insane notion that there could be winners even when both sides could blow each other to bits. Today, the Cold War seems like ancient history.

The enormous effort to sustain a campaign to end the arms race often gave way to burnout, disillusion, and despair. But the dramatic shift in geopolitics over the past decade could not have been predicted and should give inspiration and hope to grass-roots groups now working on environmental issues. The struggle to save a bit of wilderness, stop pollution, or change legislation is often difficult and disheartening, but globally, more and more people at the local level are striving to build sustainable communities and environments. Our newfound Russian friends give us hope.

Here in the north, the land and climate seem forbidding and barren. Yet life, including the most recent arrivals — human beings — has managed not only to survive but to flourish. There have been different strategies to succeed here. At the most fertile time of the year, in the long daylight hours of summer, birds arrive from distant places to exploit the sudden burst of productivity, then depart for other parts of the world.

This is a place where small is truly beautiful. Century-old trees with trunks only 5 centimetres in diameter creep along the ground while in tiny microniches behind rocks or a dip in the soil, miniature flower gardens bloom in profusion. Yet in this landscape of dwarf plants, large animals like polar bears, musk oxen, and caribou also flourish. They survive here by ranging across vast distances while armed with exquisite genetic adaptations for this climate and landscape.

But it is the presence of our species that is most impressive, a testament to the incredible ingenuity and adaptability of human beings. From rock cairns to tent rings and bone struts for tentskins, the enduring relics attest to the vigour of past human settlements. Books about the early non-Inuit explorers reveal that their success was in direct proportion to their willingness to utilize the knowledge and experience of the Inuit people.

In today's Inuit settlements, the wooden houses and concrete buildings are alien transplants, replicas of southern homes that pay little attention to the realities of the culture and landscape of the original inhabitants of the north. Here, as in so many other parts of the world, from the Americas to Africa and Australia, most new-comers and colonizers arrived without respect for the indigenous people, the local flora and fauna, and the land. They simply super-imposed their own notions of progress and development.

The Inuit are twentieth-century people, not museum pieces of a past way of life. But each new technology, from snowmobiles to syn-thetic materials and television, catapults them away from their cultural roots and traditions. An Inuk remarked to me, "When television came, young people lost the need for elders." When the communications satellite *Anik-2* broke down recently, we hardly noticed the effect in the south because signals were simply switched to other satellites. But in the north, all lines — faxes, television, computer networks, telephones — were out for a day. It was a disturbing demonstration of the extent to which northern settlements are already dependent on modern tech-nology and thus how vulnerable they have become. Yet now there is eager discussion about locking the Arctic more tightly into the infor-mation superhighway because it means progress.

In this breathtaking part of the globe, we may see with greater clarity the roots of many of our own social and ecological problems in the south.

LESSONS FROM A WALK IN A RAINFOREST

FROM CHOCO FOREST, COLOMBIA — To most Canadians the name Colombia conjures up images of coffee or drugs. But to biolo-gists, Colombia is home to one of the richest ecosystems on the planet, the Choco tropical rainforest pinched between the Pacific Ocean and the Andes mountain range. It extends from Panama through Colombia to Peru.

Chugging from Bahia Solano to Utria National Park on the *Jestiven*, a wooden boat, I am accompanied by Francis Hallé, a French expert on tropical forests. Hallé is famous for having created a huge, pneumatic platform that can be erected on the canopy where researchers can explore 600 to 800 square metres of the treetops.

Hallé points out the thick cloak of trees extending to the water line. "The first thing people do when they invade such a virgin forest," he says, "is to clear the trees along the shore." Despite the difference in vegetation, the tree-covered mountains and pristine bays remind me of British Columbia.

Utria National Park was formed in 1987 and covers 54,300 hectares of spectacular forest. In a heavy rain, I set off alone to walk across a peninsular saddle along a thin path that is a slimy ribbon of red mud. Serpentine tree roots coil along the forest floor to suck nutrients from the thin topsoil and anchor the immense trunks in place. Though impediments on level ground, the roots provide welcome hand and footholds on the steep hills.

In the forest, temperature and light intensity immediately drop. Thirty metres overhead, the canopy blocks out the sky, preventing growth of the heavy underbrush we think of as jungle. The steady rainfall is intercepted by foliage so the water doesn't pound onto the soil. Even though it has rained constantly, the water in the creeks is crystal clear.

The ground is littered with leaves. In Canada, we classify trees as deciduous or evergreens, but here the trees shed leaves year round. However, instead of building up to form thick humus, they quickly become food for insects and fungi and thus are recycled back up into the forest biomass.

It's easy to walk along creek beds or through the trees with little vegetation to hamper movement. The noise is constant, a cacophony of buzzing, clicking, and humming of insects and frogs. Walking quietly and slowly, eyes adapting to the shadows and shapes, one begins to notice movement that betrays a frog, a butterfly, a bird. A cosmos of complexity opens up.

Back on the boat, Hallé informs me that "jungle" is a word from India referring to the tangle of secondary growth that results after the initial forest is cleared. It is an insult to call a primary forest a jungle, he says. He draws my attention to trees with special properties — the hard white "tagwa" seeds, six to a cluster within an armoured shell, that can be carved like ivory; fruit trees; parasitic air-breathing plants, lianes, orchids. But when I bring a seed or leaf, he often admits he has no idea what it is. When I ask how much taxonomists know of the species residing in tropical rainforests, Hallé makes a gesture of futility and replies: "It's an impossible mess." He tells me individuals of one species are usually spaced far apart and each may house different spectra of associated species. A lifetime could be spent studying the organisms in a few square metres while an adjacent section could take another lifetime. That's the reason our ignorance is so vast.

Hallé believes the fabled diversity within a tropical rainforest gives it its stability. When one or a few trees are removed, the opening in the canopy allows light to reach the forest floor and stimulates a succession of plants. Over time, like a small nick in the skin, the opening is healed and filled in. But remove a large section of trees and like a mortal wound, the forest cannot repair itself.

Here a destructive parasite is controlled because its target species is not concentrated in an area the way species are in temperate forests. "There's no need for pesticides," Hallé tells me, "because the forest is too diverse to allow an outbreak." Similarly, an introduced exotic species can't explode like rabbits in Australia or purple loosestrife in Canada because there are too many predators able to attack them. So biodiversity is not just a descriptive property of tropical rainforests, it is the very mechanism of its stability for survival.

World demand for lumber and pulp continues to rise while forest plantations cannot deliver wood of quality or quantity. That's why deforestation continues to claim the great forests of the planet and threatens the Choco.

The Choco is the traditional home of perhaps 30,000 aboriginal people belonging to three main groups — Embera, Waunana, and Cuna — who continue to live as they have for thousands of years, depending on the forest for their food, medicines, and materials.

From the airport at Bahia Solano, we take a bus up the coast to the village of El Valle, which is populated by descendants of African slaves who were brought to mine gold more than 400 years ago. We rent a dugout with a motor and guide to take us up the Boro Boro River. After about three hours, we finally leave the plantations, cleared fields, sugar cane, and breadfruit trees to enter primary rainforest. As the river narrows, we drag the dugouts across shallow riffles and around fallen trees and logjams. At one point, we unload the boat and sink it to push it under a huge log blocking the river.

Night falls early and quickly in the tropics and as the light fades, we know we are still hours away from our destination, the Embera village of Boro Boro at the junction with the Mutata River. Five hours after nightfall, we finally reach the settlement, exhausted, wet, but exhilarated by the adventure. Hammocks and mosquito nets are slung in the tiny school, and we soon join the frog calls with snores.

Boro Boro is home for eighty-four people living under thatched huts built on supports two metres above the ground. The tiny cluster of buildings is surrounded by small fields of domesticated plants. Life here revolves around the river for bathing, laundry, food, and transportation. A three-hour hike up the Mutata ends at spectacular falls that drop 400 metres into a huge pool that is considered the source of life and power in the river. The people of Boro Boro fear the power of the place and stay away. Only the shaman goes to the pool to perform rituals to ensure the fecundity of the river and forest.

The villagers tell us they want to keep their culture and way of life. They have heard of proposals to develop the area, which one prime minister referred to as Colombia's "piggy bank." The Pan American Highway, nearly finished, was stopped only when the minister of the newly formed environment ministry threatened to resign if it wasn't. There are other proposals to build superports on the coast, a network of highways to link the ports to cities, and huge dams to deliver electricity to isolated villages. The familiar notion of "development" by extracting the resources of the forest is irresistible in Colombia too.

Colombia's forests, of which Choco is an important part, have the most known bird species (19.4 percent of all the world's known species compared to 17.6 percent in Brazil and 15 percent in Africa) and orchids, the second most amphibians, the third most reptiles, and one of every five bats. This rich tapestry of living things is beyond any scientific comprehension and, if destroyed, will never be duplicated or recreated.

There are people who have had the knowledge and expertise to make a living from these forests for millennia, but their futures are as uncertain as the fragile ecosystems that are their homes. The 1987

United Nations report *Our Common Future* stated: "It is a terrible irony that as formal development reaches more deeply into rain forests, deserts and other isolated environments, it tends to destroy the only cultures that have proved able to thrive in these environments."

Indigenous people throughout Colombia are organizing to resist incursions into their land. In the Choco, OREWA was formed to represent the Embera, Waunana, and Cuna. But in the government discussions about the future of the Choco, the indigenous people who have always occupied the forests are seldom involved.

The predicament is complicated by an Afro-Colombian population that outnumbers the aboriginal people by ten to one. After escaping slavery, they were able to survive in coastal villages for 200 to 300 years. Lacking the indigenous culture and knowledge base built around the forest, the blacks have eked out a living and are desperate for the material benefits of modern life.

In negotiations with the government, OREWA has included Afro-Colombians as stakeholders in the forest lands. But impoverished people are easy prey to the blandishments of developers. Promises of jobs, electricity, and television tempt them to welcome roads and ports. To them, the forest is a resource that can be converted to money. If we in Canada haven't been able to resist the siren's call of development, why should people who start out with far less?

Environmentalists in industrial nations of the North are concerned about the fate of tropical rainforests that have been labelled the "lungs of the planet" and the "wellsprings of biodiversity." Here in Colombia, Latin Americans demand to know why they are expected to save the forests when countries in the North haven't protected theirs. In the debate over vanishing forests, the people who live in them are often forgotten.

Travelling through the Choco rainforest along mud tracks, one can't help but wonder why magnificent forests like this are being traded for squalid towns and villages of impoverished people and of scrawny cattle grazing on barren hills. Is there no other way to create income for the human residents while preserving the forest ecosystem?

According to Francis Hallé there is. He has spent his life studying plant growth in the canopy of tropical rainforests. When I ask him whether we know enough to cut down the likes of the Choco and regrow it, he replies, "Absolutely not!" He points out that a tree plantation is not a forest and that rapidly growing species like eucalyptus or pine imported from other parts of the world seldom perform as expected. Hallé says ideas developed from northern temperate forests are inappropriate for the tropics, where vegetation and soil are completely different.

The secret to the resilience and productivity of a tropical rainforest is its tremendous variety of living forms. As long as the forest is intact, people can cut into it as the indigenous inhabitants have for thousands of years, and the cut will heal. But if the clearing is large, then like a spider web that loses too many threads, the system collapses.

Throughout tropical countries of Africa, South America, and southeast Asia, Hallé finds a sophisticated human practice called agroforestry (AF) that has sustained communities for hundreds, if not thousands, of years. Hallé has observed carvings on Indonesian temples depicting AF practices about A.D. 1000.

AF requires a profound knowledge of plants that can be used for a variety of needs. Useful plants are collected from intact primary forests and deliberately planted in a surrounding AF Buffer Zone. Here one finds small shrubs, medicinal plants, parasitic lianes for rope and furniture, and large trees that yield wood, edible leaves, and fruits.

Fifty percent of the biodiversity present in the primary forest can be found in an AF Buffer Zone. In fact, says Hallé, it has only been in the past century that foresters recognized that the AF Buffer Zone is human-created and not a natural forest. Domesticated animals are grazed in the Buffer Zone, where the huts and villages are also located. The primary forest remains intact to provide new material during collecting expeditions.

Hallé says, "Agroforesters are true capitalists; their capital is biological and it is constantly growing." Usually, they live off the interest but when they are confronted with an emergency, they may harvest more than they usually take, sure in the knowledge that over time, the forest will grow back.

Hallé's description of agroforestry makes one wonder why it

isn't being pushed everywhere as a sustainable alternative to massive clearing of tropical forests. Hallé's explanation is: "AF is always local and small-scale. People are constantly coming out of the villages with baskets of fruits, vegetables, meat, and plant products for trade or sale, but that doesn't yield the large and quick profits that governments and multinational companies want."

Since all useful organisms are harvested from the Buffer Zone, the primary forest is protected as a priceless source of genetic material. Communities practising AF don't need outside help or expertise because they depend on their own time-tested indigenous knowledge.

Hallé observes that practitioners of AF are always women. Men may be recruited to cut trees down or lift heavy things, but women are in charge. He believes it reflects women's concerns with food and children's health. "Large-scale monoculturing seems to be more of a male impulse, while diverse, small-scale ventures seem more feminine," Hallé says.

AF exposes the insanity of destroying tropical forests for a one-time-only recovery of cash. AF rests on the fundamental capital of nature, which, if protected, can sustain communities and ecosystems indefinitely. But that flies in the face of the current suicidal path of global economics that glorifies human creativity and productivity above all.

17

FINDING SOLUTIONS AND TAKING ACTION

All over the world, political and business leaders have a difficult time seeing from ecological perspectives, let alone using environmental priorities to set their agendas. But some are changing. Often they have learned lessons taught by ecological crises. Others recognize that we are heading at great speed towards a brick wall, and that it's far safer, easier, and cheaper if we put on the brakes and turn the wheel now. We are a heroically reactive species when faced with a catastrophe, but averting a crash is easier than salvaging lives after one.

The greatest cause for hope lies in the fact that at the local level, people and groups are emerging to find answers and take leadership roles.

WHY STERILE SCHOOLYARDS ARE A WASTE

When you were a child, was there a special place that evoked wonder, mystery, security? This question was posed by Gary Pennington, an education professor at the University of British Columbia, to 200 people attending a conference in Vancouver on "Learning Grounds — School Naturalization." After an interval of reflection, someone piped up with "a cherry tree," starting a torrent of answers: "a ditch," "a swamp," "my grandpa's garden," "a sand dune," and on it went. Many of those magical spots no longer exist.

It's not cities, shopping plazas, or buildings that make Canada an extraordinary land, but the haunting beauty of the Arctic, the endless horizon of grass and sky of the Prairies, rugged mountains and ancient rainforests, and spectacular autumn leafscapes. These are what inspire our art, poetry, dance, and music and evoke the envy of people abroad, who think of Canadians as people of the outdoors.

But now that most of us live in cities, we have been distanced from nature and must make deliberate·efforts to experience it. The Vancouver meeting was an attempt to find ways to bring nature into the lives of urban children by focusing on schools, where they spend a large part of their young lives.

When our children were in primary school, Tara and I would organize field trips to the beach when the tide was very low. It was the first time for many of the children to wander the beach, roll over rocks, or dip into tidepools, even though they live in a city whose beachfront is one of its proudest features. Often the children were afraid to put their hands in the water or touch an anemone or crab. But curiosity and exuberance invariably overcome reticence, and they were soon immersed in tidepools, revelling in their discoveries.

That's why schoolyards are important. They can provide an opportunity to watch the seasons change, observe the succession of plants through the year, and witness the interdependence of insects and plants and birds and soil. Students can see interconnections between air, water, and soil and note the remarkable metamorphosis frogs and insects undergo. In schoolyards, children can actually grow vegetables and flowers and compost their lunch scraps to learn about the relationship between food and soil.

But schoolyards are seldom designed for the joy of play and discovery. Instead, they are planned out of fear — fear of litigation, fear of accidents, fear of lurking strangers. These concerns must be addressed, of course, but they should not be the primary determinant of how yards are conceived.

At the meeting, a parks board member told how clover in a school field had been removed because a teacher had complained that children might be stung by a honeybee flying into the classroom. But since honeybees die after stinging, they don't pursue targets, and children can quickly learn to respect them and avoid interfering with their important work. My children's schoolyard was covered over with coarse gravel that caused far more cuts and scrapes than there were stings when there was grass. The soil is now a toxic wasteland, saturated with chemicals that will retard plant growth for years!

An outdoor environment should be a place of delight and joy, a place of surprise and constant stimulation. What could be more enchanting than a pond filled with tadpoles and chirping frogs, trees with low branches to climb, flowering shrubs and edible fruit trees, and fields of wild plants to attract butterflies and beetles? It's not necessary to sterilize schoolgrounds to avoid allergies, stings, water accidents, and assaults by drunks or perverts.

School land is constantly being taken over for more parking, new portables, sheds for tools, and specialized playing fields. The remaining space should be one of those places children will remember later in life. Right now they are learning that nature is frightening, so we nuke weeds and insects with chemicals; that soil is "dirty," so we cover it with asphalt or gravel; that wild things are tough and dangerous, so we prefer weak, dependent grass; and that children have little need for or few lessons to learn from nature.

Greening of schoolyards reflects a change in attitude that is vital in a new relationship with the rest of life on Earth. The Evergreen Foundation is one of the organizations attempting to green urban areas.

A BUDDHIST WAY TO TEACH KIDS ECOLOGY

FROM TOKYO, JAPAN — Tokyo today is a nightmare — concrete buildings and roads crammed with people and motor vehicles. The air is visible and catches in the throat. Rivers are tamed to flow within concrete walls beside the roads. This is human habitat, hostile territory for other species. Urban dwellers here are cut off from the kind of nature and wilderness most Canadians take for granted. But without intimacy with nature, we can confuse crimes against the Earth with economic and technological progress.

Eight years ago, I met a remarkable teacher of Grade 3 students in Tokyo. Toshiko Toriyama told me that most of her pupils are so disconnected from nature that they think that fish live their entire lives in Styrofoam and plastic wrap! Sadly, I have met Canadian children who are unaware that hamburger meat or wieners are the muscles of an animal or that the constituents of potato chips and bread once grew in the ground.

I met Toriyama again here in Tokyo. After teaching for thirty years, she quit in order to create a new kind of school based on the writings of Kenji Miyazawa, one of Japan's most famous poets from early in this century. He left a legacy of wonder at the mysteries and interconnectedness of nature. In Miyazawa's Buddhist universe, everything, from each grain of sand to every raindrop, insect, and plant, is interconnected by fine "threads." The destruction of any part of that elaborate web tears holes in its integrity. This image is the basis of Toriyama's lessons.

Her most useful teaching tool is each child's imagination. In Imagination Class, the children close their eyes and listen to Toriyama's voice, to music, to noises, and to silence. She lets them imagine they are eggs in a praying mantis cluster. They struggle out of the egg case, look out at a new world, and then discover the hazards of predators, the need for food, the search for a mate, and, finally, death. Through the life cycle of the insect, children come to experience challenges that are common to all living things. When the exercise is completed, Toriyama told me, the children become very energetic and read and write about their new insights.

"Children take things for granted and don't think about them enough," she said. "For example, they often lose their pencils. So I get them to imagine being a pencil." She takes each component of the pencil — wood, rubber, paint, metal, lead — and gets the children to go back to their origins. With wood, for example, they imagine the forest where trees grow, vicariously live as a tree, and then think how they are logged, transported, and processed.

The children study history through the man who first brought pencils to Japan from Paris a hundred years ago. Eventually, the lessons are reinforced by a visit to a pencil factory. Once they are aware of the true value of their pencils, the youngsters appreciate and take better care of them.

Toriyama teaches the ecology of water by getting the children to be the water of the oceans, evaporate into the sky, rain into rivers and lakes, and become part of their own body. One of the most dramatic lessons is about food. She brings a live chicken to class and then kills it, often to the consternation of many children. It is then plucked, cleaned and cut up, cooked and eaten. The children also imagine being pigs, starting as embryos in a womb, then being born, growing, and dying. They go to a farm to see how pigs are raised for mass markets and visit a slaughterhouse to witness the pigs being killed and butchered. It is a powerful experience that reveals our nutritional dependence on other living organisms.

Toriyama is fifty-two and feels desperate about the dire state of the Earth. "At my farewell class, I asked the children how many thought the air would be cleaner eight years from now. No one raised their hand. Then I asked, 'Will it be dirtier?' and they all raised their hands. It was the same when I asked about forests, oceans, and rivers. The children expressed a deep sense of despair."

Referring to environmental degradation, Toriyama said, "We human beings have never gone through this so our children are having to go through this, without being taught what to do. How painful it is. I want to tell adults to wake up. I want to tell children, 'Don't give up. We have to work together.' Adults work hard to send children to good schools but what are they struggling for? Is there anything more important than working for the health of the Earth?"

An education that prepares students for a high-tech future and competition in a global economy misses the fact that we are completely dependent for survival and the quality of our lives on the integrity of the planetary biosphere that we seem intent on destroying. Toriyama's students know what really counts.

A WONDERFUL DAY IN THE NEIGHBOURHOOD

Mother's Day and Father's Day have always struck me as oddly superfluous. When my parents were still alive, they were an essential part of my family's life and we saw them several times a week. Even now, hardly a day passes when I don't think of them several times. For me, every day was Mother and Father's day, and I feel the same way about the Earth.

But now that most of us live in cities, our dependence on and need for nature are not immediately obvious. As daily urban life speeds up and becomes more fragmented, our basic biological needs are even harder to recognize. So it's necessary to pause deliberately so we can appreciate the water, weather, energy, seasons, soil, trees — all parts of the biosphere that sustain and enrich our lives.

April 22 is one of those days set aside to remind ourselves of our continued dependence on Mother Earth. In 1995, the twenty-fifth anniversary of the first Earth Day celebration, Tom Sandborn, a writer and social activist, suggested that the David Suzuki Foundation (DSF) in Vancouver acknowledge its commitment to neighbourhoods by organizing an Earth Day celebration in the immediate area around the office. A fundamental tenet of the DSF is that a vigorous local community must be the unit of stability around which a sustainable future is built. To that end, people are encouraged to "work locally," "hire locally," "buy locally," "eat seasonally and locally."

In fact, most environmental groups spring up to resolve issues of concern to local communities. Sandborn first approached merchants who share the block-long building with the DSF, then crossed to the other side of the street. The response was immediate and enthusiastic, with every business around us participating.

Then we approached Capers, the organic food store that has become a central part of the Kitsilano community in Vancouver. Russell Precious, its founder, offered his profits on Earth Day to the event and volunteered his restaurant to hold a dinner. He then personally recruited other merchants to participate. Stores featured displays of eco-products, posters, locally made wares, and locally grown foods, as well as contributing money towards the event.

The response of local artists and musicians in the neighbourhood was equally enthusiastic. Many art pieces were donated for sale, while performers provided entertainment throughout the day. Sound systems, paper, food, and security were all contributed, and a local tent-and-awning firm donated a large piece of canvas with which Moberly Elementary School students created an Earth Day banner.

The public was invited to join in our celebration, and we suggested that they leave their cars at home and walk, bike, or take a bus.

In celebrating the wonderful nuances of local people and eco-systems on Earth Day, we were reminded to be grateful for and solicitous of the mother of us all.

GETTING BACK TO THE QUIET SATISFACTIONS

The twentieth century promised that technology and machines would free us to enjoy more leisure and quality time. But often we end up on a treadmill, slaves to the demands of telephones and voice mail, computers, fax machines, television, and the VCR.

In the flush of early love, I vowed to my wife that I would always wash the dishes. Twenty-three years later, I still keep that pledge, especially on holidays at the cottage. There, away from television, newspapers, and the telephone, life slows and follows nature's rhythms. But dishes still have to be washed and that often consumes a lot of time.

What my family doesn't know is that I actually enjoy doing the dishes! Even with the delights of the forest, beach, and ocean, the rituals of keeping the cottage in shape provide pleasure. The dish-washing routine permits the mind to disconnect from the task and roam as it pleases. It is also satisfying to transform a mess into a sparkling kitchen, however transitory that may be. And I'm not the only one who feels this way.

Adair Lara writes, in "Coming Home to Ourselves" in *Simple Living* magazine, "My mother used to wash our clothes in a wringer

washer and then hang them on the line. As she pinned up each gar-
ment, she said she thought about the child it belonged to. (It was a
wonder she knew, there were seven of us kids.) She never wanted a
dryer, even after we could afford one, because it would steal this from
her, this quiet contemplation.

"I am just as busy, or busier, than my mother was, with the job
and kids and my projects. But it's a different kind of busyness, a
faster, jerkier one, getting one task over with and then on to the next.
Thirty years after I watched my mother hang out the wash, I carry the
laundry to the basement and toss in the clothes, switching them in a
wet clump from washer to dryer. I am doing what she did — drying
the family clothes — but not getting as much satisfaction from it."

The problem of course is that we all know that we ought to
slow down and take time, as we say, to "smell the roses." But it's not
that easy given the way we live. Lara tells us: "I get caught up, like a
swimmer in a pool full of floating junk, in what's coming at me. I call
the dentist for an appointment, go to lunch, meet deadlines, throw a
load in the washer, call back a friend, and then think, later, that I
must have sounded rushed and unfriendly when that's not how I felt
at all. I fax the mail, scissor open instant meals, answer the phone
while wiping off the breakfast table."

Back in the days of horse and buggy, life was slower and simpler. But have our modern accessories liberated us? Not according to
Lara: "Now we prowl supermarket aisles in search of minute meals,
rinse out pantyhose while we're in the shower, and wear jogging gear
to the manicurist so we can take a twenty-minute run while our nails
dry. One woman told me, 'I live by lists and scribbled notes on little
yellow Post-its stuck around my house and even in my car. My home
is always messy, the clean laundry is always heaped on the pingpong
table waiting to be folded and put away, the yard is filled with weeds,
and I make dinner quickly and leave it on the kitchen counter for my
kids and husband to eat whenever they're home and passing through
the kitchen. I wonder what I'm hurrying for.'"

Lara reminds us that twenty years ago, the average person with
a full-time job worked 138 hours less than we do now. She is a
columnist for the *San Francisco Chronicle* and once wrote, "Where,

in all this hurry, do we find the quiet satisfactions of daily life that we once took for granted? When do we stop and start being?" When she asked her readers for their version of her mother's hanging out the wash, she was swamped with mail.

Just as I enjoy dishwashing, many wrote of the pleasures of doing the routine: "They write letters in longhand though they have computers. . . . One woman rubs leather shoes with mink oil until they shine, while thinking of the places the shoes have taken her. . . . They plant camelia bushes, dance with the kitchen towel, or shovel the driveway while the snowblower sits in the garage."

Many seek quiet time, a stolen moment to be alone, away from the crush of demands: "A mother decides to wait in the car during her son's guitar lesson rather than try to hit the bank, gas station, post office and supermarket and be back in an hour. A woman with grown grandchildren finally found time to watch a leaf fall all the way from the tree to the ground. Others like me are just learning how, just beginning to sample the powerful religion of ordinary life, of freshly mopped floors and stacked dishes and clothes blowing on the line. The way to slow down in a hectic world is not to find even more ways of saving time, but to look for ways to spend it."

ONE FARMER REALLY CLOSE TO THE SOIL

FROM SAKURAI CITY, JAPAN — Our relationship with food, like our need for clean air and water, should be a constant reminder that we are biological beings. But today air is often filtered, warmed, cooled, or humidified in our homes, offices, and vehicles, and we consume far more liquid in various kinds of drinks than as just plain water. Every bit of our nutrition is plant or animal, yet people today have little appreciation of the biological nature of their food.

The meals we consume today seem disconnected from the Earth where they originate. The farmer and writer Wendell Berry once told me that in North America, on average, food is consumed 3,200 kilometres from where it is produced. But because air, water, soil, and biodiversity are economic "externalities," the ecological consequences of global trade are not reflected in the cost of food. When I inquired why New Zealand–grown rather than Ontario lamb was featured on the menu of a fancy restaurant north of Toronto, the answer was "It's cheaper." The true ecological cost of fresh fruit and vegetables in winter in a northern country like Canada is never revealed in their price.

For most of human history, food was ingested close to where it grew. We ate locally and seasonally. Our severance from an immediate and intimate relationship with nutrition is a direct result of the disconnection from land that characterizes modern urban society. Food is one of the best ways to reassess the way we live.

In the farm community of Sakurai City in Nara prefecture, I encountered fifty-two-year-old Yoshikazu Kawaguchi, who practises a radically different kind of agriculture called natural farming. Kawaguchi begins with the understanding that nature is a complex community of living things that humans do not understand. Consequently, one or a few species of plants or insects can't be defined as "good" or "bad" when we know so little about their roles in the entire ecosystem.

Kawaguchi doesn't use chemical fertilizers or pesticides, and what's more, unlike organic farmers, he does not till the soil. He lets the "weeds" that are competing with his crops grow, or when he does intrude, he cuts the plants above ground and leaves their tops on the earth.

Within the plant cover, onion shoots were poking through and potatoes inserted into slits were sprouting roots. Wheat seeds are cast over the paddies and harvested in early June. Then rice is planted and harvested in November. Kawaguchi's soil is sticky, black, and pungent with decaying vegetation, in contrast to his neighbour's neat, ploughed, and weedless furrows of grey dirt.

For twenty years, Kawaguchi was a typical farmer using chemical pesticides and fertilizers. Then, about twenty years ago, his family began to get sick repeatedly and he developed a life-threatening liver disorder. He happened to read a series of newspaper articles on complex pollution, which made him realize that his family's health problems might be caused by the chemicals he was using. He then read *The One Straw Revolution*, a seminal work by Masanobu Fukuoka on natural farming, which prescribes sowing seeds onto unploughed ground. By following Fukuoka's methods, Kawaguchi lost his entire rice crop in the first two seasons! But with tenacity and observation, he succeeded the third year. "I realized that natural farming methods are not fixed. The natural farmer should be constantly flexible and must learn intimately about soil, insects, and natural conditions of the area."

Once he had changed methods, Kawaguchi looked at the world through different eyes: "It was only after I started natural farming that I felt happy to be a farmer. Before, I felt as if I was standing in a deadly world. My rice and vegetables were growing, but I watched insects dying in agony and my fields became silent places devoid of any other forms of life."

Kawaguchi believes the increased wealth created by farming with machines and chemicals is an illusion. After paying for machinery, fuels, and the ever-increasing amount and variety of fertilizers and pesticides, much of the benefit of large-scale agriculture vanishes. Furthermore, the yields may be high, but Kawaguchi calls the food tasteless and devoid of adequate nutrition. And his most pointed criticism is that modern farming breaks apart the web of life and threatens people's health.

For Kawaguchi, his farming methods have become a spiritual way of life. He has tried meditation and other forms of spiritual discipline, but he ultimately realized that farming is his vocation and that nature is his teacher. He told me, "We have been seeing other life forms as our enemies. But if we see them as friends, it changes how we act. The more we learn about what's happening in soil, the more we learn about life."

That's what is distinctive about natural farming. Instead of trying to impose a human agenda on nature, natural farmers know there is much that they still have to learn, so they try to let nature guide them. He says, "The land lets you live, the seasons give you the food from the land." Kawaguchi recognizes that humans are no longer hunter-gatherers living by the dictates of nature. The very acts of collecting seeds and planting them, whether by mimicking nature and casting them on the ground or by using large machines and chemicals, are deliberate. "I cut plants competing too much with my crops," he says without apology. "I select seeds too. I am a farmer, not a gatherer." But he begins from an understanding that categories such as "weed," "pest," "good," or "bad" are human definitions, not meaningful biological classes.

We don't know all of the constituents of soil, air, or water, nor do we understand how they interact or maintain the Earth's productivity and resilience. Thus, one must begin with respect for the 3.5 billion years during which life evolved without human intervention. Protection of the integrity of the soil ecosystem and the air and water that nourish it is uppermost in the priorities of a natural farmer because as long as they are maintained, so is human life. "We have to go along with nature, never try to impose our formula," says Kawaguchi.

But farming in Japan, as in North America, has changed. "Enjoying nature is not part of mainstream farming. It has become an enterprise designed only to make a lot of money. Farmers are removed from the philosophy of raising life. It's become totally scientific. So they are surrounded by nature but they are also removed from it at the same time."

For Kawaguchi, science has been a major cause of this change: "Scientific western thinking puts man and nature in conflict. It says nature can't do it properly without man. In natural farming, humans are seen to be a part of nature. The yield is smaller with natural farming but the food is real, it has more life. It's not artificially pumped up. You need less of it to live. The ideal situation is that you grow what you eat, [and] that you eat what is grown in your area.

"Human knowledge is so limited. So real human knowledge must achieve a kind of *sattori* [enlightenment]. What science can find is part of something, but just a part. . . . Each organism has a wide range of activities, so you can't just pull out one function; there are many more organisms than science knows and each one is complete in its existence and part of a totality. So to find just one wonderful function of one organism and bring it into the field is just disrupting the harmony of the field."

Kawaguchi pointed out that most approaches to farming focus on one or two elements of numerous possibilities. Thus organic farming emphasizes natural fertilizers and no chemical pesticides, permaculture focuses on cultivating native species, while an approach called "effective micro-organisms" uses soil microbes to counter oxidation, which breaks things down. But ultimately we have to pay attention to the whole complex of soil, air, and water and the balance of life within it. As Kawaguchi feels, "The basic thing is to trust life and let it live in the natural world."

Kawaguchi predicts, "The scientific and technological society has been developed, but life is worsening. Yet the mainstream is still blind and rushing along. It's certain this civilization has to collapse. Within this troubled world, a new civilization is already beginning. The new civilization that is sprouting is based on the value of life and chooses to live in harmony with the Earth.

"We have to get rid of our obsession with death. We must let nature do its work and trust the body. When a crisis happens, we have to respond. We take a narrow view, but we have to be calm. We must accept our mortality, but do not give in to death by disease. By accepting death, this is the only way to accept life. If we try to escape death we are actually denying life. That state works against all life. By accepting death, then you can live. So when we are ill with disease, we must accept that but not give in."

We would do well to study the philosophy of natural farming. Most of us live in cities away from the primary production of food. But his reflections about farming inform us of a different way of seeing our place in nature, a way that might guide us into a balance with the things that make all life possible.

STUDY FOCUSES ON FISHERIES THAT FLOURISH

Salmon have an exquisitely complex life cycle, beginning and ending in freshwater rivers, with years of foraging ocean waters in between. In attempting to manage these wild animals, we impose our will on them through different perspectives and priorities of our economic, political, and social categories. In the process, we ensure that they will not be dealt with as a single biological entity.

Fish on the Line, a report prepared for the David Suzuki Foundation (DSF) by the eminent fish biologist, Dr. Carl Walters, boldly stated that the management of the department of fisheries and oceans is setting up a biological disaster driven by political and economic pressures. The failure of the sockeye run in 1995 appears to support Walters's prescience. But what else can we do? Are there alternatives?

The answer is yes. *Fisheries That Work* was prepared for the DSF by Dr. Evelyn Pinkerton, a maritime anthropologist who has a long involvement with fishing communities along the Pacific Coast, and Dr. Martin Weinstein, who specializes in the socio-economic aspects of natural resource management. In case studies of fisheries around the world, they found dozens of encouraging examples of sustainable practices and focused on ten cases, in areas ranging from Peru to Australia, Japan, the U.S., Korea, and Canada.

Management by fishing villages has worked for hundreds, if not thousands, of years. Lake Titicaca in Peru has a stable fishery employing 3,000 fishers who harvest more than 8,000 metric tonnes annually. With no financial or government support, the Titicaca fishers, from communities spanning two countries, make and enforce the rules. "Perhaps the most astounding fact about this fishery is that harvest levels appear to have remained stable since the 16th century when some Spanish records are available."

Two success stories in salmon management are described in B.C. and two in Alaska. Two involve examples of co-operation between Native and non-Native fishers. In Alaska, a successful initiative was begun in the mid-1970s, when the catch had dropped sharply to 30 million salmon. As a result of state and community efforts, the catch rose to a spectacular record of 194 million salmon in 1994!

In B.C., the Skeena River Watershed Committee brings together sport, commercial, aboriginal, federal, and provincial interests to co-ordinate the various fisheries and to halt the decline in biodiversity of the fish. The committee shows that, given responsibility and account-ability, members can co-operate and be effective.

Japan's inshore fishery of non-migratory species has been dramatically successful. Dominated by small-scale operations, it contributes almost a third of Japan's 11-million-ton national catch and almost 50 percent of its value, yielding profits of more than $1.5 billion in 1988. The basic fishery is more than a thousand years old and has 22,000 local co-operative associations, each with an average of 250 members. The major thrust of this system is to funnel a maximum of the benefits of the fishery back into local communities.

From the case studies surveyed in *Fisheries That Work*, three elements emerge that are common to these successful management strategies and provide useful lessons for Canada's fisheries.

First, planning units smaller than the whole coast are needed if the project is to be effective in dealing with conflicts between different interest groups. People brought together with shared knowledge about the fish and concerns about their future can resolve conflicts, while solutions imposed from "higher" or central offices are resisted.

Second, agreements or contracts between government agencies and local or regional bodies allow a beneficial division of labour. Thus the government excels at setting general goals and standards on which it holds the line, while fishers and local bodies figure out the most practical ways to implement the goals and give themselves more fishing time. Their plans tend to be more flexible, creative, and better adapted to the local situation.

Third, local or regional committees bring specific talents and resources to the process, from knowledge of fish stocks to greater trust of local communities to access to volunteer labour. Such a committee provides more comprehensive and effective management of harvest, enforcement, enhancement, and habitat protection and restoration.

The crisis in salmon demands that we get beyond the finger-pointing and look to solid success stories from which to draw inspiration and guidance. *Fisheries That Work* is a good start.

UPDATE: The federal Department of Fisheries and Oceans' catastrophic management of northern cod on the East Coast has been matched by its equally inept approach to Pacific salmon. Perhaps the coastal symmetry is fitting, with the DFO's offices located in the centre of the country. DFO minister Fred Mifflin spent millions to reduce the fishing fleet by buying and retiring commercial licences. However, the West Coast is divided into three fishing zones and a licence is required to fish in each zone. Instead of encouraging local fishers by restricting fishing to the zone of a fisher's residence, Mifflin allowed boats to "stack" licences, that is, to buy licences for any and all of the three zones. Rather than encouraging a larger fleet of small boats, this allowed companies with large, efficient boats to buy up licences while forcing small, labour-intensive, and more job-producing boats out of business. The fleet has been reduced but the capacity to over-fish the stocks remains high. Only now, decisions and power are concentrated in a few corporate hands centred in Vancouver.

Mifflin's successor, David Anderson, has been faced with the stark reality of a catastrophic decline in coho stocks. In the summer of 1998, Anderson imposed a complete ban on commercial fishing in areas designated by red lines on the ministry's map. In yellow-marked areas, some salmon fishing is allowed. Critics point out that while Native and commercial fishers have been hard hit by the coho policy, Washington State fishers have been allowed to continue to take coho. He got a reduced American coho catch by allowing an increased catch of chinook. DFO's egregious management strategy continues even though there are better alternatives.

CLAYOQUOT PROTESTERS VINDICATED

Flying above Vancouver Island, one is confronted with a chequer-board pattern of clearcutting that has invaded most of the island's watersheds over the last two decades. But there remains one truly spectacular area that is still relatively untouched. It is called Clayo-quot Sound, an area made up of a series of coastal islands offshore from a series of valleys. Clayoquot spans 262,000 hectares of land, of which 244,000 hectares (93 percent) are forested. This is part of the traditional land of the Nuu Chah Nulth people. The fate of these forests was heatedly debated during the late 1980s and early 1990s by the First Nations, forest companies, and environmental groups.

About 160,000 hectares of the forest in Clayoquot are classified as "commercially productive." Of that area, 39,100 hectares lie in protected zones while 30,000 hectares have already been logged, virtually all of it by clearcut logging. The remaining 90,400 hectares are predominantly old-growth and thus extremely attractive to the forest industry.

Forests are a priceless treasure for all of humanity, capable of nourishing our physical and spiritual needs endlessly. But all across the planet, they are being brutally cleared with little regard for the future. Companies "liquidate" ancient ecosystems while claiming to "sustain the yield" with tree plantations that allow a "crop rotation of seventy years." It is a cruel hoax based on a short-sighted perspective. Human beings and companies cannot create forests, only nature and time do that.

In 1993, thousands of environmentalists blockaded logging roads to Clayoquot, and more than 800 protesters, ranging from children to grandparents, to doctors, lawyers, foresters, and politicians, were arrested. Foreign environmental organizations and prominent personalities offered support to what became a highly inflamed battle.

Clayoquot Sound has become a symbol of a clash between profoundly different world-views: one sees human beings as the dominant species for whom the planet is a resource. This is based on the assumption that people lie outside the natural world and are clever enough to understand and manage it. The other recognizes that we remain inextricably bound up in a nature whose complex components we barely know. Only a century ago, it didn't matter which view was predominant because human numbers and technology were still too limited to impact on the Earth. But today, we are transforming the chemical, physical, and biological features of the planet.

Responding to the protesters and the rancour of loggers and forest companies, Premier Mike Harcourt did what most politicians do when faced with a crisis — he delayed making a decision. On October 22, 1993, Harcourt announced the formation of the Clayoquot Scientific Panel, which was charged with the goal "to make forest practices in Clayoquot not only the best in the province, but the best in the world."

The panel was made up of Nuu Chah Nulth tribal leaders and eminent scientists, all of whom respected the traditional knowledge and cultural needs of the First Nations. They were also aware that Canada was a signatory to four international agreements arising from the 1992 Earth Summit in Rio. The Rio meeting released a framework Convention on Climate Change, which emphasized the importance of protecting old-growth forests and wetlands as a "carbon sink" to remove greenhouse gases. Another treaty from the Earth Summit, the Convention on Biological Diversity, committed countries to protecting biodiversity of genes, species, and ecosystems. Agenda 21 was a massive blueprint for fulfilling the conventions, and it recognized the priceless role of forests and the important function of indigenous people in developing them. Finally, the Earth Summit produced Guiding Principles on Forests, which outlined fifteen principles to manage, conserve, and sustain forests.

The Clayoquot Scientific Panel was co-chaired by Dr. Fred Bunnell, a wildlife ecologist with extensive experience in resource management, and Dr. Richard Atleo, an expert on indigenous human resources and a hereditary chief of the Nuu Chah Nulth people. It had the potential to produce an important document incorporating the deepest understanding of the limits of scientific knowledge as well as the best ecological insights on sustainability and carrying capacity.

Over nineteen months, the panel released five reports. The range of the reports is worth noting. The first lays out the terms of reference, standards, and scope of the panel's tasks. Report two reviews current forest practices and standards in Clayoquot. The third report is called *First Nations' Perspectives* while the fourth is entitled *A Vision and Its Context* and provides a global context for Clayoquot. The final report was released on May 20, 1995, and covered *Sustainable Ecosystem Management in Clayoquot Sound: Planning and Practices*.

Taken together, the documents are a stunning indictment of current forestry practices and a vindication of the thousands of people who have protested Canada's logging methods as unscientific, unsustainable, and, in the long run, uneconomic. The reports are not without weaknesses, but they provide a different perspective on forest practices that may be useful if we aspire to maintain rich, productive forests in the future.

The panel's one weakness is its demand for "forest practices that are scientifically sound," as if enough is known to manage complex ecosystems scientifically. We can't. Forests are complicated and our knowledge is minuscule and fragmented, so at best, we can try to control our activities so that nature's regenerative capacities are not impaired.

From its inception, the panel saw its mandate as "the management of forest ecosystems for their long-term health." They understood that "the world is interconnected at all levels; attempts to understand it entail analysing its components and considering the whole system. Human activities must respect the land, the sea and all the life and life systems they support. Long-term ecological and economic sustainability are essential to long-term harmony. The cultural, spiritual, social and economic well-being of indigenous people is a necessary part of that harmony."

Clayoquot Sound's spectacular, rugged landscape is slated for logging of more than 80 percent of its old-growth, much of it on steep slopes averaging 60-degree inclines. It rains a lot in Clayoquot, and the thin soil is susceptible to erosion and landslides after logging. Report two concluded: "Current planning procedures are inadequate for sustainable ecosystem management."

According to the panel, the forest department is charged with taking care of the province's vast holdings of crown land. The forests are the rightful legacy of all future generations. However, the forest department's own mandate is often contradictory. On the one hand, it is charged with maximizing the revenues from timber extraction, while on the other hand, it is to protect those same resources for the public good. Forest companies, in their pursuit of swift returns for their shareholders, have failed to "recognize sufficiently the physical and ecological connections among terrestrial, freshwater and marine ecosystems." The companies often downplay the "requirements for ecosystem sustainability," and seldom incorporate "First Nations' values and perspectives." It is public concern and pressure that have kept the protection of forests on the political agenda.

Clayoquot Sound supports a rich array of species. Of the 368 vertebrate species found in temperate rainforests from Alaska to

Oregon, 297 have been recorded in Clayoquot. The panel notes, "About 45% of the forest-dwelling vertebrates breed primarily in older forests, while less than 10% breed best in young forests."

The area of land lining rivers and creeks is the riparian zone, which is especially critical for biodiversity. Any long-term forest-management plan should be based on the understanding that "water-bodies and the immediately adjacent environment are intimately linked. . . . The hydroriparian ecosystem is the skeleton and circulation system of the biological landscape. . . . Linkages from terrestrial riparian systems to streams continue to the sea. . . . Events far upstream, well removed from spawning areas, can influence downstream characteristics and organisms. . . . Ecological integrity of the forest ecosystem is essential to meeting economic, spiritual, and recreational needs. . . . Harvesting done without planning for subsequent regeneration cannot be considered a 'silvicultural system.'"

Virtually all trees in Clayoquot (and the rest of B.C.) are logged by clearcutting, a system that "removes all trees in a given area in one cutting, after which an even-aged stand is established by planting or natural regeneration. . . . [M]ost of the opening is not shaded or sheltered by the surrounding forest." Clearcutting in Clayoquot was used exclusively from 1988 to 1994, with the exception of 1992 and 1994, when 99.5 percent and 95 percent, respectively, were clearcut.

This is not sustainable forestry, so the panel recommended variable retention silviculture, which retains forest structures and habitat elements like large old trees, snags, and downed wood. The report stresses the need to maintain the integrity of forests, recommending at least 15 percent retention of trees in all cutting areas and 70 percent where there are "significant values for resources other than timber." Logging must leave "a representative cross section of species and structures of the original stand." Removal of 85 percent of trees is still too great a loss of diversity to maintain a forest, but the report is a clear repudiation of clearcutting.

Andrew Petter, then the minister of forests, stressed that the panel's report applied only to Clayoquot Sound. It should, however, be the basis of long-term planning for *all* Canadian forests.

UPDATE: Andrew Petter is no longer the minister of forests, having been replaced by David Zirnhelt. In all, 856 were arrested at Clayoquot in 1993. In addition, children and a few elderly were taken into custody but not charged. The protesters were convicted of violating an injunction prohibiting the blocking of MacMillan-Bloedel logging trucks. They received sentences of an average of twenty-one days in jail or home confinement and a $250 fine.

Logging in Clayoquot stopped at the end of February 1998. MacMillan-Bloedel has initiated joint ventures with northern First Nations so that they can develop "conflict-free logging" programs. Another company, Interfor, claims the right to cut 53,000 cubic metres from Clayoquot. Right now the overall status of the watershed remains "up in the air."

On June 10, 1998, MacMillan-Bloedel CEO Tom Stephens announced that the company would phase out all clearcut logging of old-growth forest over the next five years. Cynics pointed out that it could still mean MacMillan-Bloedel would log most of its old-growth holdings before five years. Nevertheless, the forestry giant had been forced to act by pressure from environmental groups with their campaign to boycott paper made from old-growth trees. Stephens had presciently recognized there might be a market niche for products of better ecological logging practices.

At the grass-roots level, there continues to be a great deal of activity from both nongovernmental organizations and individuals. Around the world, people are concerned about the degradation of their surroundings and are acting against it. There are hundreds of eco-heroes. The following essays are about three of them.

AMAZON'S "TARZAN" PLANS AN EPIC SWIM

FROM LETICIA, COLOMBIA — He swaggered into the room like some kind of Latin American Crocodile Dundee. Clad only in shorts, he had a huge knife on his belt, a jaguar's tooth around his neck, and jet black hair hanging to his shoulders. With massive shoulders like a water buffalo and the look of an ageing Johnny Weissmuller, Kapax has understandably been labelled Tarzan of the Amazon by the press.

Forty-eight years ago, Kapax was born to a German father and a Native mother in the Andes mountains. Two decades ago, he moved to the tiny frontier town of Leticia, Colombia, right next to its Brazilian counterpart, Tabatinga. People move freely between the two countries without passing guards or fences. These are the western headwaters of the Amazon, and the wide, swift-flowing river dominates life here as the source of food, recreation, and transportation.

Kapax makes a living as a tour guide and he certainly looks the part. When he first approached me, I was rather put off by what seemed to me an affectation of style and attire. But as I listened to him and realized his sincerity and heard the passion of his commitment, I became caught up in his vision.

The rivers and forest are Kapax's obsession. In 1976, he became a Latin American hero when he swam down the Magdalena River from Neiva to Barranquilla on the Caribbean, a distance of 1,300 kilometres! His aim was to attract attention to the terrible pollution of the river and the destruction of the surrounding forest. This was long before the fate of tropical rainforests had become a popular global issue.

Kapax is also an ardent supporter of indigenous people. He points out that they cut down the forest and kill animals to sell because it has become a way for them to survive. Kapax wants to bring them the message that they can keep the forest intact by rediscovering traditional ways of making a living. He is particularly concerned for the Indian children living along the river: "If the children do not have a conscience to preserve the Amazon, their future will be in danger," he told me.

"We need to tell the world that the destruction of the Amazon forest is closer than ever," he went on. Kapax's message has power because it is so simple and obvious. He doesn't base his appeal on a sophisticated reasoning about the need to protect biodiversity. Instead, he points out that the Amazon, the largest river in the world, accounts for a fifth of the planet's freshwater and, for that reason alone, deserves respect.

As a calling card, he handed me a sheet with this message:

When the last river is all contaminated,
When the last tree is cut down,
When the last animal is dead,
When we are totally lacking oxygen,
We will know we have lost a great opportunity.
The world will not end,
But we are polluting and degrading it,
And we are responsible.

Now Kapax is proposing a dramatic new stunt to attract attention to the deteriorating state of the river from the governments of Peru, Colombia, and Brazil. He wants to swim from Iquitos in Peru to Manaus in Brazil, where the Amazon joins the Rio Negro — 2,200 kilometres away! On his way down the river, he intends to stop at villages where he will disseminate his message about the life-giving force of the river and the need to ensure its protection. "I want to use my popularity to defend the Amazon," he says.

He conjured up in me an almost mythic picture of a huge hulk of a man emerging from the river to tell village people about what he has seen and to warn them of what is to come if they don't change their ways. It is the kind of thing that the international media could turn into a major spectacle.

I had swum in the swift waters near Leticia the day before I met Kapax. The current was swift and threatening, with its undertow and whirlpools. I had to swim as hard as I could just to stay in the same place. Out in the middle, the river's power was awesome as it swept through ominous rapids. Dredging up visions of piranhas, crocodiles, and parasites, to say nothing of the sheer force of the waters, I asked Kapax what dangers his proposed venture would hold. He answered, "Only human-created ones. There is nothing in nature that I fear."

This is not an adventure that can be embarked on lightly. It requires an experienced person who is in superb physical and psychological condition. I couldn't help feeling inspired by Kapax's commitment and hope he is the one to do it. He needs at least $20,000 for the boats and support crews to start the first part of the swim.

UPDATE: I received several letters and calls of enquiry from people who were interested in helping Kapax. I directed them all to Kapax but have never heard from him again.

AN ECO-HERO OF OZ WRITES FROM PRISON

Dr. Bob Brown is one of my eco-heroes. He lives in Tasmania, the island state off the southeastern corner of Australia. Bob is a physician who has spent a lot of time camping and canoeing in Tasmania's fabulous wilderness areas. In the 1970s, he became concerned about the Tasmanian government's rush to exploit its natural resources by destructive logging and large dams.

More than twenty years ago, it was proposed that an area encompassing Pedder Lake and the forests and rivers around it should be flooded to generate power. Because of the area's great beauty and its unique hydrology, flora, and fauna, people began to object to the dam and became part of what we now call an environmental movement opposed to the ecological and spiritual destructiveness of mindless development.

Pedder Lake was flooded, but a movement had been created with Brown as one of its leaders. The movement grew, and Brown abandoned medicine and helped to form what was the world's first Green Party. He was elected to the Tasmanian Parliament as a Green and has been an effective politician of rare courage and integrity.

In 1995, in northern Tasmania, a 350,000-hectare area of wilderness called the Tarkine was threatened with development. The state government was building a fifty-kilometre road through it at a cost of $3.5 million (Australian). However, since the road broke the state government's own regulations, Brown says, it "gazetted a special proclamation absolving it from its own environment and planning laws." The federal government has a responsibility to intervene and enforce environmental regulations but refused to get involved, a derogation of duty that Brown labelled "inexplicable, indefensible, irresponsible."

Brown decried the lack of media coverage of what was happening in the Tarkine. To raise public awareness, he stood on the road to block it, was arrested, and was sent to Risdon Prison. From jail, he sent this eloquent statement.

"As the police vans carried us back to jail, a wedgetailed eagle stood on the buttongrass, sentinel to the Tarkine's tragic plight. She did not ruffle a feather or show the slightest fear, her head turning almost imperceptibly as she watched our noisy exit from the wild land of tireless tranquility.

"Jail is an inside-out wilderness. It awaits those who want to peacefully protest against the bulldozers but cannot gazette proclamations. . . . While the wilderness speaks of freedom and identity, Risdon's barbed wire, guard towers and cement walls shout about subjugation and the irrelevance of the individual.

"I heard the call 'Good on yer, Bob. Save the forests!' bellowed from a cellblock across the compound. . . . And the next morning, a big, cheery man . . . stuck his hand through the grill and shouted, 'Come over and shake my hand, Bob.' I knew the spirit of wilderness had no trouble permeating Risdon's walls.

"I am moving well past the equator of my migration between the poles of cradle and grave. As I move on, the sense of timelessness grows. . . . I enjoyed the features of jail which do match wilderness — no phones, no traffic, no shopping and the early-to-bed, early-to-rise routine. As I paced my little cell at night, my mind hyperactive and out divining what makes the world tick, the irony of jailing greens became clear. We are being locked up because wilderness is an affront to materialism, as the Earth is turned into a wildernessless prison.

"The goal, the 'best outcome,' is the greatest conversion of the world to human productivity, where every acre is targeted for human consumption and accounted for in the warehouses lining the information superhighway. Beyond this goal, materialism dreams of virtual reality . . . replacing the wild Earth which for so long had us in its grasp. . . . Environmentalists are locked up so that the Earth may be concreted. One by one, bit by bit, the faster the better.

"I don't want Shakespeare's line to become 'All the world's a concrete cell with all the men and women playing virtual reality.' I don't want this planet's remarkable diversity fading out of memory and grasp of future generations.

"Governments may sit on their hands or pass proclamations. Journalists may report life as the interplay of economic rationalists. Others may simply not care. But Risdon made me more defiant; I saw the eagle's eye. I want the Tarkine wild and free."

UPDATE: Former prime minister Paul Keating is no longer in politics. He makes occasional public speeches and sits on corporate boards. Bob Brown is now a Green Party senator from Tasmania and sits in the Upper House of the federal government. He was arrested twice for protesting the road into the Tarkine and was jailed for eleven days, then five days. The Tarkine is being eroded by mining and logging. The road bisecting the wilderness is completed, logging has accelerated, and a huge mine is proposed near the Arthur River. Senator Brown continues to work for the environment. He was arrested in 1997 for obstructing logging of a wild forest near Melbourne and in May, visited a blockade of a proposed uranium mine in Kakadu National Park. He tries to inspire other Greens and recently visited Party members in Taiwan, Germany, Belgium, France, and Mexico.

VILLAGE POWER WINS VICTORIES IN INDIA

FROM PUNE, INDIA — Hurtling along a road in what seems like a suicide run, I pray there are Hindu gods to look after foreigners. India is like a different planet, where one's every assumption, value, and belief simply has to be suspended. I'm here for a special program on dams for *The Nature of Things*.

Like many other nations in the less-industrialized world, India has been beguiled by the twentieth-century illusion that bigger is better and that what is modern is superior to ancient traditional ways. This attitude has been encouraged by agencies such as the World Bank.

The Narmada is the largest river flowing west in central India.

It supports rich forests and wildlife, as well as tens of thousands of tribal people, who continue to live off the surrounding land. But its most potent value to Indians is spiritual: many consider the Narmada even more sacred than the Ganges. However, the modern perspective views the river in economic terms.

With forty major tributaries, the Narmada River basin drains water from an area of almost 100,000 square kilometres. For decades, proposals had been made to harness the flow for drinking water, but especially for power and agricultural irrigation. So since the 1960s, the Indian government has pursued a plan to build two superdams and thousands of major and minor projects on the Narmada. The scheme will be the largest irrigation strategy in the world and will affect 12 to 15 million people in four states. There will be enormous economic, social, and ecological costs.

This is a country where the poor and powerless have always been pushed around by those with wealth and power. But since arriving, I have learned of two remarkable people who have given a sense of power to those at the bottom of the economic and political pile. Mehda Patkar is a Hindu woman who learned of the huge proposed Sardar Sarovar Dam, which will flood hundreds of villages of tribal people. Since the mid-1980s, she single-handedly galvanized the inhabitants of the villages into action by informing them of the government's plans. Walking hundreds of kilometres from village to village, Patkar marshalled opposition to the dam so that, by the '90s, unprecedented public demonstrations involving tens of thousands of protesters were held. Thousands have been arrested, and in 1993 police shot and killed a teenage boy. The protests created so much pressure that the World Bank eventually reneged on its promised loans.

In spite of the expense, the Indian government continued with the dam building. Opponents contended that the dams would be ecological and social disasters. But the most potent criticism was that most of the water would be used for large-scale irrigation of cash crops, which would enrich only wealthy landowners and big companies. Yet in the same part of the country, another person provided an alternative strategy that works.

During the 1965 war with Pakistan, Anna Hazare was driving

a Jeep in a convoy that came under fire. Everyone except Hazare was killed. He decided that he had been spared to be reborn again, and so dedicated his second life to serving the people of his village, Ralegan Siddhi.

Returning home, Hazare found the people and the land in a terrible state. The main sources of revenue were forty distilleries and a tobacco industry. Hazare wanted an alternative to the alcohol and tobacco industries and looked to the village's agrarian roots. But groundwater had been depleted, leaving little for crops. He recognized that when it did rain, the runoff carried away the meagre soil. To Hazare, soil is the life of the village and the village is the unit of survival that must be protected at all costs. So he began to work on "watershed development," with the aim of keeping both soil and water in the community. That involved planting trees and crops that would retain the water and digging a series of horizontal pits that would collect water and slow its flow down the hills. Within four years, Hazare could point to dramatic results — decreased soil erosion, recharged groundwater, water flowing in once-dry riverbeds, and increased crop yields.

Today the distilleries are gone. The village is surrounded by lush green fields and actually exports water to neighbouring communities. Hazare's work has been recognized and he is now co-ordinating the application of his approach to watershed development in 300 other villages.

All over the world, people like Hazare and Patkar are rallying support for community-based ideas and technology and taking charge of their own destiny. It's an inspiring lesson for us in the so-called developed world.

UPDATE: Under pressure from environmental and social justice groups, the World Bank established a committee to assess the ecological, social, and economic impact of Sardar Sarovar. Headed by Bradford Morse and Tom Berger, the committee released its report, "The Independent Review — Sardar Sarovar Project," on January 15, 1994. The report was a severe indictment of the claimed benefits of the dam and concluded, "the wisest action would be to step back from the project." The World Bank abided by the recommendation and declined to fund the dam. This was unprecedented for an organization enthralled with megaprojects and almost messianic in its faith in development. India found funding elsewhere and continues with the dam. Recently, India announced it had a vigorous nuclear program and detonated a series of nuclear bombs.

18

LEARNING FROM THE PAST TO SHAPE THE FUTURE

ℋuman beings are gifted with enormous and inventive brains. Our curiosity, creativity, and capacity for abstraction have served us very well. We have an ability to recognize patterns and regularities in nature, enabling us to develop world-views in which everything is interlinked. We learned through observation and trial and error, gradually accumulating knowledge that enabled us to anticipate the future.

In inventing the concept of a future, we recognized that we could deliberately shape that future by the choices we made in the present. In other words, faced with options, we could choose to avoid deadly sabre-toothed tigers and go instead where there were delicacies in abundance. It was a very successful strategy, one we have never needed more than we do today.

A MIND-SET GUARANTEED THE COD CRISIS

In high school in the 1950s, we learned that the oceans were a vast reservoir of protein that could feed all people on Earth. Perhaps such a goal was possible back then, when there were half as many people to feed, but today we are fishing at a rate and volume that can't be sustained. In 1994, at Dalhousie University, I was shocked by the oceanographer Bob Fournier's summary of the decline of the Atlantic cod.

He recounted that for almost 500 years, cod have been the basis of life and culture on the East Coast. In 1800, fishers took an estimated 100,000 tons a year globally, but didn't make a dent in fish populations. The yearly catch rose to 400,000 tons a year by 1950. With huge factory ships to feed an insatiable demand, the annual catch peaked at a million tons in the 1960s and then began to slide. By 1994, even with a moratorium on most of the Atlantic cod fishery, stocks were still plummeting towards extinction. Tens of thousands of jobs had already been lost and 1,300 communities were being torn apart by an ecological apocalypse.

Sadly, the story of the Atlantic cod is neither unique nor rare. Pollution in the Great Lakes has had devastating effects on human health, behaviour, and fertility. And worldwide, forests, topsoil, watersheds, wetlands, and prairies are being devastated.

There are plenty of scapegoats. In Halifax, whales, seals, cold water, environmentalists, overfishing, and poor management were blamed. But the root cause is a mind-set that is becoming globally accepted and is built into our institutions of economics, science, and politics.

The global economy into which we are being driven by our business and political leaders does not factor in long-term sustainability of communities, human and non-human. Instead, in the name of efficiency and competitiveness, the level of the playing field is set by quantity, speed, price, and profit. To compete globally, tens of thousands of inshore fishers have been displaced by a few hundred workers on giant offshore trawlers.

We are air-breathing land mammals and water is not our natural habitat. So we have only fragmentary glimpses into the habitats that cover 71 percent of the Earth, a knowledge base that is too limited to enable us to manage populations of wild organisms.

Conventional economics has little value for the sustainability of renewable resources because money is fluid and moves easily from resource to resource across political borders. That's why the great rainforests of Brazil, Sarawak, and B.C. are being trashed with little regard for the future. The commercial extinction of Atlantic cod was an inevitable result of current economic "wisdom."

Science too can be destructive when its practitioners claim to be able to "manage resources." Paradoxically, the explosive growth in our technological prowess has not been matched by our understanding of the make-up and interactions of the parts of the living world.

Scientists are often co-opted by their political masters. Those working for government see their findings massaged by bureaucrats to serve political agendas. I am told scientific data and recommendations are often unrecognizable by the time they are made public. And when scientists suggest politically undesirable strategies, they are muzzled.

Even university scientists protected by tenure feel the pressure of political priorities. They depend on research funds to do their work, but grants are not conferred solely on the basis of quality; they are spread around to satisfy political needs and government priorities. So scientists who might be studying cod, for example, are unlikely to jeopardize their support by openly criticizing government policy. Politicians seem fatally attracted to projects that are big, fast, and splashy, but ministers are seldom around long enough to be held accountable for any deleterious consequences found later. In 1977, when the federal government banned foreign ships fishing within a 200-mile zone, it was not to conserve resources. Instead, Canadian companies were subsidized to build boats and processing plants to reap a bonanza. Politicians were able to ignore the warnings that cod were being overfished and their habitat damaged until it was too late.

Today no one knows whether the fish will come back. Since all we can control is human predation and impact, we have to pull back and hope for the recuperative power of nature. But we mustn't perpetuate current economic, scientific, and political notions that are undercutting sustainable futures by extinguishing renewable resources, wiping out jobs, and destabilizing communities. When cod, forests, water, and soil flourish, so too will human beings. Then perhaps high school students will again be taught about the vast riches of the oceans.

UPDATE: Despite the moratorium, northern cod stocks have not rebounded as hoped. Sporadic reports of large populations in certain bays and areas of Newfoundland have led to vocal pressure from fishers to allow some fishing. In fact, a limited food fishery was opened, but most experts remain adamant that the fish remain in dire straits and must be left alone.

On May 15, 1994, the Atlantic Groundfish Strategy (TAGS) was initiated. It paid fishers between $211 and $382 per week. It was phased out in the summer of 1998 and replaced with a reduced program. The social and economic impact of the loss of the cod fishery has been catastrophic.

SALMON WAR AN EXERCISE IN ABSURDITY

"Fish War." "Battle Over Salmon Heats Up." These 1994 headlines describe the escalating dispute over salmon, which is an important fish on the Pacific Coast from northern California all the way to Alaska. When salmon populations declined in Washington and Oregon, Canadians were blamed for intercepting too many of the fish bound for the southern states. American fishers retaliated by increasing their catch of Canada-bound fish.

Brian Tobin, minister of fisheries and oceans, urged the completion of a Pacific Salmon Treaty to settle the controversy by setting regulations and limits. He claimed that Canadians reduced their capture of American fish by 40 percent while the Americans, especially in Alaska, increased their catch of Canadian fish by 50 percent! That translated into 9 million Canadian salmon caught in American nets and 4 million American fish taken by Canadian boats.

Responding to the American depredation, Tobin announced that all American fishing boats passing through inland waters within Canadian boundaries would be charged a fee of $1,500 one way. It was another irritant that elicited even more bellicosity.

Overlooked amid the threats and posturing is the simple fact that our claim to be able to "manage" several species of fish is preposterous. These are wild animals with complex life cycles that are only poorly understood. The fish travel over immense distances in the ocean for periods of two to five years and have no concern for the human political boundaries they cross. But we take our borders seriously and attempt to dictate the future of these species by making them conform to our priorities and needs.

The vast network of rivers that feed into the Pacific and support the five species of salmon drains the great spine of mountains paralleling the coast. Yet the Alaska panhandle cuts off half of the British Columbia coast and brings rivers originating deep in B.C. under U.S. jurisdiction. Farther south, the Columbia River has similar dual citizenship. Watersheds and ocean shores are geophysical entities that are splintered by human political domains.

The impact of different regulatory perspectives can be seen in the fate of three major river systems. In B.C., the Fraser River has been kept free of dams and now there is great concern for protecting the salmon against the ravages of pollution and development. In contrast, the Snake and Columbia rivers in the U.S. have been extensively dammed, with the consequence that one hundred distinct salmon runs have become extinct in these two river systems.

The absurdity of the squabble over quotas for each country to take the other's fish becomes obvious when we reflect on the life cycle of salmon. All of the species are born in freshwater and, after varying periods in rivers and lakes, go out to sea. Upon maturation, they return to the very river where they were born! In other words, the fish know exactly where they belong and find their way home. North American aboriginal people knew that too, so instead of intercepting the moving salmon out in the ocean, they merely waited at a river's mouth or a naturally occurring narrows for the fish to come by. There are very simple ways of estimating the size of return runs in the river, and Native people used them to ensure that a healthy number of fish was always allowed to spawn.

In Japan, fishers wait for the salmon to enter the river systems so the number taken for food and reproduction can be carefully controlled. I suspect that very few people, if any, in a blindfold taste test would be able to tell the difference between an ocean-caught fish and one taken at a river's mouth. Indeed, aboriginal people tell me they prefer the fish after they enter freshwater. Yet vast sums are invested in fishing fleets to capture fish at sea, and that creates the problem of attempting to divvy them up into Canadian and American stocks.

With sophisticated navigation and sonar technology, it is possible to intercept fish in open water and take them in sufficient numbers to be commercially feasible. Once large ships are built to take the fish at sea, there is an enormous capital investment that must be paid off. The obvious way to avoid the territorial disputes, to ensure a sustainable fishery, and to protect the salmon is to abandon fishing for them at sea.

The salmon wars are an outlandish result of fishing practices that pay little attention or give scant consideration to the geophysical and biological needs of salmon species. Instead, economics and politics are driving them towards oblivion.

RETHINKING "SUSTAINABLE" DEVELOPMENT

In 1987, after years of work, a United Nations committee headed by Norway's prime minister, Gro Harlem Brundtland, completed its report on the environment and development. Published as *Our Common Future*, it described in bleak detail the assault on the life-support systems of the planet by our species. The report urged that the Earth and its productivity be protected and nurtured for all future generations. Henceforth, economics and the environment must be linked inseparably.

Brundtland's major contribution was the phrase *sustainable development*, which was adopted and repeated like a mantra by politicians and businesspeople. The dictionary defines development as "gradual unfolding, fuller working out," which makes sustainable development a phrase full of insight and promise.

Unfortunately, in common usage, the meaning of development has been altered and is now synonymous with "economic growth," which, in turn, is frequently equated with "progress." While development in the dictionary sense has endless potential, limitless growth is impossible in a finite world.

Brundtland's insightful document then fell into the trap of a belief in both economics and our ability to manage nature; she concluded that so long as sustainable development is the operative principle in all of our actions, we could protect the environment while the global economy could increase fivefold! Economists may believe it's possible, but most scientists disagree. The demand for further economic growth in the industrialized nations is justified with the argument that wealth will trickle down to the poorer nations. Yet during the period of unprecedented economic growth from the 1950s to the 1980s, the disparity between rich and poor countries increased.

When the Brundtland report was released, Canada's first ministers, led by Prime Minister Brian Mulroney, unanimously supported it and committed themselves to sustainable development. This meant that all further economic initiatives should first be assessed for their ecological ramifications.

Upon his re-election in 1988, Mulroney promised a Green Plan that would point to a new direction. When the Green Plan finally appeared in late 1990, environmental concerns had given way to economic imperatives. The plan lacked an ecological framework for its programs, and had neither the budget nor the political clout to influence big departments like finance.

By the time of the Earth Summit in Rio in 1992, the momentum that had propelled the environmental movement through the 1970s and 1980s had faltered and governments were increasingly preoccupied with the economy. Nevertheless, the Liberal Red Book, on which Jean Chrétien based his 1993 campaign, states: "Business, labour and the general public increasingly understand that the natural environmental agenda can no longer be separated from the national economic agenda."

This is the context within which we must see a recommendation made in 1994 by the all-party Standing Committee on Environment, chaired by Charles Caccia. Caccia is a former environment minister who has remained committed to eco-issues. His committee has recommended the appointment of a commissioner of the environment and sustainable development, who would be the environmental equivalent of the auditor general.

The commissioner would not be a political appointee and would have an arm's-length relationship with government, with a budget of about $5 million and a staff of about thirty people. His or her responsibilities would be to report annually to Parliament on "federal policies, laws, regulations and programs impacting on sustainable development; the extent to which federal legislation and policies comply with Canada's international commitments; Environment Canada's capacity to lead the shift towards sustainability; and progress toward sustainable development by the government as a whole."

It's a small step towards moving from talk to the implementation of the integration of the economy with ecological sustainability. The catastrophic collapse of the Atlantic fishery might have been avoided had there been a strong environmental advocate. The fate of our forests, agriculture, and cities is equally contentious and in need of a commissioner.

The Brundtland report was published seven years ago. Since then, more than 600 million human beings have been added to the world's population, 100 million hectares of forest destroyed, 175 billion tonnes of agricultural topsoil lost, and as many as 350,000 species driven to extinction. How much longer can we make a mockery of sustainable living?

UPDATE: Remember the vaunted Green Plan promised by then Minister of the Environment Robert de Cotret and implemented by his successor, Jean Charest? It began to fall short of its claims immediately and is now deader than a doornail. The current Liberal government has downsized the environment ministry, reneged on its Red Book promise to significantly reduce greenhouse gas emissions, lobbied against the imposition of significant reduction targets at Kyoto, and now appears ready to cave in to provincial demands not to try to meet the target that was agreed to. All in all, a disgusting record.

THE PERILS OF COLLECTIVE AMNESIA

Each month I receive many letters pleading for help to save a bit of nature or wilderness from yet another scheme to develop it. Taken together, the letters become a scream to stop ecological damage occurring across the country. Why can't we recognize the magnitude of what's going on? A recent letter from London, Ontario, and another from Vancouver give a clue.

The London note contained a clipping from the *London Free Press* about a plan by developers to build a high-rise complex next to Sifton Bog. To London's nature lovers, Sifton Bog is an irreplaceable jewel that represents the last significant remnant of what was once a huge and unique ecosystem.

Bogs are said to be as biologically rich and diverse as a tropical rainforest. The London environmentalist Anne Hurd is quoted as saying Sifton Bog is home to "56 nationally, provincially or regionally rare plant species, 6 provincially rare bird species and several regionally rare animals." Nevertheless, bogs are vulnerable because many people view them as hostile, swampy "wastelands" that breed pests.

In 1971, London zoned the area around Sifton Bog for high-density residential use, but in 1991, the city council reclassified it as open space and urban reserve. Two developers, Eugene Drewlo and Donald Crich, are appealing for a return to the 1971 designation so they can build ten fourteen-storey buildings with a total of 1,800 units. That could bring up to 5,000 new residents to the edge of the bog and put such pressure on the ecosystem that it could destroy it.

The developers argue that they bought the land under the 1971 zoning laws and, having paid taxes, are entitled to reap maximum profit on their original investment. Our environmental sensitivity and concern have increased tremendously since 1971. If we must uphold standards and decisions made before the acquisition of new values, attitudes, and insights, there would be no hope of genuine progress and improvement in the way we do things.

The other letter came from Create a Real Available Beach (CRAB), a Vancouver group opposed to a megaproject that would develop the Vancouver waterfront even further. In spite of the building boom in downtown Vancouver (especially during Expo '86), the urban waters that give the city its charm still support a surprisingly rich array of animal and plant species. Toxic effluent from storm-sewer outfalls, oil spills from tankers and other ships, illicit or accidental dumping of chemicals by industries, and ocean disposal of landfill combine to put enormous pressure on the urban waterfront.

But the short-term illusion of prosperity created from the infusion of money and jobs by a large development is irresistible to politicians because it fits their time frame for re-election. The Vancouver Port Board proposal will involve at least seven acres of landfilling in the ocean, seven acres of water coverage by a pier for cruiseships, and another acre of coverage for a heliport. It constitutes a major alteration of the harbour that will change water flow and currents and increase pressure from traffic and pollution.

In London and Vancouver, each proposal calls for incremental change that by itself may be seem benign. But because change has become such a familiar part of the way we live, we develop a collective amnesia about the past. We adapt so readily to change that we soon forget what we have lost. Then when another proposal for development is submitted, we weigh its impact against the new state we have come to accept as normal. Consider this:

I grew up in London in the late '40s and early '50s. I remember abundant opportunities to bicycle to farms, woods, or creeks, where I learned some of my most important biology lessons. The swamp I loved has long been paved over for a shopping centre and apartment complex. Most Londoners today have no knowledge of the city I knew as a youth, so their standards for measuring the impact of development will not take into account what has already been compromised. And by focusing only on Sifton Bog, they will not recognize the collective effect of all the other developments on the London region.

My father was born in Vancouver in 1909 and remembers forests in what is now downtown, salmon runs in local creeks, and halibut and cut-throat trout caught on the city waterfront. They were long gone by the time I returned to Vancouver in 1963, but since then, I have seen the cancellation of the annual salmon derby for lack of fish, given up fishing below my house because of tumours in local flounders, and was horrified when dungeness crab were declared inedible because of high levels of dioxins.

Every new proposal — a pulp mill, dam, bridge, or high rise — is assessed for its impact on the environment as it currently is, not on the cumulative effect over generations of time. Without a longer memory span, our reference points are too current to see the dimensions of what is happening.

PLANET'S FATE COMPOUNDS DEATH'S STING

"Hello, David. It's Dad. The doctor says there's nothing he can do, so he's sending me home. Can you come and pick me up?"

I shuddered uncontrollably, knowing the implications of the call. His voice was trembling with shock and fear. It was November 1991. Having been diagnosed with a large tumour in his liver, he had been told that surgery was his only chance. So we had rejoiced when the surgeon had announced, "It's large, but I think I can get it." The phone call ended the jubilation.

By the time I reached the hospital half an hour later, Dad had pulled himself together and was waiting. "We all have to die," he said calmly, "and I've had a good life with no regrets. Now let's go home because I've got a lot to do." His ability to face and accept death surprised me as much as it impressed me.

When I was a boy and Dad was a young man, he always claimed to be an agnostic. As he got older, he discovered nature worship in Shinto, Japan's traditional religion. "I believe I'll always be here," he would say. "When I die, I want you to spread my ashes on the ocean-shore to return me back to nature, where we came from. And then, when you see a gull or an eagle flying in the sky, watch the fish in the water, or walk among the trees, I'll still be there."

I'm reminded of this by the recent death of a relative in England. Death informs us most powerfully of how ephemeral our lives are and of the inescapability of our demise. This knowledge is humanity's terrible burden, the price of the evolution of self-awareness. I would have given anything to shield my children from the dreadful moment of realization that they, too, like all other living things, will die.

Throughout our species' history, our comprehension that death is inevitable has invoked fear and weighed heavily on our lives. Conscious of the brevity of our existence, we strive to leave something after us, and so the major religions of the world have flourished, wars and conquests have been waged, and great architectural monuments constructed. The powerful need for children is driven by the chance to live on through our offspring.

The fact of death has been the most profound leveller. It's not just that wealth or power fail to exempt us from the same fate as the poor and the powerless, death also informs us that we are biological beings like any other species. Our immense intellect, science, and technology cannot stave off the same end that befalls all plants and other animals.

If we read the gravestones in an ancient graveyard, it is striking to note that not many generations ago, death was a familiar presence that claimed people of all ages, constantly reminding us of our own mortality. In this century, improved nutrition, antibiotics, and sanitation have made death an increasingly alien presence. The process of dying has become more protracted and managed by medical professionals, while after death, religious and funeral responsibilities are handled by other specialists. I was more than forty years old before someone I knew well died and I saw a body close up.

"Ashes to ashes, dust to dust." The invocation recalls our earthly origins and our destiny, echoing my father's faith that his atoms and molecules will be recycled endlessly throughout the ecosphere. The author and psychologist Stephen Jay Lifton once told me that our fear of obliteration through death was made tolerable by the knowledge that nature would live on, that we, who emerged from the web of life, would return to it.

Lifton recounted a powerful story. After the Second World War, a rumour spread through Japan that nothing could grow in the soil of Hiroshima because of the atom bomb. It set off a wave of terror because even though the war had been devastating, the notion that the Earth itself had lost its capacity to support life was horrifying beyond endurance. Only when plants began to sprout again was this terror relieved.

Nuclear weapons made all of nature vulnerable and this is what makes the prospect of nuclear war so intolerable. It is the same for the current spasm of ecological destruction. Throughout the existence of life on Earth, species extinction has been a necessary part of evolution. But today we are creating a high rate of extinction that is accompanied by a cataclysmic disruption of the complex interconnections of the Earth's physical and biological components. So now our fear of death has an added apprehension — that we will so upset the balance of air, water, soil, and variety of life that the productive and regenerative capacity of the Earth will have been destroyed.

My father's solace over his imminent death derived from a belief that the rich mantle of life on Earth would endure. Our continuing rush along the same ecologically destructive path adds immense sorrow to the already heavy burden of our inescapable death.

CARING FOR OUR HOME

Often journalists are reluctant to cover environmental issues because they accuse environmentalists of being too emotional. The implication that being emotional somehow diminishes credibility has never made sense to me. If our home was trashed or our child crippled by hooligans, something would be seriously wrong if we weren't emotional!

Today many believe that greed, ignorance, or short-sightedness is leading to a vandalized planet through the destruction of wilderness, extinction of species, toxic pollution, overconsumption, and population increase. We are biological beings whose real home is the Earth, which is also the source of all life. Surely the credibility of those who are not concerned or emotional about the environmental crisis must be suspect.

The global ecological emergency is not some sensational or self-serving fabrication or exaggeration. The anecdotal evidence, especially in the memories of our elders, is overwhelming. You can see it yourself in the brown dome of smog visible over every city. Skyrocketing rates of asthma, breast cancer, sex-organ dysfunctions, and skin problems are a canary's warning, as is the dramatic disappearance of many of our biological relatives — frogs, birds, trees, fish, and plants. Once-pristine rivers, lakes, and seashores are dangerously contaminated with chemicals, trash, and disease-causing micro-organisms.

The fate of Newfoundland fishers is a lesson on the consequences of failing to conserve renewable resources. Anyone who has fished or scuba-dived for fifteen or twenty years can give startling testimony about the diminution in sea life over that time. I once encountered a group of loggers who vented their anger at me openly and harshly. I finally responded that environmentalists don't oppose logging but want loggers' children to look forward to cutting trees every bit as rich as the ones currently being harvested. One of the men immediately snorted, "There's no way my kids will be loggers. There won't be any trees left"! Even angry loggers know that over-cutting is diminishing their children's future.

An extraterrestrial scientist who arrived on Earth and decided to study human beings the way I once studied fruit-flies — by watching what they do — would soon conclude that as a species, we are either suicidal or insane. With global telecommunications, computers, engineers, and scientists, we know the planet is being degraded catastrophically, yet we seem unable or unwilling to change our destructive behaviour.

Psychiatrists refer to our current condition as "cognitive dissonance" — we sense a need to change, but to do so would clash with our personal beliefs and values. It's less distressing to ignore the warnings ("It's too depressing") or discount the messenger ("She's too pessimistic," "They propose no alternatives," "He's too emotional").

Well, I don't think we can afford to indulge ourselves any longer by denying or refusing to face the facts. The future of our children is now in serious jeopardy, and each day that we carry on with business as usual reduces the range of options that will remain open to them. As time passes, the options for change diminish while the costs skyrocket.

NO WONDER OUR CHILDREN ARE BORED

My income, when today's dollars are adjusted for inflation, is many times what my parents earned while they were raising my three sisters and me. My house is more than twice as big as the one I grew up in and is crowded with products and technology — computers, freezer, television, microwave oven, breadmaker — unimaginable luxuries in my parents' time that now are affordable necessities.

Life for most of us today seems richer in experience and happier than a generation ago. My children's rooms overflow with stuff. They have access to computers, telephones, videos, and television, yet these sophisticated urban children, surrounded by technology and material goods, still often complain, "I'm *bored*!"

My memories of boyhood are filled with days spent wandering through woods, wallowing in swamps, and fishing in creeks and rivers in Southern Ontario. When my wife, Tara, came to Canada, her father had a low-paying teaching job, yet she recalls an enchanted childhood growing up in West Vancouver next door to her best friend. Their houses were separated by a stretch of brambles and bushes containing tunnels and paths to "secret" places where their imaginations let the girls play endless games. Tara and I both remember neighbourhoods where dinner time would be announced by parents yodelling for their children to come home to eat.

Our reflections on childhood are more than nostalgic self-indulgences: the memories allow us to see how much society has changed in our lifetimes. The world of my youth was radically different — far simpler, more innocent and naive — from my children's. My parents seldom worried, as I do constantly today, when I was gone for hours on end. What caused them distress was when I missed dinner or came home covered in mud. Even in a city like London, Ontario, where I spent my adolescence, there were rivers, swamps, and woods readily accessible to a child with a bike.

So why are my children bored? For one thing, cities have become hostile places for them. Cars rule the streets — there are more of them and they are faster and deadlier. Empty lots are no longer magic places to capture butterflies or play hide and seek; instead, they are heavy with the menace of possible drug dealers, child molesters, or toxic chemicals. Even our parks are too well groomed and manicured, too carefully controlled for weeds and pests to evoke mystery and awe.

My children still enjoy gardening with their grandfather or beachcombing at the cottage. They are just as receptive as I was to the astonishing complexity of the simplest things in the wild — a seed, a feather, a dragonfly's wing. Sculpted by millions of years of evolutionary experimentation and adaptation, nature has a capacity for surprise that exceeds anything created by human ingenuity and inventiveness. My children's manufactured possessions merely titillate with a novelty that quickly fades and leaves them wanting something else. And so they're bored.

More and more, we live in a simplified world, the human-created environment of cities where we are forced to seek novelty in the profusion of goods in shopping malls or in movies and electronic games. We become stupefied by the wonders of the Internet, the information superhighway, and the 500-channel television universe, and congratulate ourselves on being so creative. It is the ultimate narcissism when a species becomes so enthralled with its own cleverness and inventiveness.

And it is suicidal when, puffed up with ourselves, we concoct an economics that is based almost exclusively on human creativity and productiveness while natural capital is externalized from it. Thus currency speculators can indulge in a destructive game that has no basis in the real world — buying money and selling money to make more money. Convinced of the limitless potential of the human mind, economists cling to a dangerous faith that endless growth is both possible and necessary.

Meanwhile, there are countless tangible "services" performed by every part of nature. Take a forest tree, for example. It cleanses the air by exchanging carbon dioxide for oxygen; ameliorates weather and climate by taking up water and releasing it by transpiration; holds soil from erosion; and provides food, shelter, and habitat for microorganisms, plants, and animals — yet none of these services has value in our human-based economic system. By this kind of thinking, a tree is worth something only when we take a chainsaw to it.

In our quest for a "better life," we have been brainwashed into thinking that having more things makes us happy. Comparing my childhood with what our children have, that's clearly not true.

CONCLUSION

$\mathcal{T}$hese essays have been an attempt to make sense of the day-to-day events that assault us from the media. In this shattered world of information, it is often difficult to discern the root causes or the social context that might explain what we hear. Only when we have a sense of the context within which the disparate events and reports are embedded can we understand how we got to where we are or where we may be going.

I have used the metaphor of a car heading for a brick wall while the occupants are preoccupied with seating arrangements. In such a situation, every minute lost without turning the wheel or applying the brakes means that avoiding a collision will be more difficult. Once the threshold has been breached and the car doomed to strike the barrier, we have no choice but to respond heroically after the crash, but survival is far less assured.

In recent months, we have seen governments in Canada respond to popular concerns quite suddenly and dramatically. Ontario's premier, Mike Harris, backed down within days after a public outcry over his niggardly attempt to settle with the surviving Dionne quintuplets; Alberta's Ralph Klein capitulated similarly to protests at the meanness of his response to sterilized victims of the Eugenics Act.

In B.C., Premier Glen Clark responded very quickly to public outrage over leaking condominiums. Human tragedy that touches us emotionally and moves us to action can also move politicians. The challenge is to raise the awareness that global ecological degradation is a crisis every bit as real and potentially tragic. But that's not easy.

I have spent a lot of my life trying to raise public awareness over different issues and lobbying politicians at various ministries. Unfortunately, it usually takes quite a while to educate a new minister, and then chances are high she or he will be moved up, down, or out and be replaced with someone else who has to be educated all over again. I no longer think this is a useful way to spend my time. I now see the challenge in the following way.

I remember when I was a boy in 1941 taking a streetcar from Marpole, where I lived, to downtown Vancouver. In that streetcar was a sign that said No Spitting. At that time, there were signs in many public and private places forbidding spitting on the floor. Today there are no signs about spitting, no spit police to patrol public places, and no threats of fines or jail sentences for spitting; nor are children taught in school that spitting is frowned upon. Yet today you seldom see people gobbing on floors because it is now a deeply understood value of everyone in our society. Right now, in terms of environmental awareness, we are back in the days when we needed signs against spitting. So we have to try to elect politicians who are informed, get the right party into power, and lobby for tough laws and strict enforcement. But when *everyone* understands that clean air, water, and soil, along with solar energy and biodiversity, are critical elements for our very survival and must be protected above all else, then it won't matter whether we elect a Reform or Green government, because the accepted value system of our society will ensure that they all begin with the same fundamental understanding.

I think the difficulty in environmentalism today resides in the way that we have framed the issue. I have spent thirty-five years in battle over different causes. Often the arguments have pitted people against each other: jobs and profit versus environmental protection, clearcut logging versus parks, human beings versus spotted owls. In every battle that is resolved, there is always a loser or losing side, but when we are discussing a future for our children and grandchildren, we can't afford to have losers. I understand that those whom I have opposed are also mothers and fathers who are concerned for their jobs, their children's futures, their security — just as I am.

We have to define the issue differently. The environment isn't something "out there," something we take from, put into, and have to manage so we can continue to exploit it without damaging its productive capacity. The issue is far more profound. We literally are the Earth. There is no "out there" separated from us by our skin. Air is always inside us and fused to our lungs; we are inflated by water that makes up over 60 percent of our weight; every bit of our bodies is composed of the molecules and cellular debris of plants and animals that fed from the soil; and the chemical energy within us and that we liberate in our fuels was once sunlight trapped by plants. We are the four elements — earth, air, fire, and water — which the ancients understood very well. And the remarkable thing that modern biology has revealed is that these four elements are cleansed, replenished, and fixed by the diverse web of living things. When we define our place on this planet this way, then it's clear that our abuse of these vital elements and the extinction of so many species is a self-inflicted assault that will be suicidal. Once we have understood that, we will realize that we can't go on trying to resolve environmental problems like asthma, endocrine disrupters, breast cancer, lymphoma, and so on by finding cures after the fact. The challenge is to respect the importance of the four elements and biodiversity, and to ensure that, however we live and make a living, they are protected above all else. This is the challenge we face at this moment of transition to a new century and a new millennium.

References

The numbers at left refer to the page on which the cited material is mentioned.

PAGE

3 Sagan, Carl. 1986. *To Preserve a World Graced with Life*. Cited in *Peace: A Dream Unfolding*. Edited by Penney Kome and Patrick Crean. Toronto: Somerville House Books Ltd.

4a Hillel, Daniel. 1991. *Out of the Earth: Civilization and the Life of the Soil*. Herts, U.K.: Maxwell MacMillan.

4b Thoreau, Henry David. 1854. *Walden*. Boston: Beacon Press.

6 Harris, Michael. 1998. *Lament for an Ocean*. Toronto: McClelland & Stewart Inc.

8 Einstein, Albert. 1955. Quoted in obituary. *New York Times*. (April 19).

9a Penfield, Wilder. Quoted in George Wald. 1988. "The Cosmology of Life and Mind," in *Synthesis of Science and Religion: Critical Essays and Dialogues*. Edited by T. D. Singh and Ravi Gomatam. San Francisco: Bhaktivedanta Institute.

9b Wilson, Edward O. 1992. *The Diversity of Life*. New York: W. W. Norton & Co.

10 Odum, Howard T. 1971. *Environment, Power and Society*. New York: John Wiley & Sons.

11 Ostfeld, Richard S. 1998. *Ecology and Lyme Disease*. Presented at the conference on the Value of Plants, Animals and Microbes to Human Health. American Museum of Natural History, New York City, April 18–19.

12 Lovelock, James. 1991. *Gaia: The Practical Science of Planetary Medicine*. Sydney: Allen & Unwin.

13a   Carson, Rachel. 1962. *Silent Spring*. Boston: Houghton Mifflin.

13b   Maser, Chris. 1988. *The Redesigned Forest*. San Pedro, CA: R. & E. Miles.

14   Larking, Billian A., and Pat A. Slaney. 1997. "Implications of trends in marine-derived nutrient influx to south coastal salmonid production." *Fisheries* 22: 16–24.

15   Wilson, Edward O. 1992. *The Diversity of Life*. Cambridge: Harvard University Press.

18a   Ehrlich, Paul. 1968. *The Population Bomb*. New York: Ballantine Books.

18b   *Science Summit on World Population*. 1993. New Delhi, India, October 24–27.

19   *Population Summit of the World's Scientific Academies*. 1994. National Academy Press.

20a   Ibid.

20b   Ehrlich, Paul, and John Holdren. 1974. "Impact of population growth." *Science* 171: 1212–17.

21   *Population Summit of the World's Scientific Academies*.

22a   von Weizsäcker, Ernst, Amory B. Lovins, and L. Hunter Lovins. 1997. *Factor Four: Doubling Wealth — Halving Resource Use*. London: Earthscan.

22b   *Population Summit of the World's Scientific Academies*.

23a   "World Scientists' Warning to Humanity." 1992. Union of Concerned Scientists, Cambridge, MA.

23b   *Population Summit of the World's Scientific Academies*.

23c   *World Scientists' Call for Action at Kyoto*. 1997. Union of Concerned Scientists, Cambridge, MA.

24   UNESCO. *Sources* 58 (May 1994).

25   Franklin, Benjamin. Quoted in Herb Goldberg and Robert T. Lewis. 1978. *Money Madness: The Psychology of Saving, Spending, Loving and Hating Money*. New York: William Morrow & Co.

25   Bellah, Robert. 1975. *The Broken Covenant*. New York: Seabury Press.

27a   Chandler, Tertius. 1987. *Four Thousand Years of Urban Growth: An Historical Census*. Queenston: The Edwin Millen Press.

27b   *World Almanac*. 1996. Funk and Wagnalls Co.

27c   Thom, Bing. Architect, Vancouver, B.C. Personal communication.

28   Livingston, John. 1994. *Rogue Primate: An Exploration of Human*

Domestication. Toronto: Key Porter Books Limited.

32a Wachtel, Paul. 1988. *The Poverty of Affluence: A Psychological Portrait of the American Way of Life*. Gabriola Island, B.C.: New Society Publishers.

32b Kanner, Allen D., and Mary E. Gomes. 1995. "The all-consuming self." *Adbusters* (Summer).

32c Lebow, Victor. Quoted in Vance Packard. 1960. *The Waste Makers*, 1960.

33 Keough, Donald R. Quoted in R. Cohen. 1991. "For Coke, world is its oyster," *New York Times* (November 21).

37 Roszak, Theodore. 1986. *The Cult of Information: The Folklore of Computers and the True Art of Thinking*. New York: Pantheon.

38 *TV Dimensions '95*. *Magazine Dimensions '95*.

39a Roszak, Theodore, *Cult of Information*.

39b Kanner, Allen D., and Mary E. Gomes, "All-Consuming Self."

39c Stöll, Clifford. 1995. *Silicon Snake Oil: Second Thoughts on the Information Highway*. New York: Doubleday.

40a Ibid.

40b Postman, Neil. 1995. Quote from speech given in Town Hall in New York City. *Utne Reader* (July/August).

40c Wolf, Gary. 1996. "Steve Jobs: The Next Insanely Great Thing." *Wired* (February).

41a Kay, Alan. 1995. U.S. Congress Joint Hearing on Educational Technology in the 21st Century, Science Committee and the Economic Opportunities Committee, U.S. House of Representatives. October 12.

41b Clinton, U.S. President Bill. 1995. Quoted in *New York Times* (September 23).

41c Shenk, David. 1994. "Investing in our Youth." *Spy* (July/August).

42 Shenk, David. 1997. *Data Smog: Surviving the Information Glut*, 167–68. San Francisco: HarperEdge.

43 Novak, Philip. 1988. Commencement address at Dominican College, San Rafael, CA. Published in *Dominican Quarterly* (Summer).

44 George, Susan. 1997. Interview for the David Suzuki Foundation. Broadcast on the British Columbia Knowledge Network.

45 Simon, Julian. 1981. *The Ultimate Resource*. Princeton, NJ: Princeton University Press.

46a Schumacher, E. F. 1974. *Small Is Beautiful: A Study of Economics as if People Mattered*. London: Abacus.

46b Daily, Gretchen, ed. 1997. *Nature's Services: Societal Dependence on Natural Ecosystems*. Washington: Island Press.

46c Baskin, Yvonne. 1997. *The Work of Nature: How the Diversity of Life Sustains Us*. Washington: Island Press.

47 Pimentel, David. 1994. "Natural Resources and an Optimum Human Population." *Population and Environment* 15, no. 5.

47 Constanza, Robert, et al. "The Value of the World's Ecosystem Services and Natural Capital." *Nature* 387: 253–260.

48a Simon, Julian L. 1994. *A Debate on the Environment*. New York: W. W. Norton & Co.

48b Daly, Herman, and John Cobb. 1989. *For the Common Good: Redirecting the Economy Towards Community, the Environment and a Sustainable Future*. Boston: Beacon Press.

49a Schumacher, E. F., *Small Is Beautiful*.

49b Daly, Herman. 1994. Farewell lecture to the World Bank, Washington, DC, January 14.

49c Keynes, John Maynard. 1933. "National Self-Sufficiency," in *The Collected Writings of John Maynard Keynes*. Vol. 21, edited by Donald Moggeridge. London: Cambridge University Press.

50 Gorbachev, Mikhail. 1990. Quoted in *The Guardian* (January 19).

51 Reed, Christopher. 1989. Quoted in *The Guardian* (September 8).

52 Standing Committee on Environment. 1993. "No Time to Lose: The Challenge of Global Warming," in *Our Planet . . . Our Future*.

53a Gore, Al. 1992. *Earth in the Balance: Ecology and the Human Spirit*. New York: Houghton Mifflin Co.

53b Powell, Enoch. 1989. Quoted in *The Guardian* (September 8).

54 World Commission on Environment and Development. *Our Common Future*. 1987. New York: Oxford University Press.

57 Einstein, Albert. Quoted in *Peace: A Dream Unfolding*. Edited by Penney Kome and Patrick Crean.

58 Eiseley, Loren. 1970. *The Invisible Pyramid*. New York: Scribner's.

59a Lewis, C. S. 1947. *The Abolition of Man*. Macmillan.

59b Prigogine, Ilya, and Isabelle Stengers. 1984. *Order Out of Chaos: Man's New Dialogue with Nature*. New York: Bantam.

68 Cassidy, John. 1995. "Who Killed the Middle Class?" *New Yorker* (October 16).

70   UNESCO. *Sources* 58 (May 1994).

72   Faraclas, Nicholas. 1997. "Critical Literacy and Control in the New World Order," in *Constructing Critical Literacies*. Edited by Sandy Muspratt, Alan Luke, and Peter Freebody. Creeskill, NJ: Hampton Press.

76   Barnet, Richard J., and John Cavanagh. 1994. *Global Dreams: Imperial Corporations and the New World Order*. New York: Simon and Schuster.

79   Daly, Herman. Farewell lecture.

83   *Wall Street Journal*. 1995. "Bankrupt Canada?" (January 12).

88a   Kennedy, Robert, Jr. Quoted in Clifford Cobb and Ted Halsted. 1994. *The Genuine Progress Indicator: Summary of Data and Methodology*. San Francisco: Redefining Progress Institute.

88b   Cobb, Clifford, and Ted Halsted, ibid.

89   Conable, Barber. Quoted in Clifford Cobb and Ted Halsted, ibid.

95   New Road Map Foundation. 1994. *All-Consuming Passion: Waking up from the American Dream*.

97   Brown, Lester. 1994. "Who Will Feed China?" *World Watch* (September/October).

100   Brown, Lester, and Hal Kane. 1994. *Full House: Reassessing the Earth's Population Carrying Capacity*. New York: W. W. Norton & Co.

101   Quinn, Daniel. 1993. "On Investments." Address to the Minnesota Investment Forum, June 7.

109a McKibben, Bill. 1998. "A Special Moment in History." *Atlantic Monthly* (May).

109b Vitousek, Peter, Paul Ehrlich, Anne Ehrlich, and P. Mason. 1986. "Human appropriation of the products of photosynthesis." *BioSciences* 36: 368–73.

110   Wackernagel, Mathis, and William E. Rees. 1996. *Our Ecological Footprint: Reducing Human Impact on the Earth*. Gabriola Island, B.C.: New Society Publishers.

111a Wackernagel, Mathis. 1994. "How Big Is Our Ecological Footprint?" Pamphlet may be obtained from Janette McIntosh, Dept. of Family Practice, University of British Columbia, Vancouver, B.C.

111b For information on the Task Force on Planning Healthy and Sustainable Communities, contact the Dept. of Family Practice, University of British Columbia, Vancouver, B.C.

115 Pimentel, David. 1994. "National Resources and an Optimum Human Population." *Population and Environment* 15, no. 5.

121a Hansen, James. 1988. Testimony before a Congressional subcommittee. Cited by Al Gore in *Earth in the Balance.*

121b Appeal by American Scientists to Prevent Global Warming. 1990. Union of Concerned Scientists, Cambridge, MA. February 16.

122 Standing Committee on Environment, *Our Planet . . . Our Future.*

123a Intergovernmental Panel on Climate Change. 1995. Second Assessment Report. New York: United Nations.

123b *World Scientists' Call for Action at Kyoto.*

123c Kendall, Henry, and David Pimentel. 1994. "Constraints on the Expansion of Global Food Supply." *Ambio* 23.

130 *Maclean's.* 1994. (April 25).

131a Kaplan, Robert D. 1994. "The Coming Anarchy." *Atlantic Monthly* (February).

131b Gee, Marcus. 1994. "Apocalypse Deferred." *Globe and Mail* (April 9).

134a Levy, Stephen. 1995. "Technomania." *Newsweek* (February 27).

134b Sale, Kirkpatrick. 1995. *Rebels Against the Future.* Reading, MA: Addison-Wesley.

142 Pratt, Larry, and Ian Urquhart. 1994. *The Last Great Forest: Japanese Multinationals and Alberta's Northern Forests.* Edmonton: NeWest Publication.

145 Nikiforuk, Andrew. 1998. "Taking the Axe to Alberta's Forests." *Globe and Mail* (June 22).

151 Urud, Anderson Mutang. 1992. Address to the United Nations General Assembly to launch the UN Year of Indigenous People, New York City, December 10.

156 Suzuki, David T., and Keibo Oiwa. 1996. *The Japan We Never Knew: A Journey of Discovery.* Toronto: Stoddart Publishing Co. Limited.

160 Jacob, François. 1970. *The Logic of Living Systems: A History of Heredity.* London: Allen Lane.

164 Wilson, Edward O. 1996. *Naturalist.* Washington: Island Press.

169a Wilson, Edward O. 1984. *Biophilia: The Human Bond with Other Species.* Cambridge: Harvard University Press.

169b Dubos, René. 1990. *The World of René Dubos: A Collection of Historical Writings.* Edited by Gerard Piel and Osborn Segerberg, Jr. New York: Henry Holt.

169c Kellert, Stephen R., and Edward O. Wilson, eds. 1993. *The Biophilia Hypothesis.* Washington: Island Press.

173   Carlsen, E., A. Giwercman, N. Keidling, and N. Skakkebaek. *1992.* "Evidence for decreasing quality of semen during the past 50 years." *British Medical Journal.* 305: 609–13.

174   Colborn, Theo, Dianne Dumanoski, and John Peterson Myers. 1996. *Our Stolen Future.* New York: Plume/Penguin.

185   Mowat, Farley. 1985. *Sea of Slaughter.* Toronto: Seal.

192   Tilman, David, and John Downing. 1994. "Biodiversity and Stability in Grasslands." *Nature* 367.

195   Devall, Bill, and George Sessions. 1987. *Deep Ecology: Living as if Nature Mattered.* Salt Lake City: Peregrine Smith Books.

206   Hallé, Francis. 1990. "A Raft atop the Rainforest." *National Geographic* (October).

210   World Commission on Environment and Development, *Our Common Future.*

215   Suzuki, David T., and Keibo Oiwa, *The Japan We Never Knew.*

219   Lara, Adair. 1995. "Coming Home to Ourselves." *Simple Living* (Winter).

221   Suzuki, David T., and Keibo Oiwa, *The Japan We Never Knew.*

222   Fukuoka, Masanobu. 1978. *The One Straw Revolution: An Introduction to Natural Farming.* Emmaus: Rodale Press.

225   Mollison, Bill, and Reny Mia Slay. 1994. *Introduction to Permaculture.* Tyalgum, Australia: Tagari Publications.

225   Higa, Teruo. 1994–95. *Chikyu o sukuu daihenkaku* (EM: *The Revolution that will Save the Earth*). 2 vols. Tokyo: Sanmaku shuppan.

226a Walters, Carl. 1995. *Fish on the Line: The Future of Pacific Fisheries.* A Report to the David Suzuki Foundation, Vancouver, B.C.

226b Pinkerton, Evelyn, and Martin Weinstein. 1995. *Fisheries That Work: Sustainability Through Community-based Management.* A Report to the David Suzuki Foundation, Vancouver, B.C.

230   Reports can be obtained from Cortex Consultants Inc., Victoria, B.C. Phone # 250-360-1492.

245   Harris, Michael, *Lament for an Ocean.*

247   World Commission on Environment and Development, *Our Common Future.*

CREDITS

The following sources have given permission for quoted material:

From "Who Killed the Middle Class?" by John Cassidy, *New Yorker*, October 16, 1995. Reprint by permission of the author.

From "Farewell Lecture to the World Bank" by Herman Daly, January 14, 1994. Reprint by permission of the author.

From "Who Will Feed China?" by Lester R. Brown, World Watch, September/October 1994. Reprint by permission of the author.

From "On Investments" by Daniel Quinn, address to the Minnesota Investment Forum, June 7, 1993. Reprint by permission of the author.

From "How Big Is Our Ecological Footprint?" a pamphlet by Mathis Wackernagel, 1994. Reprint by permission of the author.

From "Constraints on the Expansion of Global Food Supply" by Henry Kendall and David Pimentel in *Ambio*, volume 23 (1994). Reprint by permission of the authors.

From *Rebels Against the Future* by Kirkpatrick Sale, 1995, Addison-Wesley. Reprint by permission of the author.

From an address to the United Nations General Assembly to launch the UN Year of Indigenous People, by Anderson Mutang Urud, December 10, 1992. Reprint by permission of the author.

From *Naturalist* by Edward O. Wilson, 1996, Island Press. Reprint by permission of the author.

From *Biophilia: The Human Bond with Other Species* by Edward O. Wilson, 1984, Harvard University Press. Reprint by permission of the author.

From "Coming Home to Ourselves" by Adair Lara, *Simple Living*, Winter 1995. Reprint by permission of the author.

Every reasonable effort has been made to contact the holders of copyright for materials quoted in this book. The author and publisher will gladly receive information that will enable them to rectify any inadvertent errors or omissions in subsequent editions.

THE DAVID SUZUKI FOUNDATION:
WORKING TOGETHER FOR A SUSTAINABLE FUTURE

The David Suzuki Foundation was established to work for a world of hope in which our species thrives in balance with the productive capacity of the Earth.

Our mission is to find solutions to the root causes of our most threatening environmental problems. Then, we work with our supporters and their communities to implement those solutions for a sustainable future.

Our mandate is broad, ranging from projects on climate change, air, soil, water, fisheries, forestry, energy, and liveable cities, to defining the foundations of sustainability, how social change occurs, and the potential of new economic models.

We can only accomplish this with the support of concerned citizens who care about the environment. We invite your help.

JOIN OUR PARTNERSHIP . . . JOIN THE FOUNDATION!

NAME   ADDRESS

CITY/PROVINCE   POSTAL CODE   TELEPHONE

Here is my donation of:　❑ $30　　❑ $50　　❑ $100　　❑ $500
　　　　　　　　　　　❑ $1000 National Sponsor　❑ $5000 Founder

❑ Cheque　　❑ Money Order　　❑ Visa　　　　❑ MasterCard

CARD NUMBER   EXPIRY DATE

SIGNATURE

Yes, I'll become a Friend of the Foundation. I authorize the Foundation to receive the following amount from my chequing account on a monthly basis. I understand I'll receive a tax credit and the benefits of becoming a Foundation Supporter.

❑ $10 a month　　❑ $15 a month　　❑ $25 a month　　❑ $_____ a month

I understand I can change or cancel my pledge at any time.
I enclose a sample cheque marked VOID for bank coding.

SIGNATURE

Please return this reply memo with your tax-creditable donation. Cheques can be made payable to The David Suzuki Foundation. Thank you very much for your support.

 THE DAVID SUZUKI FOUNDATION
219–2211 WEST FOURTH AVENUE
VANCOUVER, B.C., CANADA V6K 4S2
Phone (604) 732-4228; Fax (604) 732-0752

Charitable Registration Numbers: Canada 0873299-52; U.S. 94-3204049